63354

P9-CMV-391

SB
457.6
.R67
1998

Ross, Stephanie.

What gardens mean.

$40.00

DATE			
WITHDRAWN			

BAKER & TAYLOR

FASKEN LEARNING RESOURCE CENTER

9000063354

What Gardens Mean

Sun tunnels (detail), by Nancy Holt. Photograph courtesy of Nancy Holt.

63354

WHAT
Gardens
MEAN

STEPHANIE ROSS

The University of Chicago Press ❧ Chicago and London

STEPHANIE ROSS is associate professor of philosophy at the University of Missouri-St. Louis. She has published articles in various areas of aesthetics; an airedale and a bassett hound thwart her attempts to garden.

The University of Chicago Press, Chicago 60637
The University of Chicago Press, Ltd., London
©1998 by The University of Chicago
All rights reserved. Published 1998
Printed in the United States of America
04 03 02 01 00 99 98 1 2 3 4 5

ISBN 0-226-72822-6 (cloth)

Library of Congress Cataloging-in-Publication Data
Ross, Stephanie.
    What gardens mean / Stephanie Ross
        p. cm.
    Includes bibliographical references and index.
    ISBN 0-226-72822-6 (cloth : alk. paper)
    1. Gardens, English—Philosophy—18th century. 2. Gardens,
English—Philosophy. 3. Gardens—Philosophy. 4. Art—Philosophy
I. Title.
SB457.6.R67 1998
712'.2'094209033—dc21   97-22441

This book is printed on acid-free paper.

63354

To my parents
Rhoda and Sidney Ross

Contents

Illustrations

Preface

Gardens yield prodigal pleasures. Their bounty includes not only fruits and flowers, vegetables and herbs, but also beauty, respite, and reflection. Gardens delight the senses, prompt thought, evoke feeling and emotion, and engage the imagination.

Gardening dates back at least to Neolithic times.[1] Garden historians can document the gardens of Mesopotamia and Egypt, ancient Greece and Rome. Distinctive gardening styles are also attributed to the world of Islam, to the Far East, and (in more recent ages) to Italy, France, and England.

What I am interested in here is a particular moment in garden history. A unique garden style evolved in eighteenth-century England—the English landscape garden. Moreover, English amateurs, critics, and connoisseurs alike united in declaring gardening to be a bona fide art, a full sister to painting and poetry. I propose to use this episode in the history of taste as a springboard for investigating important and enduring philosophical issues.

To introduce some of these issues, consider the following: first, a natural landscape—rolling hills, green fields, a tree-lined road winding into the distance; next, a garden in the English landscape style with lush lawn, a central lake, clumps of trees, and grazing sheep; next, a French formal garden with fountains, statues, hedges, knots; next, a Baroque stage setting depicting a garden, with illusionistic scenery and convincing props; next, an amateur's photograph of the scene with which we began; and finally, a realistic painting of that same scene. In traversing this series, we move from three dimensions to two, from reality to representation, from nature to art. Yet each element in the series is a landscape. According to Webster, the term "landscape" denotes (1) those portions of land which the eye can comprehend in a single view, and (2) representations of such land.[2] What, then, differentiates the items in our series? What, to borrow a phrase from Kenneth Clark, makes landscape into art?

The items in the continuum prompt a myriad of more specific questions as well. Among them are these: What is involved in creating a garden? What roles are played by change and chance? How are gardens described and notated? Can gardens from the past be preserved? How are gardens experienced by those who view them or walk through them? Does perceiving a garden differ from perceiving a landscape? Does perceiving a garden differ from perceiving a landscape painting? How does imagination enter in? What sorts of meanings can gardens possess? What sorts of messages can they convey? Can gardens express deep-felt feelings and emotions? Can they have moral force? What artistic tasks can they perform? What distinctive pleasures can they yield? What patterns of influence linked gardening and her sister arts in the eighteenth century? What institutions arose to train gardeners and educate the garden-going public? What philosophical and aesthetic theories supported eighteenth-century gardening practice? What explains the prevalence of distinct national styles in gardening and in the other arts? Why isn't gardening considered a full-fledged art today?

The questions just listed vary greatly in scope. They involve the psychology of perception and the history of ideas as well as straightforward philosophical analysis. But they all bear on a fundamental question of aesthetics, namely, "What is art and what does it do for us?" I believe that the study of gardens provides a fruitful and original way to approach this age-old issue.

In what follows, I shall try to address and answer some of the questions posed above. I have chosen to focus on England in the eighteenth century for three reasons. First, at that time in England the art of gardening was considered every bit as noble as the arts of painting and poetry. The traditional comparison between the arts expressed in Horace's simile *Ut pictura poesis* ("As is painting, so is poetry") was expanded to include comparisons between gardens and poems, and between gardens and paintings. These new comparisons prompted cross-fertilization among these arts and a blurring of their boundaries. Eighteenth-century gardens were expected to perform the tasks of their sister arts, to offer messages visitors could "read" and scenes they could savor.

Second, eighteenth-century English garden history is of interest because gardening styles changed dramatically in the course of the century. The emblematic garden characteristic of the early 1700s was complex and allusive. It gave way to the English landscape garden, which was carefully cultivated to resemble untouched nature. Garden history here reflects a larger change in taste—a shift from neoclassical to romantic sensibility. The fact that gardening responded to these intellectual and artistic currents shows gardening to be an ideological enterprise. During this period in England, gardening also evolved from a largely amateur endeavor to one practiced by professionals. This too had consequences for the significance of garden design and the status of garden designers.

Finally, the study of eighteenth-century gardens raises one more aesthetic issue, that of art's demise. Gardening does not flourish today. While a great many Americans claim gardening as a hobby, few garden in the manner of the eighteenth century. We do not consider gardening a high art, and artists do not make major statements in this medium. Hegel theorized that art would one day come to an end, to be superseded by religion and philosophy. Gardening's decline invites us to reconsider Hegel's dark claims about the death of art.

I have organized my book around a quotation from Horace Walpole (1717–97), author of *Anecdotes of Painting* (1762–71) and *The History of the Modern Taste in Gardening* (1771–80). Walpole's wide-ranging interests are summed up by one author who describes him as a "connoisseur, dilettante, letter-writer, novelist, art-historian, amateur artist and architect."[3] Walpole was deeply interested in garden history and in England's distinctive contribution to garden style. In a marginal annotation to a poem by William Mason, Walpole wrote that "Poetry, Painting, and Gardening, or the Science of Landscape, will forever by men of Taste be deemed Three Sisters, or *the Three New Graces* who dress and adorn Nature."[4] This quotation introduces three crucial issues around which my book is organized: what it is to experience a garden; gardening's relation to her sister arts; and the status of gardens today.

The seven chapters that follow consider gardens in general and the claim that they are works of art (chap. 1), provide background material relevant to the eighteenth-century appreciation of landscape (chap. 2), explore two aspects of Walpole's claim about gardening's sister arts (chaps. 3 and 4), examine an aesthetic category—the picturesque—which arose from eighteenth-century debates about gardens (chap. 5), consider what is distinctive about experiencing a garden (chap. 6), and argue that certain contemporary works of art—earthworks and environmental art—should be viewed as the descendants of the eighteenth-century landscape garden (chap. 7).

Some portions of my book borrow from papers I have published previously. Chapter 5 is based on my article "The Picturesque: An Eighteenth-Century Debate," published in the *Journal of Aesthetics and Art Criticism* 46, no. 2 (1987): 271–89. Chapter 7 was drawn from two papers of mine, "Philosophy, Literature, and the Death of Art," which appeared in *Philosophical Papers* 17, no. 1 (1989): 95–115, and "Gardens, Earthworks, and Environmental Art," which was published in *Landscape, Natural Beauty, and the Arts,* ed. Salim Kemal and Ivan Gaskell (Cambridge: Cambridge University Press, 1993), 158–82. I am grateful to the respective publishers for permission to reproduce this material. An earlier article, "Ut Hortus Poesis: Gardening and Her Sister Arts in Eighteenth-Century England," which appeared in the *British Journal of Aesthetics* 25, no. 1 (1985): 17–32, contains my first, tentative exploration of the topic of garden aesthetics.

I have accrued many debts of gratitude over the long time that I have been working on this book. I first began the project while spending a sabbatical year in New York City. I thank the New York University Institute for Fine Arts and the Columbia University Philosophy Department for their hospitality. I did additional research while holding a NEH research fellowship at the Huntington Library and Museum in San Marino, California, and a short-term research fellowship at the Yale University Center for British Art. Both were delightful places to think about gardens. I also obtained valuable released time from my own university in the form of a University of Missouri Research Board fellowship.

A generous grant from the Graham Foundation for Advanced Studies in the Fine Arts made possible the inclusion of color plates in this volume. The black and white illustrations were supported by an additional grant from the University of Missouri Research Board.

And I have of course received help from many colleagues. The American Society for Aesthetics has been a wonderfully nurturing and supportive organization, a source of many friendships and a place to try out and strengthen ideas. I owe special thanks to Donald Crawford, Susan Feagin, Stan Godlovitch, Peter Kivy, and Jenefer Robinson for suggestions made and recommendations written. I have benefited greatly from the voluminous writings of John Dixon Hunt and from the ground-breaking book by Mara Miller, *The Garden as an Art.* I thank Mara too for her exceptional generosity in encouraging other writers. Even where I disagree with her conclusions, much of my own view is animated by its engagement with her claims. In addition, I thank David Conway and Jennifer Judkins for their support and encouragement, Dominic Lopes for reading over the finished manuscript, and Henry Shapiro for repeated readings and invaluable suggestions for improving arguments and polishing style.

Finally, I want to thank Karen Wilson, former art editor at the University of Chicago Press, for her faith in my project, and Bruce Young, retired managing editor of the Press, for his extraordinarily attentive and helpful editing of my text.

GARDENS AND ART,
GARDENS AS ART

I. GARDEN VARIETY

Just what is a garden? It is unlikely that we can come up with any precise definition in terms of necessary and sufficient conditions—that is, one listing a set of properties possessed by all and only by all gardens. For consider the variety at hand. Gardens can be large or small, unbounded or enclosed, terraced or flat, natural or geometric, with flowers or without. They can contain blossoms, trees, lawns, and shrubs, lakes, canals, streams, and fountains, statues, rocks, paths, and benches, follies, grottoes, ruins, and temples. Contrast the endless expanse of Versailles with an intimate Moorish courtyard, an English landscape garden with a suburban perennial bed, the hanging gardens of Babylon (actually, terraced, planted ziggurats)[1] with that limiting case, a Japanese Zen garden consisting of nothing but rocks and raked sand.

Not only do gardens differ in features and appearance; they also differ in purpose. Historians today trace gardens to two ultimate sources: (1) sacred groves and nymphaea dedicated to particular pagan deities, and (2) utilitarian kitchen and medicinal gardens.[2] Thus gardens are linked with magic and religion as well as with practical needs. Consider some of the benefits of a garden. First and foremost, gardens yield produce—fruits, vegetables, flowers, and herbs. These in turn contribute to products as varied as brandy, opium, perfume, shampoo, textiles, tisanes, and dyes.

The Court of the Lions at the Alhambra. Reproduced by permission of the MacQuitty International Photographic Collection.

The Dry Garden, or *kare sansui,* at Ryoan-Ji. Reproduced by permission of the MacQuitty International Photographic Collection.

Gardens also answer our aesthetic needs. Above all they provide visual delights (see color plate 1). These include vast vistas as well as the more concentrated beauty of a particular bloom or bed. Flowers enchant us with their varied colors and shapes, but we also take pleasure in flowerless gardens—the soothing patch of green in a vest-pocket city park or the subtle patterns and textures of a traditional Japanese *kare sansui* (dry garden). Garden delights aren't limited to the sense of sight. Fragrances mingle with the splash of a fountain, the buzz of a bee, the warmth of the sun, the cooling touch of a breeze. Finally, gardens provide the general kinesthetic pleasures of moving in and through a space.

In addition to these sensory pleasures, gardens also evoke complex trains of thought and feeling. All gardens carry with them certain associations. For example, in Western culture, gardens inevitably suggest paradise, the bounty and bliss of the Garden of Eden. These Judeo-Christian connotations coexist with more primitive associations—sexuality and fertility, death and regeneration, the cycle of the seasons[3]—as well as with more recent overlays ranging from the tradition of courtly love to the awareness of ecological crisis. Absolutely anything can be caught in this net of associations. For example, a lush garden might make one person think biblically, another lecherously, and remind a third of garden tasks awaiting her at home. By summoning up ideas and associations, a given garden glimpse can bring to mind similar scenes, recall paintings and poems, prompt imagination and reflection. Different people will also associate different feelings and tones with the same garden scene or feature. Here too all depends on the wealth and shape of the viewer's past experience.

Beyond this sensory and intellectual bounty, gardens provide arenas for activity—places to play or stroll or converse. Think of all the eighteenth-century novels in which a key scene unites hero and heroine on a garden path. In many cultures, particular games and sports are at home in the garden. For example, eighteenth-century English gardens often contained a bowling green;[4] later, badminton and croquet became usual garden sports.[5] Regattas and races were staged on the canals of seventeenth-century French gardens.[6] The sumptuous fetes and fireworks displays held by Louis XIV at Versailles are an extreme example of gardens' use for socializing, and that legacy lingers in our familiar phrase "a garden party."

Possession plays a prime role here. Elaborate gardens testify to the wealth and power of their owners. For example, the vastness, opulence, and regularity of Versailles symbolized the greatness and glory of Louis XIV's autocratic reign. And in fact Louis moved his court to Versailles as a calculated means of occupying and neutralizing opposition of the French nobles. Eighteenth-century English lords spent vast sums improving their estates, and they often commissioned portraits of themselves and their families in their houses and on their grounds. This tradition evolved to include portraits of the gardens alone. Thus Lord Burlington commissioned Pieter Andreas Rysbrack to paint a series of pictures of the gardens at Chiswick. These hung in Burlington's London townhouse to remind him of the pleasures of his country seat.[7]

Not only did the most illustrious eighteenth-century gardens feed their owners' sense of pride; they excited popular interest as well. This is evidenced by the practice of engraving sets of garden views and offering them for sale by subscription. Chiswick, Stowe, and Claremont were among the first gardens to be recorded in this manner.[8] In addition, visiting estates and viewing their gardens became a popular pastime late in the century. Many

A View of the Orangerie at Chiswick / Lord Burlingtons Garden   *Vüe de l'Orangerie a Chiswick / Jarden du Comte de Burlington*

The orange garden at Chiswick, painted by Pieter Rysbrack about 1730 (engraver unknown). Reproduced by permission of the Yale Center for British Art, Paul Mellon Collection.

guidebooks and first-person accounts were published to aid tourists in appreciating their splendors. Stowe was the most visited of all gardens.[9] The guidebook to Stowe was first published in 1744 and was continually revised and updated through the next hundred years.[10]

Private gardens and the pride and pleasure they promote are complemented by public gardens. These reach an even wider audience. Eighteenth-century London boasted public gardens of two sorts. The first were areas that had originally been royal parks, many of them set aside for hunting. From these evolved London's famous green areas—Hyde Park, Green Park, St. James's Park, and, somewhat later, Regent's Park. The second category were pleasure gardens open to the public for a nominal fee. Some featured medicinal springs (Tunbridge Wells, Islington Spa, etc.), others functioned as tea gardens, and the grandest of all offered meals, concerts, dancing, and fireworks (Ranelagh, Vauxhall, Marylebone).[11]

While gardens can serve worldly ends, there is also a long tradition linking gardens to retreat, contemplation, and repose. Gardens serve such nonworldly purposes in the Bible, in the Chinese tradition of the scholar-recluse, and in Virgil's praise of the life of retirement in the *Georgics.* In the Judeo-Christian tradition gardens recall paradise, and the abundance and glory of the Garden of Eden. There is a darker resonance as well, since the Garden of Eden was also the site of man's fall, and another garden, the garden of Gethsemane, was the site of Christ's agony and betrayal. In addition, the opposition between wilderness and civilization links gardens with darkness and with Satan.[12] Yet clearly the brighter associations triumph. Gardens' negative connotations are counterbalanced by their medieval ties to trysting and love, their role as "bowers of bliss."

2. DEFINITION

So far I have been trying to document the great variety in gardens. They differ strikingly in features and functions. How does this affect our definition of gardens and their status as art? The *American Heritage College Dictionary* defines "garden" as follows: "a plot of land for the cultivation of flowers, vegetables, herbs, or fruits." Clearly this leaves out many of the types of garden mentioned above—water gardens, public pleasure gardens, and Moorish courtyard gardens, among others. Mara Miller, in her recent book *The Garden As an Art,* offers this preliminary definition: "A garden is any purposeful arrangement of natural objects (such as sand, water, plants, rocks, etc.) with exposure to the sky or open air, in which the form is not fully accounted for by purely practical considerations such as convenience."[13]

Miller's proposal certainly accommodates greater variety in gardens than the dictionary definition quoted above. Yet her demand that all gardens contain at least some natural objects rules out some contemporary candidates. One she mentions is I. M. Pei's sunken plaza adjoining Yale University's Beinecke Rare Book Library. I would be willing to deem this space, as well as the building's central courtyard, with striking geometric marble sculptures by Isamo Noguchi, gardens. Miller will apply the term to these spaces "only in a metaphorical sense."[14] I find Miller's requirement of exposure to sky or air equally ad hoc. Can't conservatories and greenhouses sometimes contain gardens? Finally, consider an example which violates both of Miller's first two requirements. *Bloomer,* a video work by Matthew McCaslin recently on display at the St. Louis Art Museum, consists of twelve

Isamu Noguchi's marble courtyard at Yale's Beinecke Rare Book and Manuscript Library can be viewed but not entered. Photograph courtesy of the Isamu Noguchi Foundation, Inc., New York.

video monitors showing flowers exploding into bloom via time-lapse photography. The monitors are grouped in various clumps and stacks, and the tangle of wires and cables snaking along the floor (and rising occasionally to overhead outlets) forms the perfect electronic undergrowth. Is it possible that *Bloomer* should count as both mechanical garden and modern art?

I shall take up these questions again in chapter 7. For now, let us turn to the last part of Miller's definition, what she goes on to call an "excess of form." This too is troubling. At first glance, it threatens to privilege formal or geometric gardens over their more natural competitors. Miller hastens to note that the concept is not quantitative, since minimalist art can possess the requisite excess of form. She concludes that it "is 'more' only in the sense that more decisions, planning, consideration, perhaps measurement or study, went into it."[15] But this will not do either, since it suggests that works created by meticulous, or merely careful, or even halting and stumbling, designers have more form, and are thus more clearly gardens, than those produced by more slapdash or more intuitive artists.

Can we do anything to repair these—or similar—definitions of the term "garden"? While the terms of some disciplines can be given strict definitions, this is not the case with most of our language. We can characterize bachelors as unmarried men, cousins as children of a parent's sibling, triangles as closed three-sided plane figures, but no such tight definition is available for even the common word "chair." No physical feature is common to armchairs, kitchen chairs, rocking chairs, and beanbag chairs, and the "functional" definition, "intended to accommodate one person sitting," can't distinguish chairs from toilets, milking stools, or tractors without a host of ad hoc qualifications.

Wittgenstein made this same point in his discussion of the word "game."[16] He argued that the items all correctly named by a general term were united not by a core of essential properties possessed by all, but by a looser relation which he called family resemblance. Thus all games are united in the same ways that members of a large family pairwise resemble one another. I recall a family with five children I knew when I was growing up. Seeing any two of them together, one immediately knew they were siblings, but different characteristics supported the judgment in each case. Joanie, Mark, and Barbara shared the family freckled nose, Barbara and Rocky the family laugh, Rocky and Carol the family walk. Rocky, Joanie, and Carol were redheads, Barbara and Mark were dark. Such disparate games as chess and Monopoly, football and jacks, hopscotch and hide-and-seek, poker and Russian roulette, are linked in a similar way. Any two share identifying traits yet there are no properties common to all members of the class.

Adapting Wittgenstein's suggestion, it may well be that gardens, like games and chairs, are united by family resemblance. For if we include amongst our examples formal gardens, landscape gardens, vegetable gardens, water gardens, Zen gardens, and more, there is no feature or set of features that they all share. Nevertheless, any *group* of gardens has traits in common. For example, French gardens are rectilinear and architectural, like Islamic gardens, and expansive, like English landscape gardens, while the latter are naturalistic, like Chinese gardens, and flowerless, like Egyptian gardens.

One might insist that at the very least all gardens are cultivated. Consider the following example: I find a pretty area in the woods ablaze with trilliums and lady's slippers. Does admiring it or putting a fence around it make it a garden? The advocate of cultivation would say that unless I *do* something to that bit of land, it remains just nature observed or nature possessed. The intuition here is that a garden must be worked. It needn't be enclosed; it needn't have flowers; it can even look exactly *like* untouched land.[17] But unless someone has shaped and cultivated that land, it isn't a garden.

Counterexamples are sure to be proposed here. Suppose I want a very natural-looking garden behind my house, one that resembles a meadow full of wildflowers. And suppose further that there happens to *be* such a meadow in just the proper place. To make it a garden, must I first dig up the meadow and then sow it with wildflower seeds?[18] Why not acknowledge instead a category "found garden" akin to the category "found art"? Further problems arise if I gradually alter the meadow, at first just enjoying the wildflowers, but then adding to the array by transplanting other blooms. Does the meadow at some point *become* a garden, and if so, when?

Two elusive concepts figure in the examples above: change and artifactuality. Let me discuss them in turn. Though gardens are enduring entities, they are constantly changing. Plants grow, winds blow, pests ravage. Many eighteenth-century gardens that delight us today are not at all as their designers intended them. For example, some of the trees at Stourhead have grown for over two hundred years; they now tower over and shade the garden, while at Blenheim majestic avenues of chestnuts have succumbed to blight and it will be decades before replacements can grow. How much change can a garden sustain before it is no longer the "same" garden? Two months' unkempt growth? Two years' such? Twenty years'? What if every plant in a garden is dug up overnight and replaced with one identical in size and shape? Do we have two different but indistinguishable gardens?

Mara Miller has recently suggested that the criterion according to which gardens are identified and individuated is spatial location.[19] Though gardens are constantly changing in appearance, they occupy a fixed site. This allows us to treat them as persisting and self-identical. Thus Miller remarks, "The garden at Stowe today is the same garden as the garden at Stowe in 1728 precisely because it is *at Stowe*."[20]

I believe Miller's claim is mistaken. Stowe today is a conglomeration of several different gardens created by different garden designers over the course of a century.[21] Bridgeman's Stowe, Kent's Stowe, Brown's Stowe, and more can be reconstructed from contemporary plans and documents.[22] Since we can distinguish successive gardens on a single site, spatial location alone is not sufficient to determine garden identity. A second factor comes into play here, the intentions of the garden designer. Gardens are shaped by their makers, and often a designer who *re*shapes an existing garden in fact creates a new one.

This response to Miller's claim still leaves problems of identity. How much change and what sorts of change are required to generate a new entity? Philosophers have long debated such questions. Their examples range from Theseus's raft, in which every plank is replaced while the raft remains afloat, to science-fiction scenarios in which brain transplants put one person's mind, memories, and character into another's body.[23] The story of the altered meadow told above resembles the old Sophist puzzle "When does a man become bald?" Both cases concern identity in the face of continuous change. Moreover, both show our ordinary intuitions to be inadequate. There is no one right answer to either puzzle. They must be settled by stipulation, and what we stipulate is determined by our interests and by the complexities of the case at hand. Thus different criteria of baldness would be selected by an adman selling hair tonic, a scientist researching male-pattern baldness, and a casting director seeking a double for Telly Savalas. Similarly, a garden historian, an agent selling a venerable English estate, and a philosopher doing metaphysics might propose quite different criteria for the concept "same garden."

This situation does not show our language to be unacceptably vague. Once again we can learn from Wittgenstein, who cautioned against viewing natural language as a calculus.[24] Most general terms have a penumbra of vagueness, and flowery meadows are no less problematic for a lexicographer than balding men or beanbag chairs. That is, the puzzles posed above about change are not unique to the word "garden"; they apply to most general terms in our language.[25]

Artifactuality is a second concept that figures in many definitions of a garden. I considered above the suggestion that gardens must be made. On this view, "art"—in the sense of human shaping and control—must combine with nature in the creation of a garden. It follows that gardens must be artifacts. Some theorists also claim that artifactuality is a necessary condition of art in general.[26] Are at least some gardens then works of art? Let me pause here and consider the age-old question "What is art?" and then return to gardens in section 4.

3. ART

Philosophers have offered a number of competing answers to the question "What is art?" For the ancient Greeks, the answer had to do with *mimesis*, or imitation: art imitates life. This was Plato's reason for rejecting art as doubly removed from reality (an imitation of an imitation)[27] and Aristotle's reason for demanding, in the *Poetics,* that the highest art imitate serious actions and noble characters. Yet some works of art don't seem imitative at all (for example, Mozart's symphonies), while others seem to perform important tasks in addition. Accordingly, a number of alternative theories have been proposed.

Among other theories that have been offered in answer to the question "What is art?" are these: art expresses emotion, art communicates feelings, art expresses intuitions, art exhibits significant form. These theories are associated with Suzanne Langer, Leo Tolstoy,

Benedetto Croce, and Clive Bell, respectively. Each theory brings about a sort of gerry-mandering, for each in effect "redraws" the map of what is and isn't art. For example, in his work *What Is Art?* (1898), Tolstoy denied the title "art" to the novels that earned his fame as well as to many other classics of Western music, painting, and literature. All failed to meet Tolstoy's criterion for true works of art, for he stipulated that such works must communicate their artists' significant religious feelings in the strong sense of infecting the audience with those very same feelings.[28]

Compelling objections can be found to Tolstoy's theory—as well as to those of Plato, Aristotle, Croce, Bell, and Langer. What has gone wrong? Overall the philosophical debate about the nature of art is misguided. There *is* no one single task which all works of art perform. Instead, different works fulfill different ones of the criteria proposed above. Some express emotion, others exhibit significant form, others accurately represent the world. Since these functions are not mutually exclusive, it is also possible for a given work to fulfill two or more of them at once, to express *and* exhibit *and* represent.[29]

Horace in his *Ars poetica* declared that art ought to instruct *and* delight. All manner of functions fit between these two poles. Works of art can offer clear-cut moral exhortation, exhibit truths about human nature, amuse, provide mere sensory surface. For an example of each of these functions, consider Picasso's masterpiece *Guernica,* short stories by Ann Beattie or Bobbi Ann Mason, the films of Woody Allen, Ravel's shimmering string quartet. We today find artworks of each of these types worthy of admiration. It may seem that very few of these functions have anything to do with gardens, but I shall argue in the course of this book that gardens can instruct and delight and do many things in between. In fact, I think gardens can perform each of the functions canvassed above.

One problem remains, however. Much modern art fails to fit any of the theories just mentioned. Environmental art, found art, conceptual art, aleatory art, seem to fulfill none of the functions which confer the status "work of art." Consider the urinal which Marcel Duchamp submitted to the Society of Independent Artists' show of 1917 under the title *Fountain by R. Mutt.*"[30] It may well be the item most written about by twentieth-century aestheticians. Yet it does not seem to represent, teach, express, or enchant. Then how or why is it art?

In response to cases like these, some philosophers have tried to formulate theories of a radically different sort. They proposed that an object's status as a work of art depends not on properties manifested by that object—those that can be read off directly from it—but on nonexhibited relational properties—for example, the way in which we treat the object in question.[31] George Dickie developed this insight into the institutional theory of art. Dickie's definition of art runs as follows. "A work of art . . . is (1) an artifact, (2) a set of the aspects of which has had conferred upon it the status of candidate for appreciation by some person or persons acting on behalf of a certain social institution (the artworld)."[32]

Clause 1 of Dickie's definition requires some loosening. The category of found art suggests that works of art needn't be created, nor even altered or shaped, by the artist; the category of conceptual art suggests that works of art needn't be physical. And note that it is not just contemporary works that create difficulties for Dickie's artifactuality condition. However we explain the ontology of novels, plays, ballets, and symphonies—that is, of multiple arts and performing arts—works do not turn out to be artifacts in the sense of physical objects that the artist has created or shaped. I would support a revision of Dickie's artifactuality condition along the lines of that proposed by Vanda Bozicevic. She replaces his summary demand that a work of art be an artifact with a broader disjunctive requirement: the work may be produced or selected, object or event. Bozicevic does, however, insist that the work be perceptible.[33]

Turn now to clause 2 of Dickie's definition. Dickie defines the artworld in terms of a bundle of systems (i.e., the various arts: poetry, painting, dance, music, theater, and so on), and a core personnel ("artists, producers, museum directors, museum-goers, theater-goers, reporters for newspapers, critics for publications of all sorts, art historians, art theorists, philosophers of art, and, [ultimately] every person who sees himself as a member").[34] Something is art if it is sponsored and presented in the appropriate way against the background of this pervasive institution. Thus Dickie's answer to the question "What is art?" emphasizes complex external or contextual factors rather than intrinsic features of a given work; the anti-essentialism recommended above is built into the very structure of his view.

Dickie's theory is quite ingenious. It explains how certain objects (like pre-Columbian bowls or Early American quilts) which were created to fill entirely utilitarian needs can change their status and become works of art. They are transformed once they become the recipients of the proper sort of interest and attention. The theory also accommodates readymades like Duchamp's urinal and controversial acts and events like Vito Acconci's installation *Seedbed* (in which the artist lay under a false gallery floor and masturbated in response to viewers' walking above him).[35]

Is it just context, literally construed, that determines an object's status as art? Those cases which inspired Dickie's theory—most notably Duchamp's Fountain, but also junk sculpture, found driftwood, primitive pots—seem to involve objects which are transfigured in being carried over the museum threshold. Yet an object's presence in the museum is neither necessary nor sufficient to make it art. Consider the art of architecture. Utilitarian buildings from the past like Boston's Fanueil Hall and St. Louis's Union Station are now considered to be architectural masterpieces, bona fide works of art.[36] On the other hand, the urinals in the men's room at the Museum of Modern Art are *not* works of art, though they are within the museum precincts and indistinguishable from Duchamp's urinal (or from newer models displayed in the design galleries). Perhaps then our attention is directed in a special way toward those utilitarian objects which we elevate into art, and this both brings about and explains their altered status.

This last suggestion would be embraced by aesthetic-attitude theorists; also by theorists who recognize aesthetic experience or psychical distance. Proponents of such views maintain that a distinctive attitude or experience characterizes our (appropriate) encounters with works of art. This experience is generally defined in terms of distance or disinterestedness. Disinterestedness here does not mean boredom or lack of interest. Rather, it is something akin to the lack of bias our legal system requires of judges or members of a jury. The people in such roles can have no personal stake in the matters they decide. They are disqualified from a case if they stand to gain in any way, or if they have a strong emotional involvement in the outcome. Aesthetic-attitude theorists desire something similar in aesthetic situations. Thus Edward Bullough speaks of the distance "obtained by separating the object and its appeal from one's own self, by putting it out of gear with practical needs,"[37] while Jerome Stolnitz defines an attitude of "disinterested and sympathetic attention to and contemplation of any object of awareness whatever, for its own sake alone."[38] If there really is a distinctive aesthetic attitude which we adopt toward works of art, then it may also be that adopting that attitude towards nonart *produces* art. But is there such an attitude, a qualitatively distinct mental set associated with aesthetic situations?

The most obvious way to address this question is to examine our experience. But introspection alone does not establish the existence of an aesthetic attitude. Accordingly, theorists have sought to delimit it in a more roundabout way. They examine cases in which the aesthetic attitude fails, then try to pinpoint what is missing. For example, J. O. Urmson, in the paper "What Makes a Situation Aesthetic?" proposes ways in which a play may provide its viewer with varieties of satisfaction that are not aesthetic: "A play may give me moral satisfaction, because I think it likely to have improving effects on the audience; economic satisfaction because it is playing to full houses and I am financing it; personal satisfaction because I wrote it and it is highly praised by the critics; intellectual satisfaction because it solves a number of difficult technical problems of the theatre very cleverly."[39] In a much-anthologized paper, "The Myth of the Aesthetic Attitude," George Dickie builds on such examples. Dickie argues that cases which attitude theorists would offer as examples of viewers paying *interested* attention to a play (for example, proud parents watching their daughter in a leading role, or any of Urmson's cases outlined above) "turn out to be just different ways of being distracted from the play and, hence, not cases of interested attention to the play."[40] If interested attention, which exemplifies the failure of the proper aesthetic attitude, turns out to be just so many varieties of *in*attention, then, suggests Dickie, disinterestedness or disinterested attention is nothing but successful attending, attending closely. ("This does seem to be all that is left after the aesthetic attitude has been purged of *distancing* and *disinterestedness*. The only thing which prevents the aesthetic attitude from collapsing into simple attention is the qualification *closely*."[41])

Dickie proposes, then, that we dispense with such hothouse notions as disinterestedness or the aesthetic attitude and content ourselves instead with degrees of attention. He admits that we can attend from a variety of motives, but he denies that different motivations make our attention itself interested or disinterested. There is a pleasing simplicity here, in that Dickie's theory eliminates a distinctively aesthetic mental set that we would have to treat as sui generis. In trendy terms, we might say that he advocates "naturalizing" the aesthetic attitude posited by Bullough and Stolnitz, replacing it with varieties and modes of attention. But questions remain about the nature of attention. Surely the attention we owe works of art is not rapt absorption or frozen fascination. Such states are too passive. We want to be engaged by works of art, perhaps even engrossed by them. But we also want to be able to think about these works, relate them to our experience, profit from them in various ways.

This much seems right about Dickie's critique of aesthetic-attitude theory. Our encounters with works of art are quite unlike the experiences Bullough and Stolnitz describe. Instead of concentrating on the work itself, we relate it to an increasingly wide array of objects: other works by the same artist, other artists' works similar in appearance, technique, style, or theme, natural objects which the work resembles or recalls. We also puzzle over the meaning of the work, ponder the artist's intentions, monitor our own responses and observe the reactions of others. In short, understanding and appreciating a work of art requires an *interested* attitude, one which reaches out to place the work in its artistic, social, historical—and personal—context. This expansive and integrative approach involves more than narrowly focused attention, and it is adopted in various situations besides aesthetic ones. Accordingly, it does not seem promising to delimit art or the aesthetic in terms of some mental set its audience enters.

I conclude that no given mental set characterizes our rich interactions with works of art. Nor does an aesthete make the world over into art merely by enjoying that world. It follows that the contextual features highlighted by Dickie's theory cannot simply be modes of attention. Rather, they are more complex institutional traits. Dickie indicates these very broadly when he describes the personnel and the subsystems that comprise the artworld. To spell out the details of his theory, he must specify the roles and responsibilities that pertain to or animate the various artworld personnel—also the practices and traditions that distinguish the different artworld systems. Dickie must offer constraints in both these areas if he is to avoid problems of permissiveness. That is, he must limit both who can declare herself to be an artist and what objects she can promote; otherwise his theory allows just *anything* to be art.

Such limits could be most plausibly introduced by incorporating references to the past practices of the framing social institution. Someone is an artist only if her interests and activities bear some relation to those of artists of the past; similarly, an object, concept, or event becomes a work of art only if it bears some relation to works of the past. Clearly, the relations in question cannot be anything so simple as similarity, or we would never have progress or evolution in art. Yet I believe that both categories—artist and work—can be defined by reference to a range of relations in which they must knowingly stand to their predecessors.[42] These might include repetition, variation, expansion, challenge, undermining, refutation. On this view, new art need not resemble art of the past, but it must somehow make reference to it—comment upon it, amplify it, sabotage it, and so on.[43]

While such connections are compatible with the artworld as Dickie describes it, they are not mandated by Dickie's account. These proposals should, I think, be treated as friendly amendments to Dickie's theory. Moreover, they are in keeping with some other recent attempts to answer the question "What is art?" In *Art and its Objects,* Richard Wollheim speaks of "the essential historicity of art." Arthur Danto remarks, "Not everything is possible at every time, as Heinrich Wölfflin has written, meaning that certain artworks simply could not be inserted as artworks into certain periods of history."[44] Answering the question "What is art?" then, requires explaining just what *is* possible at any given time, and why.

Why are works possible at some times and not at others? The claim I was defending above was this: while art evolves and our conceptions of art continually change, new works (and entire new *arts*) are introduced on the coattails of existing ones. The newly established art is seen and conceptualized in terms of works that are already entrenched. For example, abstract painting, modern dance, serial music, and performance art would all have been rejected by the artworld of the 1870s, yet today we treat them as accepted modes and styles. This is so in part because we can situate them with regard to what came before, see them as developing latent trends towards flatness, informality, atonality, and so on. The question then becomes how to determine the limits of this sort of vision. Can a given item be seen in terms of literally any other? Can just anything be seen as a poem, a painting, a play, a melody, a narrative, or a garden?

These last questions are very broad. Answers to them would fuel a theory of metaphor as well as an account of art. I will take them up again in my account of representation in chapter 5. But let me close by briefly describing one last theory, proposed by Noel Carroll, that suggests ways of framing and thinking about such questions. Carroll's theory, like Dickie's, provides a contextual account of art, but one that does more to acknowledge art's "historicity." Carroll argues that recent philosophy of art, at least in the Western analytic tradition, has been driven by the avant-garde.[45] Experimental and avant-garde works are viewed as "mutations" that theory must explain (314). The explanation takes the form of "identifying narratives" (315). Such narratives "tell . . . a story that links the contested work to preceding art-making practices and contexts in such a way that the work under fire can be seen to be the intelligible outcome of recognizable modes of thinking and making of a sort already commonly adjudged to be artistic" (316).[46] Thus Carroll's identifying narratives chart the sorts of connections between past and present art that, I argued above, need to be acknowledged in a revised and strengthened version of Dickie's theory.

Carroll emphasizes that "Identifying narratives are genetic accounts of the provenance of artworks; they do not simply track manifest resemblances" (318). A good Aristotelian, he insists that each narrative must have a beginning, a middle, and an end. The beginning describes some state of the artworld preceding the production of the work in question;[47] the end recounts the introduction of the work; and the middle gets us from here to there. Carroll's theory takes into account an artist's intentions in making a work and also her assessment of the art-world context in which the work is created. Overall, identifying narratives indicate "the artist's conception of what must be done in order to rectify, reform or revolutionize pre-existing practices" (320). Identifying narratives thus vet shocking or avant-garde works by showing their connection to acknowledged works that preceded them. Using these techniques, Carroll legitimates not only Alfred Jarry's 1896 play *Ubu Roi,* but also a recent lurid example of "that sub-genre of Performance Art often called Body Art . . . Rudolf Schwarkolger's fatal self-castration" (324).

Where do we stand now in our pursuit of the question "What is art?" Overall, any acceptable answer to this question must, I suggest, accommodate the following six problems or puzzles:

> 1. Art and Nature. Any acceptable theory must allow us to respond aesthetically to a broader range of phenomena than works of art, narrowly construed.

Yet it should not permit an aspiring avant-garde artist to appropriate some chunk of nature—say, a spectacular sunset over Key West.

2. Found Art. We're probably all sick of hearing about Duchamp's urinal, but any acceptable theory must explain how ordinary objects that were not art—Danto's "mere real things"—can become art.

3. The Historicity of Art. Not every work of art could be art at just any time. Try inserting a Jackson Pollock into the artworld of 1810, or a Max Beckmann into that of the Renaissance. So, any acceptable theory must allow our concept of art to expand and change, but it must also establish that what counts as art at any given moment depends in crucial ways on what has been art heretofore.

4. Originality. Particularly in the modern era, artists outdo one another seeking to break the rules that constrained their predecessors. Any acceptable theory must allow room for revolutionary change, yet stop short of simply saying, "Anything goes."

5. Interpretation. Not only do styles of art change over time; so too do our understandings of individual works. An acceptable theory must explain works of art so that they are variously interpretable and so that the meaning of a given work can change for successive generations.

6. Bad Art. No acceptable theory should include a normative dimension that judges all art as good. The category of art should be defined broadly enough that some art will be exemplary, some will be execrable, and much will remain in between.

The first two of these puzzles concern the scope of our concept of art; the next two concern relations between past and present art; the final two concern a topic I do not take up here, the evaluation of art. While Carroll's account of identifying narratives remains quite skeletal, the structure he outlines brings it about that individual works are knowingly inserted into the history of art by those who create them or those who promote them. I have outlined Carroll's theory here because I think it exemplifies the sort of elaboration needed to shore up Dickie's institutional theory. I believe that a theory *like* Dickie's—but more fully elaborated and historically buttressed—will solve the six puzzles sketched above.[48] I also believe that it will provide the best available account of the nature of art. It will not be a simple account, nor will it take the tidy form of a real definition, that is, one that comprises a set of necessary and sufficient conditions. Nevertheless, it will be sensitive to past goings-on in the artworld of our own culture as well as to the diversity of art across cultures and the continual changes over time in our very concept of art.

4. GARDEN RIDDLES

The relevance of all this for the aesthetics of gardens is this: we want to know when and whether gardens are art. Perhaps more than any other art, gardens belong in and partake of the everyday world. Looking at paintings is not qualitatively like looking at literal landscapes, nor is watching a play or reading a novel much like thinking about or observing the misadventures and crises of our friends. Yet our responses to gardens and to natural landscapes are similar in many respects. Compare and contrast the experiences of enjoying a garden and enjoying a natural scene. We scan each, attending to similar aspects: the beauty of particular plants and flowers, the arrangement of larger masses of color, the variety of textures, the play of light and shade, the appeal to our other senses, and so on.[49] It doesn't follow, however, that all nature is a garden or that all nature is a work of art. Compare two other cases where artists *have* succeeded in elevating nature into art: Christo and Jeanne-Claude's "wrapping" Florida islands in bright pink skirts, and James Turrell's reshaping Roden Crater, an extinct volcano in Arizona. The latter enterprises are self-consciously performed *as* art; they are offered *to* the artworld and commented on *by* the artworld. Examining them, we ask ourselves questions about meaning, artistry, design, and control that don't arise when we contemplate unadorned nature but that often are relevant when we examine gardens.

Of course not all gardens are works of art. The vegetable plot in my backyard consists of four unruly tomato plants, some wilting basil, and patches of volunteer arugula. One lone gaillardia blooms toward the front. The garden is unattractive and offers no reward beyond an abundance of tomatoes. Even a flower garden can fail to be art. A casually planted border of marigolds, pansies, bachelor's buttons, and geraniums flanking a walk or porch delights the senses and refreshes the spirits without aspiring to that higher status.

One contemporary aesthetician suggests some more complex cases of gardens that fail to be art. In his book *The Transfiguration of the Commonplace,* Arthur Danto proposes various pairs of indistinguishable objects where one is a work of art but its twin is not.[50] His paired examples include (1) a blue necktie which Picasso has mottled green and one similarly defaced by a finger-painting three-year-old and (2) a five-by-eight-foot monochromatic red canvas by a left-leaning abstract painter and an exactly similar sample of a paint company's brightest available red. Note that we can construct garden versions of Danto's cases. Compare a carefully cultivated woodland garden with a sunny glade deep in the woods which just happens to be filled with wildflowers; or a vast park landscaped by Capability Brown—central lake, smooth hills, clumps of trees—with a rolling cow pasture identical in layout and grazed until smooth.

Such examples help us to see just what factors contribute to something's being a work of art. Danto's point is that artworks are objects that *say* something, that are about the world. It follows that such works require interpretation. Their *esse* is *interpretari,* and an *art* world is, for Danto, "a world of *interpreted things.*[51] I think this view is ultimately quite compatible with the revised version of Dickie's theory proposed above. The sorts of considerations that explain when and how an object or event is interpretable would, I think, be just the sorts of historical, institutional, and contextual facts with which we were going to supplement Dickie's initial account of the artworld.

I will argue in the course of this book that at least some gardens can "speak" in the way Danto prescribes. Yet Mara Miller appears to contest this claim. She offers some reasons to think that *no* garden is a work of art. Danto's doppelganger examples just discussed show the importance of an artist's self-conscious intention to create a work of art. Miller maintains that a garden designer's intentions are much less efficacious than those of other artists. Gardeners are always battling nature, struggling against the effects of climate, soil, weather, pests, disease. Moreover, a garden is never a finished work, since it is always growing, dying, changing. As Miller points out, "Much of what we see in a garden . . . is being actively resisted by the gardenist, who spends exorbitant amounts of time weeding, pruning, mowing, raking, and otherwise counteracting the changes taking place in his design against his will."[52] The result is that much that occurs in a garden is beyond the gardener's control. Miller speculates that a garden "probably demands more unremitting effort and attention from its creator than any other art" (71), and she concludes that "we must acknowledge a radical difference between gardens and other arts as far as the degree of control . . . of the artist" is concerned (77).

Miller goes on to note further ways in which gardens differ from other works of art. There is no final form to a garden, no "unchanging *inert* core" (76); gardens cannot be moved or forged (74); they cannot be replicated or mass-produced (74). We might summarize Miller's position with the claim that gardens are "hyperunique," for she asserts, "At this point we may conclude that the garden is *too unique* to be a work of art."[53]

Miller's discussion of uniqueness highlights some unique garden features. Gardens can't be notated, moved, forged, or replicated because they are ever-changing and because they are site-specific.[54] Replicating a given garden in a new location cannot succeed even if exactly the same plants are placed in exactly the same array. The views and vistas from each spot would necessarily be altered in the duplicate garden, and these are an essential part of the overall aesthetic effect.[55] Even the notion that there is some fixed "target" garden to replicate can be called into question. We have already admitted that gardens are constantly changing. In a perennial bed where the first tulips and daffodils are supplant-

Above and on facing page: Christo and Jeanne-Claude, *Surrounded Islands, Biscayne Bay, Greater Miami, Florida, 1980–83.* © 1983 Christo. Photographs by Wolfgang Volz.

ed by clusters of iris, then by frothy columbine and astilbes, next by coneflowers and gaillardia, and finally by hostas and mums, what counts as "the" garden? Successive time slices? The entirety of whatever occurs (grows?) on that site? Whatever occurs on that site over time as intended or designed by some one garden designer? And finally, what might we do to notate this or any garden? To start, we would need something like a contour map of the site. But then how would we indicate the pattern of plants succeeding one another, the series of blooms, their different heights, colors, textures?

Note that none of these difficulties removes gardens from the realm of art. There are aleatory arts which are just as indeterminate as gardens. Consider improvisational music, Merce Cunningham choreography, or even a Calder mobile shifting in the wind. And, there are environmental works which are just as site-specific as gardens. Consider the

earthworks of Robert Smithson, Michael Heizer, Walter de Maria, and Nancy Holt. (Such works will be discussed in more detail in chapter 7.) In sum, since much present-day art is site-specific, uncontrolled, and without final form, Miller's argument does not disqualify gardens as works of art.

Even granting that some gardens are works of art, we need to say more about the possibilities of changing status. One of the virtues of Dickie's institutional theory of art outlined earlier is its provision for the elevation of quotidian objects from nonart to art. If we grant that not all gardens *are* art, then there are two garden parallels to the cases Dickie considers. A purely utilitarian garden might be transformed into art; and, there might be "found" gardens akin to found art. Here something not a garden at all would become both a garden *and* a work of art. I think both cases present difficulties. Examining them will help us appreciate the ways in which gardens differ from other types of art.

Consider first the case where a Georgian kitchen garden, planted for entirely utilitarian ends, comes to be treated as a work of art. (If this seems outlandish, compare our treatment of primitive pottery or colonial American tools.) Kitchen gardens had a traditional layout which remained unchanged for many centuries.[56] High walls enclosed a rectilinear plot bisected by paths running north-south and east-west. The paths were bordered with parsley and strawberries and the walls supported espaliered fruit trees and vines. Modest gardens would supply cabbages, artichokes, spinach, fennel, and asparagus, as well as a considerable variety of greens and herbs.

What would it take to come to see such a garden as art? Merely judging the garden overall, or particular parts or plants, to be beautiful would not suffice. Beauty is not necessary for art, and the discovery of natural beauty is not sufficient. On Dickie's view, judging something to be beautiful differs from treating it as a work of art because only the latter requires an institutional background—that dauntingly complex compilation of all the arts, all the roles connected with them, and all the conventions and practices their interaction begets, which Dickie dubbed the artworld.[57]

To appreciate this institutional involvement, compare the case of Early American quilts. Originally created above all to provide warmth, such quilts are now displayed in art museums, discussed appreciatively in books, and collected by connoisseurs. Seeing these quilts on display, we are struck by how much their bold patterns resemble and anticipate modern-day abstract expressionist paintings. It is just such judgments that indicate these quilts' entry into the artworld. We no longer attend to their practical features (inches of loft) or to their historical import (what they tell us about eighteenth-century American needlework, housekeeping, and sleep habits) but to their formal and semantic properties (color, pattern, texture, meaning). In many ways, then, our treatment of such quilts is affected by our treatment of paintings. The two certainly don't become indistinguishable—we don't ignore the differences between pigment and cloth, between brush and needle and thread. But our experience of the one informs our experience of the other, primes our judgments and expectations.

Return now to the garden case. What might prompt the apotheosis of the lowly kitchen garden into a work of art? To parallel the quilt example, it seems that two things are required: (1) kitchen gardens are not initially considered works of art, and (2) people come to regard them in terms of some other art form, such that attitudes, expectations, and judgments are transferred from the one realm to the other. It is an open question what that other art form might be—perhaps other gardens with more clear-cut aesthetic intent, perhaps some three-dimensional and highly textured art like embroidery, low-relief sculpture, or collage. To say that a kitchen garden could become a work of art is simply to leave open the possibility of this sort of integrative vision. We can no more imagine or predict the details of this vision today than nineteenth-century art lovers could imagine or predict such features of the twentieth-century artworld as environmental art, conceptual art, or "cunt art."

Almost anything can count as art in the twentieth century. Does the same license extend to gardens? Can *anything* be a garden? What is to prevent me from declaring the room in which I'm now writing—a small sunporch with tiled floor, lawn furniture, and a dog's bed and bowls—to be a garden? Perhaps an answer can be modeled on Dickie's and Carroll's accounts of art. Within each culture, ongoing conventions determine what sorts of things can count as gardens. These conventions evolve and change, influenced by goings-on within and without the culture. At present there is no precedent in our culture for declaring the room of a house—a room, moreover, without a single growing thing—to be a garden in any but a metaphorical sense. We could of course apply that metaphor and come to see the room *as* a garden. This would involve considerable strain as the room is, in summer, hot and barren. Nor does it bear any functional resemblance to the atrium of a Moorish palace or a Mediterranean villa. The room is not central, not at the heart of the house, and it is neither cool nor refreshing. In sum, to declare the room a metaphorical garden is to make a bad metaphor.[58]

Note that the notion of family resemblance, which Wittgenstein introduced to explain the workings of general terms like "game," "chair," and "garden," is itself metaphorical. While I am here asking what can count as members of the family "garden"—siblings, if you will—I shall in my closing chapter take up the question of more distant relations, asking what might count as, say, cousins of the gardens we now know, and how we might identify relatives several generations removed from the grand gardens of seventeenth- and eighteenth-century Europe.

In discussing our changing concept of art, I suggested that new arts are introduced on the coattails of existing ones. The newly established art is understood in terms of one that is already accepted. In that context, and in the context of the room-as-garden example, it becomes important to know the limits of such inter-art comparisons. Just as metaphors can range from illuminating to awkward to misleading, so too the assimilation of one art to another can be varyingly successful. There is a long tradition of such comparisons, dating back at least to Aristotle. Much of this book will be devoted to exploring this issue in the case of gardens. In asking what gardens can do and what they can be, I am really asking in what ways they can resemble their sister arts.

In what follows, I propose to look at eighteenth-century gardens which were clearly and consciously created *as* works of art and see how those two worlds—the world of art and the world of gardens—come together.

SOME EIGHTEENTH-CENTURY
BACKGROUND

My aim at this point is to sketch some of the background to the philosophical and aesthetic issues raised by eighteenth-century English gardens. My topics will include the gardening style of seventeenth-century France, which predominated in England at the turn of the century, the institution of the grand tour, which acquainted so many Englishmen with the artistic and cultural achievements of Italy and France, and finally, the academies of art established in Paris and London in the seventeenth and eighteenth centuries.

I. THE FRENCH FORMAL GARDEN

While eighteenth-century English gardens can be traced back to Italian Renaissance models, and ultimately to the gardens of ancient Greece and Rome, I would like to examine their more proximate ancestors, the gardens of seventeenth-century France. French gardens were themselves deeply indebted to Italy; when Charles VIII led his army to Italy and conquered Naples in 1494, Frenchmen saw for the first time the glories of Italian Renaissance civilization. Delighted by the gardens he saw adjoining Italian villas, Charles brought back with him twenty-two Italian artists and four tons of artistic booty.[1] A distinctively French gardening style was to develop from these Italian borrowings.

By the time of Louis XIV France was all-powerful. Her hegemony extended beyond politics and warfare to include culture and the arts. French style was imitated in all things, and French gardens sprang up throughout Europe. Since eighteenth-century English gardeners were clearly influenced by and reacting to the predominant French style, I would like to give a brief account of a paradigmatic French formal garden—Louis XIV's estate at Versailles as it evolved from the 1660s until the king's death in 1715.

It is well known how André Le Nôtre came to design the gardens at Versailles. Louis's finance minister, Nicholas Fouquet, hired a trio of artists—the architect Le Vau, the painter Le Brun, and the gardener Le Nôtre—to create his new chateau at Vaux-le-Vicomte. There was no preexisting structure to improve or renovate. The entire complex was built from scratch. It was an undertaking on an unprecedented scale, employing some eighteen thousand men.[2] As William Howard Adams reports, "three offending villages were leveled and the river Angueil marshalled into a canal over three thousand feet long. Earth was moved to form massive terraces, parterres, and ramps, followed by tree planting on an imposing scale."[3] A grand fete was held in 1661 to celebrate the completion of the ensemble. Offended by the conspicuous extravagance of his underling, Louis had him arrested and shortly hired away his trio of artists to improve the small hunting lodge he had inherited at Versailles.

The gardens at Vaux (considered by some Le Nôtre's masterpiece) and at Versailles exhibit the quintessential traits of the French formal garden: symmetry, grandeur, and great expanse. These gardens are rectilinear and architectural, unified by recurrent geometry and relentless axial symmetry. Their design relates house to garden and each garden part to every other.[4] The broad alleys crossing at right angles or radiating outwards in a patte d'oie (goose foot) pattern mark the gardens' structure. While earlier French gardens were often centered on some architectural feature which closed off the view, Le Nôtre swept the alleys to the very horizon, appropriating and controlling all the visible landscape.[5] The rectilinear areas within the intersections of these alleys were often given over to *parterres*. These were low gardens (the word comes from "par" and "terre," meaning on or along the ground), in which clipped boxwood, flowers, and colored gravel traced ornate patterns recalling Venetian lace or elaborate brocade. Hence the term *parterre de broderie*, in reference to the art of embroidery. The parterres were designed to be viewed from a lofty vantage point, often one within the chateau itself.[6]

The symmetry and axiality of such views helped to unify the garden. These traits also allowed French gardens to be expanded and added to indefinitely simply by extending the axes and incorporating more land into the garden grid. Le Nôtre did just this in his fifty years of continuous work at Versailles. Comparing a series of garden plans from different

The Orangerie and Parterre du midi at Versailles, engraved by Perelle. Reproduced by permission of the Bibliothèque Nationale de France, Paris.

A boxwood parterre at Courances. Photograph by Edwin Smith.

years, F. Hamilton Hazlehurst shows how the gardener would first work in one area of the garden, say the northern parterres, then enlarge the southern sections to balance the transverse axis.[7] The chateau also played a role in this give and take. At times the gardens overwhelmed the building, awaiting intended architectural improvements that would bring the two back into harmony; at other times expansion of the building rendered the existing garden inappropriate and necessitated further work there.[8]

Water was another crucial feature of the French formal garden. The medieval moat gave way to canals traversed by pleasure boats, and fountains and waterworks abounded. The Grand Canal at Versailles was nearly a mile long, with cross canals every half mile. At various times Dutch sailors and Venetian gondoliers were hired to ply its waters.[9] Christopher Thacker claims that "Versailles was in Louis's reign a water garden, one of the great water gardens in the world."[10] At their zenith, the king's gardens contained fourteen hundred fountains.[11] This imposed considerable hardship, however, for water was always in short supply. Despite the construction of the machine of Marly in 1688, whose fourteen water wheels raised water from the Seine to reservoirs serving the gardens, and despite ambitious plans to divert local rivers, the fountains could not all play simultaneously. A scheme of signals was devised so that when the king toured the gardens, various water effects could be turned on and off in step with his progress.[12]

As Christopher Thacker notes, Versailles lacked the temples and follies associated with so many gardens from the Renaissance on (153). There were, however, sculptural ensembles throughout the park, and these contributed to a unified iconographical program, one assimilating Louis XIV to the sun god Apollo. André Félibien, a contemporary visitor, commented on this conceit as follows: "Since the Sun is the king's device, and since the poets identify the sun with Apollo, there is nothing in this superb edifice which is not linked to this divinity."[13]

A final ingredient in Le Nôtre's ensemble were the *bosquets*, or groves. These intimate wooded areas provided a relief from the formality and monumentality of the garden as a whole. They were often entered by a single path, and the surrounding greenery cut off any views of the larger ensemble. Within, each enclave contained virtuosic waterworks and places for conversation, dining, and entertainment. The bosquets were altered often during the years Le Nôtre worked at Versailles. For example, the Bosquet des Sources, created in 1675, was replaced by the Colonnade some ten years later,[14] while in 1677 two earlier bosquets, the Pavillon d'Eau and the Berceau d'Eau, gave way to the Arc de Triomphe and the Trois Fontaines.[15] Thus the bosquets were treated much as an art collector treats his paintings, constantly altering the selection open for view.

Let me briefly describe two of the bosquets. I am drawing heavily throughout this sec-

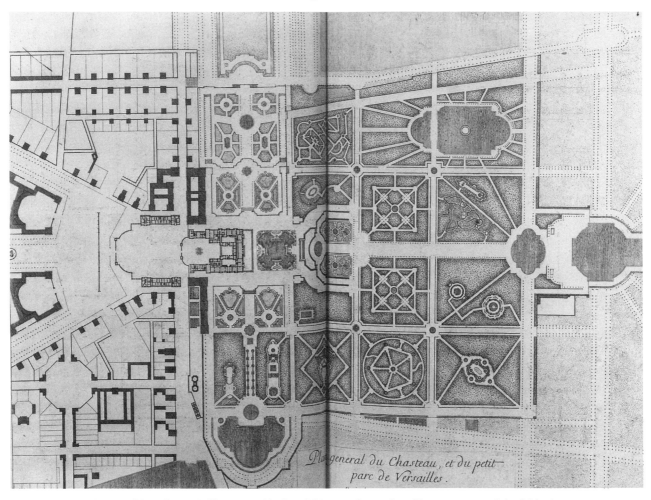

A plan of Versailles in 1689, engraved by Israel Silvestre. Reproduced by permission of the Bibliothèque Nationale de France, Paris.

tion on F. Hamilton Hazlehurst's superb book *Gardens of Illusion*. One bosquet, the Marais, was proposed by Louis's mistress, Louise de La Vallière (91). At its center was a rectangular pool containing a metallic tree. The tree was in fact an elaborate fountain, and water sprayed from its branches and leaves. The border of the basin was lined with metallic ferns and flowers. These too were fountains, as were the gilded swans gracing each corner. White marble tables at each end of the pool supported baskets of gilded flowers from which jets of water streamed. And finally, along each side of the pool stood two *buffets d'eau.* These were tiers of red and white marble bearing a "mock feast"—urns and vases spewing water in fanciful and diverse forms.

Hazlehurst criticizes the Marais as fussy (91) and claims that later bosquets were nobler in scale and conception. Jean Cotelle's painting of the Trois Fontaines (reproduced on page 119 of Hazlehurst's book) shows a long, sloping site divided into three terraces. Each terrace is occupied by a fountain of a different geometric shape—an octagon at the bottom, then a square, then a circle. Water plays from the fountains in myriad ways forming vertical jets, arching crowns, and sparkling liquid tunnels. The three levels are joined by subtly varied stairways and rocaille cascades. When the entire ensemble is viewed on axis, the various fountains align: the arch of the middle level frames the jets of the uppermost pool, and water seems to spill down the upper cascade and flow to the square pool below (111-12). These carefully crafted illusions add to the joy of the bosquet.

To get some sense of the unity and power of Le Nôtre's creation, consider the view west along the main garden axis in the 1670s, shortly after the elongation of the Grand Canal. The garden facade of the chateau extended for more than six hundred feet. A viewer standing there, or looking down from Le Vau's recently completed *envelope* which enlarged and balanced that facade, first saw a complex water parterre which mixed water, green borders, plants in vases, and sculpture (79). Its basins were swirling and complicated in form, with a round central pool flanked by four cloverleaf basins (81).[16] Beyond the water parterre stairs led down to the Jardin Bas, a large area of parterres culminating in the Latona Basin. This basin contributed to the garden's iconography for it honored Latona, the mother of Apollo. Legend had it that Latona, banished by the jealous Juno, was jeered by peasants while trying to drink at a spring. As punishment her lover Jupiter turned them into frogs.[17] The Latona Basin features the goddess at the center. Spouting frogs ring the pool's periphery, while various figures in between, writhing and spouting water, are shown midway in their transformation from human to amphibian form (82).

West of the Latona Basin began the Allée Royale, a majestic avenue with broad walks enclosing a central green sward, the *tapis vert*. Beyond the allée was the Grand Canal, which continued along the western axis for nearly a mile. At the juncture of the allée and the canal lay another magnificent fountain, the Bassin d'Apollon. Apollo, the horses which pulled his chariot, and various tritons and whales filled the large quatrefoil basin (83).

The Grand Canal was enlarged in 1671 in order to balance the newly renovated western front of the chateau and to match in scale and grandeur the growing gardens (83). Le Nôtre carefully adjusted the proportions of the canal and the Allée Royale so that they would appear equal in width when viewed from the chateau's second-story terrace. This

Bosquet des Trois Fontaines, painted by Jean Cotelle. Musée de Versailles. Photograph from Réunion des Musées Nationaux.

A view along the main garden axis of Versailles with the Latona Fountain in the foreground and the Grand Canal in the distance. Photograph by Edwin Smith.

illusion was accomplished only by making the canal in fact much wider than the allée, and by increasingly elongating the three basins marking the beginning, middle, and end of the canal so that they would all three appear equal and square when viewed from afar (84). From different vantage points, parts of the western garden axis would come in and out of view,[18] thus adding further subtleties to Le Nôtre's scheme.

Le Nôtre devoted great energy to optical effects of the sort just described. Versailles was a garden which constantly controlled and manipulated its viewers' perceptual experience. The vista I have been describing, which stretched westward from the chateau to the visible limits of the horizon, both constituted and expressed Louis's absolute control over a vast stretch of land and, symbolically, over an entire nation. Thacker puts this aspect of Versailles into context, noting that such "conspicuous use of land to adorn one's residence, without any return of crops or fattening of cattle was a sign of power, and a proof of wealth—English landlords, and even the English monarch, could not afford this ostentation" (152).

Versailles makes a statement not only through its extent, the vast *amount* of land which is put to such use, but through the manner in which that land is leveled, tamed, and regularized, emblazoned with features and designs which everywhere testify to the glory of the Sun King. The magnificence of the gardens of Versailles can be appreciated all the more if we keep in mind how inappropriate and inhospitable the site was to begin with. The swampy and marshy terrain was described by the duc de Saint-Simon as "that most dismal and thankless of spots, without vistas, woods, or water, without soil, even, for all the surrounding land is quicksand or bog."[19] He went on to complain that though the gardens were magnificent, enjoying them was difficult: "To reach any shade one is forced to cross a vast, scorching expanse. The broken stones on the paths burn one's feet, yet without them one would sink into sand or the blackest mud." We should note that Saint-Simon's assessment of the gardens of Versailles is belied by their extraordinary popularity. Visitors crowded the grounds on the rare occasions when they were open to the general public, special tours were arranged for visiting nobility, and Louis himself wrote a guide-book or itinerary, *La manière de montrer les jardins de Versailles,* to aid visitors in appreciating the garden's splendors.

2. THE GRAND TOUR

Before the death of Louis XIV, England (and all Europe) was under the cultural sway of seventeenth-century France. Critics and theorists read French treatises in translation, playwrights debated the Aristotelian unities, painters honored the strict hierarchy of genres established by the Académie royale (see below), and gardens were laid out in the French formal style. France's political power waned with the death of the king, but further factors contributed to the decline of her aesthetic hegemony. One of these was the development of the grand tour—the practice of young English gentlemen completing their education with a tour of the Continent.

Englishmen had long traveled in Europe. For example, Sir Philip Sidney made such a journey in 1572 in preparation for a diplomatic career; John Milton and Robert Boyle were among those who made tours in the seventeenth century; and the gardener and diarist John Evelyn spent the years 1643–47 traveling on the Continent in order to avoid the turmoil following the Civil War.[20] However, travel became easier after the Peace of Utrecht in 1715, and the eighteenth century marked the heyday of the tour. (B. Sprague Allen notes that the word "tourist" was coined toward the end of the eighteenth century.)[21]

Young Englishmen were typically accompanied by tutors or "bear leaders" whose purpose was to instruct their charges and also to safeguard their moral and religious development. Among the distinguished Englishmen who served at one time or another in this capacity were Thomas Hobbes, Adam Smith, and Joseph Addison. Italy was the ultimate destination of the grand tour. The usual itinerary took travelers across the Channel, then to Paris where the pupils applied themselves to the study of French. A frightening journey across the Alps led to Italy. After venturing as far south as Naples, most English tourists returned home through Germany and the Low Countries.[22]

The grand tour just described was fraught with dangers and discomforts. Banditti roamed the Italian countryside, and those who attempted a sea passage to Italy were threatened by the Barbary pirates. Roads were primitive and most inns, wretched. Tourists crossed the Alps in precarious sedan chairs, their coaches dismantled and packed on mules.[23] Horace Walpole's pet spaniel was snatched by a wolf when his party entered Italy by way of Mont Cenis.[24] Despite such difficulties, the tour became more and more routinized. J. H. Plumb writes that "the flow of young men, tutors, and servants had become so large by the 1760's that the structure of modern travel gradually came into existence— printed guidebooks containing maps, road conditions, money and conversion tables; phrase books in every language; coach-hire systems; lists of recommended hotels; couriers; foreign exchange facilities; and specialized guides to beauty spots."[25] The most popular guidebook was Thomas Nugent's *The Grand Tour: Containing an Exact Description of Most of the Cities, Towns, and Remarkable Places of Europe*, first published in 1743.[26]

Not all young men profited from the grand tour. Many looked back with regret at the laziness and dissipation that had attended their travels. The pursuit of prostitutes and love affairs figures prominently in James Boswell's memoirs of his tour of the Continent. For a time in Rome he set himself the challenge of having a different woman each day.[27] Sir Francis Dashwood, whose garden at West Wycombe will be discussed below, disgraced himself in various ways on his tour. He wooed the Princess of Russia while disguised as Charles XII (then deceased), and he was banished from the Vatican for setting upon flagellants at St. Peter's with a horsewhip.[28]

Many Englishmen also earned criticism for their constant complaints and their intolerance of foreign customs and manners. One Frenchman wrote in 1785 that "In a hundred there are not two that seek to instruct themselves. To cover leagues on land or on water; to take punch and tea at the inns; to speak ill of all the other nations, and to boast without ceasing of their own; that is what the crowd of English call travelling."[29] Walpole declared Paris "the ugliest beastliest town in the universe . . . a dirty town with a dirtier ditch calling itself the Seine," while Hazlitt objected to Rome's "almost uninterrupted succession of narrow, vulgar-looking streets, where the smell of garlick prevails over the odour of antiquity."[30] Lord Chesterfield mocked those English tourists who rose late, breakfasted at length with other Englishmen, spent the day at the English coffee house, and after dinner and a play retired "to the tavern again, where they get very drunk, and where they either quarrel among themselves, or sally forth, commit some riot in the streets, and are taken up by the watch."[31]

Despite such complaints, England benefited immensely from the institution of the grand tour. Important artistic and cultural changes were sparked by the experiences of the travelers. Above all, the tour awakened Englishmen to the legacy of Greece and Rome. Italy was unlike anything they had ever seen. The Roman campagna was imbued with the spirit of antiquity and dotted with actual ruins—reminders of classical civilization. Plumb writes that "the young aristocrats, whether artistically inclined or not, were taught to revere not only the arts but also the past which enshrined them, and so the classical heritage became a vital force in their lives. . . . They saw themselves as the heirs of a great tradition."[32]

The practical effects of this legacy were many. Architecture, for example, came increasingly to reflect ancient models.[33] In the seventeenth century Inigo Jones traveled twice to Italy. He studied treatises (by Vitruvius, Alberti, Serlio, Vignola, and Palladio) as well as Roman ruins and Palladian villas. Jones's designs revolutionized English architecture. He "broke with the current fumbling Jacobean style and revealed how profoundly he had assimilated the spirit of Italian classicicism."[34]

In the eighteenth century, Richard Boyle, third earl of Burlington, became the chief patron of the Palladian revival. An amateur architect, Burlington made two trips to Italy. In Rome he met the painter, architect, and garden designer William Kent who became his friend and protege. Among the architectural projects directly influenced by Burlington's travels were the remodeling of Burlington House in Palladian style and the construction of a country house at Chiswick based on Palladio's Villa Rotonda.[35] The formal gardens at Chiswick were also altered in ways clearly indebted to the Renaissance gardens Burlington and Kent had viewed in Italy. In addition, Burlington supervised the English publication of Palladio's writings on architecture, and in 1728 he sponsored Robert Castell's work *Villas of the Ancients*, which reconstructed accounts of Pliny's villas and gardens in Rome.

The Society of Dilettanti exemplifies further ways in which the grand tour fostered awareness of Europe's classical heritage. The society was founded in 1732 to encourage interest in art and antiquities. Membership was restricted to those gentlemen who had completed a grand tour. The Dilettanti met regularly in various London taverns (prompting Horace Walpole's sarcastic remark that "the nominal qualification for membership is having been in Italy, and the real one being drunk").[36] The society sponsored archeological expeditions and scholarly publications. The latter ranged from James Stuart and Nicholas Revett's *The Antiquities of Athens Measured and Delineated* (published in four volumes from 1762 to 1816) to Richard Payne Knight's treatise on the worship of Priapus.[37] Richard Chandler's five volumes on *Ionian Antiquities* (also sponsored by the Society of Dilettanti), the excavations of Herculaneum and Pompeii under the patronage of Charles VII, King of Naples,[38] and Piranesi's popular etchings of romanticized ruins all provide further testimony to the eighteenth century's engagement with its classical past.

England also received more concrete benefits from the grand tour. For instance, Burlington returned from his first trip to Italy with 878 pieces of baggage.[39] This is an extreme example of the booty taken home by eighteenth-century tourists. A contemporary of Burlington's, Thomas Coke, spent six years on the Continent. He purchased antique sculpture and, as B. Sprague Allen reports, "on one occasion he was actually arrested for attempting to smuggle a fine headless figure of Diana out of the country. Four other precious pieces of antique sculpture were lost at sea on their way to England."[40] It was generally expected that Englishmen would return from their tour of Italy with valuable souvenirs. (Hibbert gives the following elaborate list: "books of prints, medals, maps, paintings and copies of paintings at Rome, as well as scent, pomatums, bergamot, imperial oil, and *aqua di millefiori;* snuff-boxes and silk from Venice; glasses from Murano; swords, canes, soap and rock-crystal from Milan; mosaics of dendrite, and amber, musk, and myrrh from Florence; point lace, sweet-meats and velvet from Genoa; snuff and sausages from Bologna; fire-arms from Brescia; milled gloves from Turin; masks from Modena; spurs and toys from Reggio nell'Emilia.")[41] Soon a network of picture jobbers sprang up to aid travelers with their purchases. Hogarth described them as "importing, by shiploads, Dead Christs, Holy Families, Madonnas, and other dark, dismal subjects, on which they scrawl the names of Italian masters."[42] A present-day writer adds that "behind these dealers were the native Italian painters and sculptors, 'restoring' Greek and Roman statues, faking Leonardos and Guido Renis, or sometimes, as with the immensely successful Pompeo Batoni, painting portraits of visiting Milords."[43]

Despite the dangers of fraud and deception, Englishmen like Robert Walpole, Thomas Coke, and William Cavendish built up art collections of major importance in the eighteenth century.[44] And less wealthy tourists still acquired an interest in the appreciation and acquisition of art. This was the second great legacy of the grand tour.

Landscape painting did not flower in England until the eighteenth century. Earlier, portraiture had been the most popular genre, followed by the solemn historical and religious paintings prescribed by French theorists and academicians (see below). The grand tour changed all this by exposing English travelers to new sorts of natural landscapes—the Alps and the Roman campagna—and to the landscape paintings of the French and Italian masters. In her book *Mountain Gloom and Mountain Glory,* Marjorie Hope Nicholson documents the change in taste that occurred in the eighteenth century with regard to mountain scenery. While seventeenth-century poets and theologians conceived of mountains as "warts, wens, and blisters" that mar the earth, travelers in the eighteenth century sought them out as sources of the sublime. The arduous journey across the Alps primed English tourists to appreciate the landscape paintings of Salvator Rosa. His romantic scenes of fearsome banditti amid craggy, fir-clad hills fed the growing taste for rugged scenes. At the same time, the experience of Italy's classical heritage allowed tourists to enjoy the arcadian landscapes painted by Nicholas Poussin and Claude Lorrain. These two aesthetic poles, represented by the Alps on the one hand and Rome on the other, were codified in Edmund Burke's work *A Philosophical Inquiry into the Origin of Our Ideas of the Sublime and Beautiful* (1757). A third aesthetic category, the picturesque, was added later in the century. It was associated with the painter Gaspard Dughet (see chap. 5).

Works by Claude, Poussin, Rosa, and Dughet were brought back to England by returning tourists. The paintings functioned as personal and affecting reminders of the tourists' travels. The wide dissemination of prints and engravings also did much to increase the popularity of these four artists.[45] In the end, the works of Claude, Rosa, and Dughet became so closely associated, respectively, with the aesthetic categories of the beautiful, the sublime, and the picturesque that the artists' names became a shorthand for describing certain sorts of scenes. For example, Horace Walpole, recording a journey over the Alps, wrote: "Precipices, mountains, torrents, wolves, rumblings, Salvator Rosa!"[46] Later in the century, a tourist guide promised to conduct the traveler "from the delicate touches of *Claude,* verified on *Coniston* Lake, to the noble scenes of *Poussin,* exhibited in *Windermer*-water, and from there to the stupendous romantic ideas of *Salvator Rosa,* realized in the Lake of *Derwent.*"[47]

This last quotation indicates one final legacy of the grand tour. Beginning with the final decades of the eighteenth century, the new attitudes toward travel and tourism cultivated on the tour were turned toward Britain herself. English men and women began to travel in pursuit of their native land's beauties, antiquities, and culture. The Wye Valley,

Landscape with Hermits, by Salvatore Rosa. Denis Mahon collection. Photograph courtesy of the Witt Library, Courtauld Institute of Art, University of London.

the Lake District, the Welsh mountains, and the Scottish Highlands were favorite desti-
nations, and guidebooks to these areas proliferated. For example, William Gilpin published the first of his series of *Observations Relative Chiefly to Picturesque Beauty* in 1782;
it was a report of a tour of the Wye Valley taken twelve years earlier. In 1799, Charles
Heath published *Excursion down the Wye,* a compendium of extracts from Gilpin and
other authors together with "copious historical and topographical information."[48]

In addition to providing practical advice and arcane facts, the guidebooks encouraged
travelers to cultivate aesthetic responses to the landscapes they viewed. Tourists not only
described natural scenes in terms of the paintings of Claude, Rosa, and Dughet; they also
attempted their own sketches. Drawing pads, pens and pencils, watercolor sets, and a
"Claude glass" were among the standard accoutrements of the picturesque tourist.[49] Many
guidebooks furthered this enterprise by identifying "station points" where the tourists
should pause and produce their sketches (see chap. 5).

As a result of the grand tour and its British extensions, English gentlemen aspired to
be amateurs of the arts, men of taste. Hussey writes that the eighteenth century saw a new
class emerge in English society, the connoisseur.[50] Another author notes that "the fash-
ionable young man of the day not only tried his hand at nature poetry but he copied landscape paintings, sketched from the out-of-doors, and designed gardens in delightful self-
confidence."[51] We are left with the picture of the enlightened amateur who returned from
his tour of the Continent, built up his cabinet of paintings and prints, read treatises on the
arts, improved his estate, and traveled the British countryside seeking out picturesque
scenes. Overall, the institution of the grand tour did much to heighten interest in both
landscape and landscape improvement—the art of gardening.

3. ACADEMIES AND THEORY

While the grand tour was responsible for the creation of countless amateurs of the arts, the
seventeenth and eighteenth centuries also saw an important change in the status of art
professionals. During the reign of Louis XIV French artists broke away from the medieval
guilds and formed the Académie royale de peinture et de sculpture. The development of
the Académie—and of the dogmatic doctrines associated with it—helped to elevate painting from a mechanical to a liberal art. It also vastly improved the social status of artists.

In France at the beginning of the seventeenth century, the art of painting was under
the control of the medieval guild known as the Maîtrise. The guild's privileges, confirmed
repeatedly by monarchs dating back to Philip the Fair in 1260, included setting the terms
of apprenticeship, regulating the importation of works of art, and barring nonmembers

from keeping an open shop.[52] In 1646 the Maîtrise tried to extend its power by limiting the number of independent artists who could be employed by the crown. The court artists (members of the royal *Valets de chambre* and *Brevetaires*), angered by this move, began to plan an organization to rival the Maîtrise. Their plan won royal approval, and in 1648 the Royal Academy of Painting and Sculpture held its founding meeting.

The arguments offered in support of the fledgling Académie and the rules laid down at its first meeting show that the institution was intended to serve a number of complementary purposes. Like every other royal institution in seventeenth-century France, the Académie had a political task—to glorify the reign of Louis XIV. But its founders also hoped to ennoble the art of painting and to raise the social status of painters. Finally, the explicit charge to the Académie was that of educating young artists. Its primary focus was pedagogical. But the doctrines and values at the core of the curriculum did much to further the larger goals just listed.

The Académie did not provide the entirety of a young artist's education. Students still lived with their masters and learned the skills of painting, carving, and the modeling of figures in their masters' workshops. To gain admission to the Académie, each student had to present a certificate from his master.[53] The Académie, however, held a monopoly on life drawing,[54] and the academic program was built around a set progression: drawing from drawings, drawing from plaster casts (and originals) of antique sculpture, drawing from live models. These activities were supplemented by lectures on perspective, geometry, and anatomy.[55]

In addition to the traditional course of study just described, the Parisian program offered one important innovation. Beginning in 1667, members of the Académie presented a series of lectures or *conférences* on theoretical and practical problems of art. These lectures were first proposed in the academy's founding statutes of 1648,[56] but except for a series of "pompous harangues" in 1653, intended to humiliate the members of the Maîtrise and drive them from the academy,[57] nothing was done to implement the plan. It was not until Colbert, the king's finance minister, was named vice-protector of the Académie that the founders' ambitious intentions were realized.

Colbert saw that the Académie could contribute in important ways to the splendor and glory of Louis's regime. For the last nineteen years of his life, Colbert carefully monitored the academy's activities. He insisted that the long-awaited lecture series commence, he attended the sessions, and he chided the academicians when they tried to wriggle out of this obligation.[58] Most important of all, Colbert stressed the educational benefits of the lectures. He demanded that each discussion yield a rule, or *précepte positif,* that would be inscribed in the academy's official register. In 1667 Colbert declared that "the decisions of the Académie should be accompanied by the reasons used to determine each resolution . . . and not offered naked to the public like oracles one is obliged to believe. Since these matters are all subject to reasoning, anyone whose opinion differs from that of the Académie will surrender once he considers the reasons and demonstrations and responses to the objections he might make."[59]

This reliance on reason shows that Colbert and the academicians were eager to formulate a theory of art, a science of beauty. Convinced that the arts of music and poetry had "infallible rules" leading to each art's perfection, they sought to create an equivalent set of rules which would guarantee the perfection of painting.[60] The historian Louis Hourticq emphasizes this point: "Of all the arts, it is only painting and sculpture which lack, among their rudiments, a doctrine which is certain. The poet obeys the imperious demands of grammar; the musician studies harmony and counterpoint with their mathematical rigor; the architect absorbs geometry and mechanics which are the most exact of sciences. Is it only the painter who must rest content with an empirical apprenticeship? . . . The fundamentals of his art, drawing and painting, don't go beyond the practical. . . . The Academicians didn't want this."[61]

Colbert believed that the "laws of beauty" were best discovered by closely scrutinizing the works of the masters rather than by talking in generalities about art.[62] Accordingly, he proposed a format for the lectures. Each month one of the best paintings in the king's collection would be explained by an expert in front of the entire academy. For eleven years the *académiciens* adhered conscientiously to Colbert's scheme.[63] When first initiated, the monthly lectures were extremely popular. Various entries in the official proceedings of the Académie note measures taken to alleviate the clamor and confusion as the public flocked in to attend the sessions.[64] Most present-day readers, however, are shocked in looking over the texts of the *conférences*. They seem puerile and petty, greatly removed from what we consider today to be legitimate art criticism. Although writers today criticize the academy's doctrines and deplore their effect on seventeenth-century French painting,[65] the Parisian *conférences* become less puzzling when we assess them in light of the academy's overall goal. Above all the academicians were concerned to put painting on an equal footing with the two most established and respected arts of the time, literature and theater.[66]

The theory which emerged from the Académie's discussions and debates can be reconstructed from the lectures themselves and from the writings of two of the academy's secretaries, André Félibien and Henri Testelin. Félibien's long preface to the 1667 *Conférences* emphasizes two norms for painting: beauty and nobility.[67] The standard of beauty was set by the art of ancient Greece. The academicians reserved their highest praise for

Greek painters and sculptors; Raphael and Poussin were the only modern artists admitted into this pantheon, precisely because they came so close to replicating the antique ideal. Thus in his lecture on Poussin's *The Israelites Receiving Manna in the Desert,* Charles Le Brun describes how Poussin based each of the major figures on some famous piece of classical sculpture. This is offered as praise and not as a condemnation of Poussin's lack of originality. Instruction was similarly backward-looking. Students learned by copying ancient models. Overall, the goal of painting was not to imitate nature but to improve her by appeal to the canons of antiquity.

The second academic ideal, nobility, was sought through a comparison with the literary arts. The academicians declared that painting shared the subject matter of poetry and drama. They enforced a strict hierarchy of genres which placed history painting at the top, followed by portraits, animal pictures, landscapes, and still lifes. History paintings took their themes from the Bible, classical myth, and epic poetry. Accordingly, they shared the grand actions and noble subject matter praised by Aristotle in the *Poetics.* Such paintings had moral import. They expressed deep truths about human nature since they showed a group of people united by and responding to a heroic action. By contrast the lesser genres like portraits and landscapes could aspire only to achieve verisimilitude or decorative value.

Those *conférences* which focused on a single painting generally analyzed it in terms of a fixed set of categories. These included composition, proportion, design, color, expression, and light and shade. All too often, however, the lecturers got sidetracked by issues that were not straightforwardly aesthetic. For example, Philippe de Champaigne's discussion of Poussin's painting *Eliezer and Rebecca* quickly descended into a debate about the artist's faithfulness to the Bible. According to the Old Testament story Eliezer had ten camels, but Poussin failed to show them. The *Académiciens* came up with a tortured defense of this artistic license.[68] Similarly stilted debates occurred regarding a number of other biblical scenes.[69] Occasionally, however, the lectures were more general, addressing a particular practical or theoretical issue rather than analysing a given painting. Le Brun's discussion of the relative merits of color vs. line is one such case. This lecture took up the longstanding Italian debate between *colore* and *disegno.* Le Brun resolved the debate in favor of line by appeal to a number of Cartesian principles—the supremacy of mind over matter, of the rational over the sensory, of the essential over the accidental.[70]

The atmosphere of theory and discussion extended beyond the halls of the academy, for the academy lectures were published, often with summaries by the secretary. In 1680 Testelin's *Tables de préceptes* presented in synoptic form the academy's views on composition, expression, proportions, chiaroscuro, *ordonnance,* and color. Other art treatises were also available. The most influential were those of Fréart de Chambray (1662) and Charles Du Fresnoy (1667). These emphasized roughly the same doctrines as had the academicians. All in effect reprised standard aesthetic views going back to Alberti's treatise *Della pittura* of 1435.

I have described the organization and activity of the Académie royale de peinture et de sculpture in considerable detail. This arrangement was replicated in a number of other academies established under Colbert's guidance. These included the academies of Dance (1661), Inscriptions and Belles-lettres (1666), Science (1669), Music (1669), and Architecture (1671). And of course the earliest and most influential of all was the Académie française, founded in 1635 in order to protect and preserve French language and literature.

Let me briefly contrast the situation in England. While there was some awareness of the artistic currents at work in France (for instance, in 1695 John Dryden translated Du Fresnoy's *De arte graphica,* and Le Brun's treatise on expression was translated in 1701), no English counterpart to the French academy of art was proposed until the middle of the eighteenth century. Art instruction at that time took place in various private schools. Sir Godfrey Kneller opened a private studio academy in 1711, and James Thornhill established another after Kneller's death in 1723.[71] Various artists of note were members of these schools. They gathered regularly for life drawing. By 1750, Hogarth's academy in St. Martin's Lane "became the chief practising ground for artists in need of models."[72]

Some of the factors that precipitated the formation of France's Académie royale were not present in England. In particular, guilds did not threaten individual artists' freedom, and there were no limitations on the importing of artworks from abroad. Nevertheless, different groups tried at various times to form an academy on the French model.[73] The Royal Academy of Arts in London was finally founded in 1768.

England's Royal Academy differed from that of Paris in two crucial respects. First, the British academy had from the start two purposes—educating young artists, and staging an annual exhibition. The annual exhibitions (which evolved from earlier ones connected with the Academy's precursors) were immensely popular. They were also highly profitable, and this led to the second difference between the two academies. The London academy was private from the very start. It was supported by revenues from the annual exhibition and was not in any way dependent on the crown. The Academy's income was sufficient not only to run the school but also to sustain various charitable commitments—in particular, the support of indigent artists and their families.

While the organization of London's Royal Academy was strikingly different from that of its Parisian counterpart, the academies promulgated very similar doctrines. In 1769 Sir

Joshua Reynolds, first president of the Royal Academy, initiated the practice of delivering a discourse at the prize-giving ceremony that concluded each academic year. In all Reynolds delivered fifteen such discourses. Together they comprise a full statement of the Academy's official position. Reynolds's views were decidedly reactionary. He endorsed the hierarchy of genres established a century earlier in France. And he championed those paintings which exemplified the grand style. Such works were not merely ornamental. Rather, they pursued a general, abstract notion of beauty. Such beauty was only achieved when the artist "got above all singular forms, local customs, particularities, and details"; this in turn was accomplished through "reiterated experience and close comparison."[74] Reynolds did inform students of one familiar shortcut in their pursuit of this goal—he advised them to study the works of the ancients.

4. GARDENS

The theories of painting proposed by the Paris and London academies posited certain affinities between the arts of painting and literature. The founders of the Académic royale, in particular, were carrying out a self-conscious plan to elevate the art of painting by appropriating the theory, subject matter, and status of her sister art. Great emphasis was placed on the two arts' similarity of content. Thus history paintings, like epic poems, tell tales from classical or biblical sources, embellished with allegory and myth, and replete with didactic and moral messages. Considerable knowledge—classical, historical, and scientific—is needed to create successful paintings *or* successful poems. And finally, painters practicing Reynolds's grand style pursue an ideal beauty outlined by ancient philosophers and exemplified by antique art, much as epic poets pursue the ideals set out in Aristotle's *Poetics.*

Such comparisons ennoble painting by emphasizing its moral and literary content and its debt to classical canons and sources. Given that the academies served the art of painting in this way, why couldn't a similar campaign be mounted for the art of gardening? That is, since many eighteenth-century gardenists had an equally elevated view of the art of gardening,[75] why didn't they pursue a similar strategy, establishing academies of gardening whose curricula would demonstrate gardening's affinities to both painting and poetry and thereby elevate that pursuit from a mechanical to a liberal art?

In some sense, this enterprise was a possible one. Consider the ways in which an academy of gardening might parallel the academies of painting discussed above. The theory of painting, as formulated by seventeenth-century French theorists, was inspired by a set of paintings they had never seen. The writers of the time rhapsodized about the lost works of Zeuxis and Apelles, telling familiar tales of painted grapes so real that birds tried to eat them, painted draperies so convincing that viewers tried to pull them aside. Certain lost gardens of antiquity were also known through description. For example, in his *Georgics* Virgil describes a garden in Corycus given over to beekeeping, in the *Odyssey* Homer describes the gardens of King Alcinoüs,[76] and Pliny's letters contain accounts of the gardens at his Laurentian villa and his Tuscan villa. It is easy to imagine these gardens revered and mythologized, grounding and inspiring the nascent garden theory. Secondly, a scientific curriculum could be devised for academies of gardening, featuring courses in botany, agronomy, genetics, and meteorology, just as students in academies of painting studied geometry, optics, anatomy, and perspective. And of course general aesthetic principles of gardening, grounded in a philosophical analysis of such concepts as balance and harmony, unity and multiplicity, form and content, nature and art, could be proposed and defended (as in fact they were late in the eighteenth-century by Sir Uvedale Price, Richard Payne Knight, and Humphry Repton). A foundation of this sort would link gardening theory with classic works in the western philosophical tradition.

Two more points of similarity could guide the creation of an academy of gardening. Promising painters in the seventeenth and eighteenth centuries made an obligatory trip to Rome to study the artistic treasures of the classical and Renaissance eras. A similar pilgrimage could acquaint aspiring gardenists with Italian Renaissance gardening treasures— the villa gardens of Rome, Tivoli, and Frascati. Finally, there is a body of gardening literature going back before the seventeenth century. Consider, for example, the following works: Thomas Hill's *Briefe and Pleasaunt Treatyse* (1563),[77] Jacques Boyceau's *Le traité du jardinage* (1638), André Mollet's *Le jardin de plaisir* (1651), Claude Mollet's *Théâtre des plantes et jardinages* (1652), René Rapin's *Of Gardens* (1665), Sir William Temple's *Gardens of Epicurus* (1682), Dezallier d'Argenville's *Théorie et pratique du jardin* (1709), Joseph Addison's *Spectator* essays on the pleasures of imagination (1712), Pope's *Guardian* essay on topiary (1713), Stephen Switzer's *Ichnographia Rustica* (1718), Batty Langley's *Principles of Gardening* (1728), William Shenstone's *Unconnected Thoughts on Gardening* (1759), Thomas Whately's *Observations on Modern Gardening* (1770), and Horace Walpole's *History of the Modern Taste in Gardening* (1771). These texts could have been part of the classroom curriculum for an academy of gardening, all of which could have been supplemented by an apprentice system which provided young aspirants practical training under the guidance of master gardeners.

I have been arguing for the possibility—indeed the conceptual coherence and the pedagogical utility—of academies of gardening. I claim that such academies could have been constructed in seventeenth-century France and eigheeenth-century England so as to mirror very closely both the purpose and practices of the academies of painting described above. But of course Colbert never did establish an Académie de jardins,[78] nor, to the best of my knowledge, did the eighteenth-century English critics who praised gardening so highly attempt to establish academies, societies, or clubs of gardening.

Some features of gardening may explain its recalcitrance with regard to the pedagogy I have proposed. In seventeenth-century France, gardening operated as a manual trade, passed down from father to son. There are famous families of French gardeners—the Mollets, the Boyceaus, the Le Nôtres—who designed and maintained the royal gardens, wrote gardening books, and traveled to spread French-style gardens to other European nations. For example, Pierre Le Nôtre (1570–1610) was appointed one of the chief gardeners in Catherine de Médicis's newly created Tuileries Garden in 1571; he was succeeded in this post by his son Jean in 1618, who was in turn succeeded in 1637 by his son André, the renowned designer of Vaux and Versailles.[79] Members of the Mollet family comprised an even lengthier gardening dynasty. Jacques, head gardener to the duc d'Aumale, was the father of Claude, the author of *Théâtres des plans et jardinages,* gardener to Henri IV, and designer of gardens at Fontainebleau, Saint-Germain-en-Laye, and the Tuileries. Claude's son André (d. 1665), author of *Le jardin de plaisir,* designed gardens abroad—in England, the Netherlands, and Sweden. In 1644 he was named *premier jardinier du roi.* His sons Pierre and Claude held positions at the Tuileries, while their brother Jacques was head gardener at Fontainebleau. Claude was succeeded by his son Charles, who was in turn succeeded by his son Armand-Claude Mollet.[80] Clearly, the traditional system brought security to many French gardening professionals; some also achieved wealth and recognition. (There is a touching story about André Le Nôtre as an old man touring Versailles in a sedan chair alongside the king.) But the profession continued to operate like a manual trade or mechanical art throughout the seventeenth century, and the gardeners themselves didn't band together to seek the higher status that might come through guilds, societies, academies, and the like.

In England, gardening developed along two quite different paths—amateur and professional. Those gardens that came to define the English landscape style were not associated with the crown, as had been the case in France. Instead, Englishmen like Alexander Pope, William Shenstone, and Henry Hoare designed their own gardens. Later in the century, a new phenomenon emerged—professional gardeners with their own identifiable style (Capability Brown, Humphry Repton, and (perhaps to some extent) William Kent). Along both these lines of development, gardening differed from painting in significant ways. While many English amateurs and connoisseurs painted, drew, and sketched, they remained avid collectors of works by acknowledged masters; they didn't aspire to paint all the paintings that would hang in their homes. They often did, however, aspire to design their own gardens and improve their own estates. Moreover, though gentlemen would amass art collections featuring many noted painters, there seemed to be no sense that their gardens should be a collection displaying individual garden designers' styles. Many gardens were indeed worked on successively by different garden designers, but they would often simply tear up and redo one another's work. Compare hiring Richard Wilson to paint over a landscape by Claude! By the end of the eighteenth century, new attitudes were in place that would have lessened some of these differences between gardening and painting. A growing romantic sensibility encouraged the recognition of genius in any creative endeavor, supporting the notions of individual style and individual fame in gardening as well as in the more traditional arts.

Various objections could be raised to my contention here, that academies of gardening resembling the seventeenth- and eighteenth-century academies of painting could have been established. For example, one contemporary garden designer, Russell Page, writes in his aptly titled book *The Education of a Gardener*, "I know now that one cannot be taught to design gardens academically or theoretically. You have to learn the ways and nature of plants and stone, of water and soil at least as much through the hands as through the head."[81] This objection can be deflected. Academies of gardening would *teach* gardening no more—and no less—than academies of painting taught painting. Recall that the students of the Académie royale were apprenticed to particular painters and did all their practical training with them. The academy curriculum included only theoretical subjects plus the course in life drawing. Garden academies would have been arranged similarly. Historical, scientific, and aesthetic programs of study would be supplemented by hands-on work in actual gardens.

A more serious objection to the possibility I have been promoting concerns the underlying assumption that gardens can be assimilated to the arts of poetry and painting. How could mere gardens share the subject matter of epic poems and mythological paintings? Such comparisons were indeed made in the eighteenth century. Although the first pairing—gardens and poetry—seems especially unlikely, recent scholarly accounts of eighteenth-century gardens bear it out, showing that such gardens conveyed moral, religious, political, and philosophical messages to viewers strolling through them. In the next chapter, I shall explore in more detail gardens' ability to articulate such messages.

THREE

THE SISTER ARTS I

Gardens and Poems

I. THE SISTER ARTS

In this chapter I want to examine critically one aspect of Horace Walpole's claim that "Poetry, Painting, and Gardening, or the Science of Landscape, will forever by men of Taste be deemed Three Sisters, or *The Three New Graces* who dress and adorn Nature,"[1] namely, the link between gardening and poetry. Clearly, Walpole's conceit builds upon the sister-arts tradition, the association of poetry and painting. This tradition is generally traced to two venerable sources (1) a remark by the Greek poet Simonides (556–467 B.C.): "Painting is mute poetry, and poetry a speaking picture;" and (2) a phrase from line 361 of Horace's *Ars poetica* (13 B.C.): *Ut pictura poesis* ("As is painting, so is poetry").[2]

While the saying from Simonides is suggestive, the quotation from Horace needs to be put in context. In this section of his epistle, Horace is arguing that critical standards should be flexible and that some faults should be forgiven in a worthy poem. To illustrate his claim he turns to the example of painting and points out that different paintings please in different circumstances. Some reward close scrutiny, bright light, repeated encounters; others do not. Ben Jonson's verse translation of the passage reads as follows:

As painting, so is poesy. Some man's hand
Will take you more, the nearer that you stand;
As some the farther off: this loves the dark;
This, fearing not the subtlest judge's mark,
Will in the light be viewed: this, once, the sight
Doth please: this, ten times over will delight.[3]

These casual, unsystematic remarks about artistic criticism were taken up and elaborated by countless painters, poets, critics, and theorists. They transformed them into a set of rigid precepts, thus generating the tradition of the sister arts.

Jean Hagstrum traces this tradition in his book *The Sister Arts.* He shows how occasional remarks by Horace, Simonides, Plato, and Aristotle were elevated by Renaissance thinkers and used to ground dogmatic theory. Writers who contributed to this tradition include Alberti, Leonardo, Dolce, Dryden, Dufresnoy, Pope, and Reynolds. Its influence waned after the publication of Lessing's *Laokoon* (1766), which argues that painting and poetry serve separate tasks.[4]

The link between painting and poetry can be put to varied purposes. The sister arts can be celebrated in order to encourage literary pictorialism, on the one hand, or to establish the nobility of painting, on the other. While Hagstrum takes the first tack in *The Sister Arts,* tracing the pictorial tradition in neoclassical English poetry, Rensselaer Lee takes the second in his monograph *Ut Pictura Poesis,* which traces the rise of the humanistic theory of painting. Dean Tolle Mace, however, seeks a common thread. He argues that the doctrine of the sister arts "came into being not because poetry and painting sought out one another's pictorial devices, but because both arts became equally concerned with developing powers of expression."[5] Writing about Dryden's "Parallel of Poetry and Painting" (1695), Mace says that "it grew out of [Dryden's] conviction and the conviction of the age that all great art must treat great human subjects. This being so, all great art must thus be parallel in some way to poetry, the art which had been perfected through the ages to deal with great human subjects."[6] For Mace, then, the crucial commonality between painting and poetry is the ability of each to represent significant human action.

Given this reading of Horace's simile, it may seem puzzling that Horace Walpole proposed gardening as a sister to both poetry and painting. Gardens do not seem well suited to the tasks Aristotle sets out in the *Poetics* as definitive of the arts of poetry and drama. In particular, how can gardens deal with great human subjects and represent significant human actions? In what follows, I shall show that some eighteenth-century gardens did indeed accomplish such tasks. Gardens such as Stowe and Stourhead contained complex iconographical programs that visitors could "read" as they strolled through the grounds. Garden historians have amply documented the powers of such gardens, and I shall draw on their research. But before describing particular gardens and their messages, I want to say something about how an arrangement of plants, earth, and water—augmented by architecture and sculpture—can become articulate.

2. GARDENS, POEMS, AND EMBLEMS

Those gardens from the first half of the eighteenth century which most resemble poems have been variously labeled. Ronald Paulson calls them poetic gardens, and John Dixon Hunt calls them emblematic gardens, while others simply speak of the English landscape garden. A number of these gardens are laid out as a circuit. The visitor strolls along a path which brings him past a series of monuments, scenes, and vistas. The viewer's experience is carefully controlled. Benches and inscriptions indicate special points of interest—striking views or sculptural or architectural ensembles with complex charged meanings.

One of the most frequently made comments about such gardens is that they must be read, that walking along the path in many ways resembles seeing successive pages of an emblem book.[7] For example, Ronald Paulson says of Lord Cobham's garden at Stowe that "the visitor . . . saw a carefully prepared scene with statues, temples and other objects of a high degree of denotation arranged to express a *topos*—a philosophical or literary commonplace—on which he could meditate or converse. . . . What he saw was virtually a page from an emblem book, and page followed page as he strolled along the garden path."[8] John Dixon Hunt says of the same garden that it offered "constant examples of visual exhibits, often accompanied by inscriptions or mottoes, the full meaning of which depends upon the exact encounter of word and image that we find in the emblem book."[9] Paulson remarks of another eighteenth-century garden, Henry Hoare's estate at Stourhead, that Hoare "makes his garden almost literally a poem, creating a series of emblems whose statement at its most general is about the course of man's life on earth."[10]

Let me pause here to describe in a bit more detail the emblem books with which these eighteenth-century gardens are being compared. Emblem books, common from the 1500s on, were handbooks combining images, mottoes, and inscriptions drawn primarily from classical literature.[11] Alciati's *Emblemata,* published in 1531, and Cesare Ripa's *Iconologia,* published in 1593, were frequently reprinted and translated. These handbooks were intended to assist the inspiration of poets, painters, and orators, and their association of word and image soon became common cultural coinage. Educated people, seeing a particular phrase or image, would know its traditional meaning and associations.

The subjects Ripa treated included virtues and vices, temperaments and humors, arts and sciences, continents and nations. Later editions of his work considerably expanded the range of emblems. For example, Jean Baudoin's 1644 Parisian edition offers emblems of the five senses, the nine muses, the twelve months of the year, as well as a host of items that come in groups of four—the four elements, the four seasons, the four winds, the four types of poems, the four parts of the day, and the four ages of man.[12] Hagstrum writes that a typical page of Ripa shows "a single figure, usually female, wearing her iconic symbols and representing an emotion like love, melancholy, or anger, an idea like perfection or literary mimesis, an art like poetry or music, a city like Rome, or a river like the Tiber,"[13] while Hunt describes the 1709 London edition as containing "Various images of virtues, vices, passions, arts, humours, elements, and celestial bodies."[14]

Consider two images from Ripa. (1) Art is portrayed as a woman in a flowing green robe. In her right hand she holds a hammer, a pencil, and a burin, three tools needed for the artist's imitation of nature. In her left hand she holds a stake supporting a climbing plant. The commentary explains that "the Stake supplies Nature's Defects, in holding up the tender plant."[15] The emblem thus expresses a neoclassical ideal endorsed by writers as diverse as André Félibien and Alexander Pope, namely, that art does not just copy nature but improves her. Note that a "garden" (a plant guided and supported by a stake) symbolizes this relationship. (2) Delight is portrayed as a young boy in a green suit holding violin and bow. A book on Aristotle and one on music lie open at his feet. Two pigeons stand kissing nearby. This image is glossed as follows: "The Green signifies the Vivacity and Delightfulness of green Meadows to the Sight: the Violin, Delight in Hearing; the Book, Delight in Philosophy; the Doves, amorous Delight."[16] Both the green suit and the green meadows symbolize the growth and fecundity of the natural world, while various ones of the props indicate the importance of the senses through which we take in and appreciate that world. Once again gardens are relevant here. Thinking about the unique place they occupy between nature and art helps us understand and amplify the emblem.

By 1709 Ripa's *Iconologia* had been translated into English, but a number of English authors had already furthered the emblematic tradition. Both George Wither and Francis Quarles published books titled *Emblemes* in 1635, and Henry Hawkins's *Parthenia Sacra* appeared in 1633. Wither's texts are much more discursive than Ripa's. Each image is accompanied by a motto (in Latin), a couplet, and an extended poem. The books by Quarles and Hawkins are more religious than classical in orientation. Each of Quarles's emblems takes its inspiration from a Bible verse, while Hawkins, who was a Roman Catholic, devotes his entire text to an emblematic celebration of the Virgin Mary. The garden is the unifying image of Hawkins's book. *Parthenia Sacra* is in fact a devotional man-

The emblem for art from Cesare Ripa's *Iconologia* (Padua, 1630). Reproduced by permission of the Huntington Library, San Marino, California.

ual which invites its readers to meditate upon twenty-two emblems drawn from the fictional garden of Parthenia. These include the garden itself, the rose, the lily, the heliotrope, the iris, the olive, the palm, the fountain, and the mount.

Despite the differences between the early emblem books with their ties to classical sources and the later ones with more narrowly religious agendas, they all would have inculcated in their readers certain habits of mind: a readiness to associate word and image and a tendency to interpret the sensory world as rife with implication and in need of exegesis. Thus emblem books employed associations like the following: the pelican is an emblem of self-sacrifice, the peacock of pride, the bee of flattery, the crocodile of luxury, the crab of irresolution, and so on. Many of these pairings originated in contemporary lore—for example, it was thought that when food was scarce the pelican would feed its young with blood from its own breast—but they came to attain the status of a conventional code. Plants entered into this lexicon as well. Alciati concluded his emblem book with a list of various trees and their significance,[17] and flowers too were associated with particular virtues and traits of character. Thus ivy was an emblem of constraint, the oak of long life, the vine of lust, laurel of victory, cedar of mercy, the violet of humility, the marigold of charity, the hyacinth of hope, the sunflower of contemplation, the tulip of beauty, the lily of chastity, and the narcissus of stupidity. By Elizabethan times the so-called language of flowers was well developed; nosegays and bouquets contained messages that could be decoded by reference to the flowers they contained.[18]

In sum, the emblematic tradition integrated references to classical culture, the Bible, and more primitive lore and superstition. Together these sources provided a wealth of character and incident whose significance would have been instantly recognized by "cultured" people—those who formed the audience for the arts of painting and poetry. Furthermore, because the emblematic tradition assigned conventional significance to particular visual images, it could be transferred to the art of gardening. Using a combination of resources—inscriptions, sculpture, architecture, plants, even topography—a garden designer could recreate an image from an emblem book or highlight certain elements whose significance would be immediately appreciated. This explains one way in which gardens, in the absence of alphabet, syntax, and grammar, could convey meaning.

In comparing scenes from a garden to pages from an emblem book, however, I haven't yet got to the heart of the sister-arts claim that I mean to explore. As Hunt noted, emblem books present a succession of "encounters" between words and images. Each image is accompanied by a title and a written elucidation. Thus emblems straddle the divide between the visual and the verbal arts. Poetry, by contrast, is a predominantly verbal art.[19] How then can a garden approximate a poem? Visual resemblance is certainly not the key here. I suggest the relevant overlap is one of function: a garden can often convey the same content as a poem; furthermore, it can do so in part by exploiting the fact that gardens, like poems, are experienced over time.

Let me briefly review the way poetry functions. Poems are, first and foremost, composed of words. And, with the exception of onomatopoetic words like "murmur," "buzz," and "slither," whose sounds mirror their meanings, linguistic meaning is conventional or arbitrary. We could have called cats "dogs" and dogs "cats" without any loss of efficiency. Thus part of the force of poems comes from the conventional meaning of their component words, however that is construed.[20] But semantic properties don't exhaust poetry's force. Readers must also take into account more "remote" aspects of meaning—images presented, metaphors employed, associative and expressive properties conveyed—as well as syntactic features like rhyme and rhythm and such cumulative effects as narrative line and temporal relations. On the basis of this sketch, a garden would count as poetic if it had denotative content, if the individuals, concepts, properties, and events referred to were related in ways conveyed by the garden's structure, and if these relationships became apparent to visitors as they viewed or strolled through the garden.

In what follows, I shall describe and discuss four gardens from the first half of the eighteenth century: Twickenham, Stowe, Stourhead, and West Wycombe. In each case I shall argue that, in important ways, these gardens function like poems.

3. POPE'S TWICKENHAM

Alexander Pope was the preeminent poet of Augustan England; he also wrote about gardens, advised his friends on the disposition of their estates, and created his own garden at his estate at Twickenham, beginning in 1719. He is an especially appropriate figure to discuss in connection with the comparison between gardening and poetry because he helped to formulate the doctrines of both disciplines. Yet Pope was also an amateur painter, and so his writings and his garden are relevant as well to the second of Walpole's two comparisons.

Pope's garden at Twickenham has an interesting commercial connection to poetry. The poet acquired his estate with profits derived from his successful subscription translation of Homer's *Iliad.* He leased a small villa on the Thames and eventually cultivated a surrounding five-acre plot.[21] The villa was about fifteen miles from London, and the area was decidedly rural in feeling. In creating a garden there, Pope was clearly and self-consciously echoing themes and forms from his poetry.

Though Pope wrote poems of many kinds throughout his career, all his writings are distinguished by their ties to the classical world. Never schooled in a systematic manner, Pope acquired his learning first at the hands of a Catholic tutor, and then through a self-guided course of reading. He told his friend Joseph Spence that during his "great reading years" he read "all the best critics, almost all the English, French and Latin poets of any name, the minor poets, Homer and some of the greater Greek poets in the original, and Tasso and Ariosto in translations."[22] During this time Pope also exercised himself with projects of translation and imitation.[23] He thus emerged familiar with the great authors of antiquity and conversant with a variety of genres. One critic lists the many kinds of poetry Pope attempted as follows: the mock epic, the georgic, the pastoral, the dream vision, the didactic, the heroic epistle, the elegy, the familiar epistle, the formal verse satire, the moral epistle, the prologue, the epilogue, the ode, the epigram, and the epitaph.[24]

Many writers see parallels between Pope's poetry and his gardening. Just as Pope's poems treat classical themes, utilize classical forms, and imitate classical exemplars, so too his garden combines themes from classical poetry and forms from classical architecture with the learned allusiveness of the arts of its day. Consider the features of Pope's estate. His three-story house was set alongside the Thames, a grassy lawn running down to the river. Behind the house, the main road to London separated the house from the garden. An underground tunnel—Pope's grotto—ran beneath the road and led to the garden, which occupied a rectangular plot about twice the width of the front lawn. Maynard Mack, in his study *The Garden and the City,* lists the garden's features as follows: "a grotto, three mounts (one of these quite large), some quincunxes, groves, a wilderness, an orangery, a vineyard, a kitchen garden, a bowling green, a shell temple, and an obelisk."[25] He also calls attention to the poet's "striking use of openings, walks, and vistas, each terminating on a point of rest, supplied by urn or statue."[26]

Stylistically, Pope's garden combines both forward- and backward-looking features.[27] The entire ensemble was arranged axially, though not in line with the underground passage leading from the Thames. Upon emerging from this passage (i.e., the "grotto,") the visitor passed the shell temple and a large mount, traversed first a wide alley flanked by groves and then a circular bowling green, walked between two smaller mounts, and finally approached the obelisk to the memory of the poet's mother, which Mack describes as the "visual and emotional climax" of the garden.[28] The linearity of the garden was countered by its bowers, hills, and thickets, as well as by the surrounding "wildernesses"— quincuncial groves penetrated by serpentine paths. Urns were arrayed in various parts of the garden, and over the grotto entrance was inscribed a line from Horace, "Secretum iter, et fallentis semita vitae," translated by Spence as "A hid Recess, where Life's revolving Day,/ In sweet Delusion gently steals away."[29]

Two other features of Pope's garden must be described before we can consider its likeness to a poem. The first is Pope's grotto—more technically, a *cryptoporticus,* or subterranean portico.[30] It consisted of several chambers through which trickled a small stream. The walls and ceilings were decorated with a collection of rocks, spars, flints, and shells, which Pope had gathered on his travels or been given by friends. The poet had also attached small pieces of mirror to the pebbled surfaces, and so his grotto multiplied both sounds and sights, the murmur and splash of the stream and the flash of flames and lamps. From the grotto, a view extended in two directions. Visitors glancing up into the garden could see the shell temple, while turning the other way, they could glimpse boats sailing on the Thames. In a letter to Martha Blunt, Pope explicitly mentions how the grotto func-

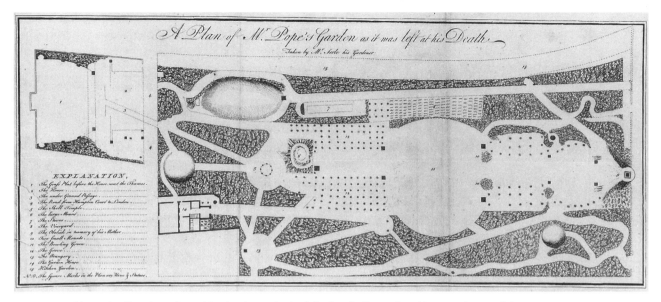

Alexander Pope's garden at Twickenham, plan by John Searle. Reproduced by permission of the Beinecke Rare Book and Manuscript Library, Yale University.

tioned like a camera obscura once its doors were shut: "on the Walls . . . the River, Hills, Woods, and Boats, are forming a moving Picture in their visible Radiations." [31]

Grottos are associated with creativity and contemplation. Inhabited by nymphs, oracles, divinities, and muses, the grottos described in classical literature are loci of poetic inspiration. Maynard Mack links Pope's grotto to caves described by Homer and Ovid; he also situates Pope's move to Twickenham and his creation there of garden and grotto against the tradition of retirement stemming from Virgil's *Georgics*.

Though Pope's entire garden is allusive, recalling both literature and ideals from the classical past, one section of his estate bore an even stronger likeness to a poem. This was a plan for a series of monuments to adorn the riverfront. The sculptural ensemble, as described by Pope's friend Joseph Spence, combined a swan flying into the river, two reclining river gods holding inscribed urns, and busts of Homer, Virgil, Marcus Aurelius, and Cicero. Explaining the significance of this ensemble, Mack states that it is "a more elaborate work of the associative instinct than at first appears. Like some of the allusions in Pope's verse, it spreads in circles of analogy that one hardly knows how to follow." [32] One of the inscriptions is from Politian's *Ambra*. It reads: "Here softly flows the Meles, and

Pope's grotto, a perspective view by John Searle. Reproduced courtesy of the Print Collection, Lewis Walpole Library, Yale University.

silent in its deep grottos listens to its singing swans."[33] As Mack explains, this alludes to the poetic enterprise (the singing swans), as well as to the preeminent poet associated with the river Meles, namely, Homer. The second inscription—"Where the Mincius wanders with great windings"—is drawn from a passage in Virgil's *Georgics* where the poet writes of taking home spoils and trophies from conquered Greece to his Italian home. In using this quotation, Pope alludes to his own career. He too has brought home artistic "spoils," namely, the poetry and learning of the ancient world which, through his imitations and translations, he has secured for Augustan England. Hunt writes "This elaborate contrivance, properly decyphered, would lead the spectator to recall the birth of Homer from Politian and the poetic conquest of Greece from Virgil and so to identify Pope's own role in rededicating this classical literary heritage to his own age."[34]

To "read" Pope's garden ensemble requires the very same skills as reading a poem. The viewer must recognize the quotations, recall the context from which they are drawn, and realize their relevance to Pope's situation. Considerable background knowledge is required, not only about *Ambra* and the *Georgics* but also about conventions in the various arts—for example, the fact that in classical times rivers were often personified by reclining figures pouring forth water from urns. Viewers must also understand that the meaning to be extracted from the riverside ensemble is cumulative—that is, that the busts of Homer and Virgil reinforce and complement the meaning to be teased out of the statues and inscriptions. How such meaning is conveyed by ensembles of the sort just described is a problem for art in general, not one newly raised by gardens and by the claim that gardens must be read. Paintings and poems are allusive in similar ways—thus the doctrine of the sister arts—and the example of Twickenham shows that gardens can function in just the same manner.

I said earlier that Pope's garden combined innovative and traditional elements. If the sculptural ensemble placed on the banks of the Thames must be unpacked much like Pope's denser poems, the meaning of Pope's grotto can be viewed differently. The shells and minerals affixed to the ceiling and walls evoke personal rather than emblematic associations,[35] while the implicit connection between the flowing spring and the poet's (and viewer's) mind anticipates later romantic conceptions of artistic creativity. John Dixon Hunt argues that the varied acquatic effects in Pope's grotto—pools, rills, torrents, fountains—"provide a machinery of meditation, various landscapes where the expressive character of water determines mental activity."[36]

4. STOWE

I have been arguing that portions of Pope's small landscape at Twickenham give striking support to Walpole's claim that poetry and gardening are sister arts. One of the most famous of all eighteenth-century gardens, Richard Temple, Lord Cobham's estate at Stowe, is another that is frequently cited in support of Walpole's claim. Like Pope's garden, Stowe cannot be easily forced into a single stylistic category. A succession of gardeners worked there in the course of the century, among them Charles Bridgeman, Richard Kent, and Capability Brown, and different parts of the garden exhibit quite different styles. I would like to start, however, by briefly recounting the features to be found in the Elysian Fields, an area of the garden designed by William Kent in the 1730s.

The Elysian Fields occupies a wooded glade fed by a small stream known as the River Styx. Three structures are crucial to the overall meaning of this area: The Temple of Ancient Virtue, the Temple of Modern Virtue, and the Temple of British Worthies. The first of these is (color plate 2A) a round classical building modeled after the Temple of Vesta at Tivoli. The Ionic structure houses statues of Socrates, Homer, Lycurgus, and Epaminondas—the most famous philosopher, poet, lawmaker, and soldier, respectively, of the classical world. Next to this was the Temple of Modern Virtue, which no longer stands. It was built in the Gothic style and was, moreover, built as a ruin. Downhill and across from these stands the Temple of British Worthies (color plate 2B), a semicircular building with sixteen niches, each containing the bust of a British notable. Included are philosophers, poets, scientists, and statesmen.[37] Architecture carries much of the meaning in Stowe's comparison of ancient and modern virtue. The juxtaposition of Gothic and classical styles creates the visual pun between a ruined temple and ruined virtue. But the very topography of the garden contributes to the meaning as well, for the British worthies are placed downhill, looking up to their ancient predecessors.

The three temples of the Elysian Fields make a moral statement, but Kent and Cobham added further layers of subtlety to give the ensemble political and religious dimensions as well. John Dixon Hunt declares the Temple of British Worthies to be an "ideological building." He states that "the message of these figures is anti-Stuart, anti-Catholic, pro-British."[38] Lord Cobham had been dismissed from Queen Anne's army and was among those Whigs who came to oppose Sir Robert Walpole's ministry. The choice of figures for the temple—in particular, the omission of Queen Anne—underscores this point. In addition, a quotation from Virgil is presented with a crucial line omitted. Hunt explains: "This particular religious hostility is reinforced by a quotation from the sixth book of the *Aeneid* . . . in which a line praising priesthood is omitted. . . . Such is the learned subtlety of [this building] that we must not only identify our Virgil but recognize how and why it is incomplete."[39]

Note that the Elysian Fields are as demanding intellectually as the section of Pope's garden described above. Hunt and Willis sum up the challenges this section of the garden presents to its "reader":

> The Elysian Fields present a much more ambitious scheme of associations; they require a visitor to compare ancient virtue with its modern counterpart . . . to register the political significance of the British Worthies, which in turn required noticing that a line was missing from a Virgilian quotation, and to appreciate that the Temple of Ancient Virtue called to mind the Roman Temple of Vesta . . . at Tivoli, and the Temple of British Worthies some other modern Italian examples.[40]

While writers discussing the poetic powers of eighteenth-century gardens tend to fixate on the small sector of Stowe containing these three temples with their political and religious connotations, other iconographical programs could be found in other parts of the garden. Ronald Paulson writes that the rotondo was the focal point of the garden, since it could be seen from all parts of the estate. This structure originally held a gilded statue of Venus; later this was replaced by a statue of Bacchus. Since the grounds also boasted a Temple of Venus (which, the current Stowe guidebook reports, contained "indelicate murals") and a Temple of Bacchus, Paulson argues that the overall theme of the garden was love in all its varieties. He states, "The temples thus tell of wives running away from their jealous husbands to consort with satyrs, Dido seducing Aeneas, and even a saint who finds it hard to resist sexual temptation in his grotto."[41]

One further argument that is supported by the gardens at Stowe is John Dixon Hunt's claim that eighteenth-century English gardens progressed from the emblematic to the expressive. In his book *Observations on Modern Gardening* (1770), published some fifty years after Pope began laying out his Twickenham estate and some thirty-five years after Bridgeman and Kent commenced the creation of Stowe's Elysian fields, Thomas Whately rails against the demands of emblematic gardens. He writes:

> Statues, inscriptions, and even paintings, history and mythology, and a variety of devices have been introduced [into gardens]. . . . All these devices are rather *emblematical* than expressive; they may be ingenious contrivances, and recall absent ideas to the recollection; but they make no immediate impression, for they must be examined, compared, perhaps explained, before the whole design of them is well understood; and though an allusion to a favourite or well-known subject of history, of poetry, or of tradition, may now and then animate or digni-fy a scene, yet as the subject does not naturally belong to a garden, the allusion should not be principle; it should seem to have been suggested by the scene: a transitory image, which irresistibly occurred; not sought for, not laboured; and have the force of a metaphor, free from the detail of an allegory."[42]

A section of Stowe which answers to this new antiemblematic taste is the Grecian Valley, the last of the areas created during Lord Cobham's lifetime. The Grecian Valley was a rolling green expanse surrounded by thick woods but lacking the denotative apparatus—temples, statues, inscriptions, and so on—so common elsewhere at Stowe.

Hunt suggests that the emblematic garden from the first half of the eighteenth century went out of favor in part because garden owners and designers wanted to create landscapes which would answer to the new Lockean theory of the mind, that is, landscapes that would support and promote a train of private associations, answer to viewers' changing moods. He says of Stowe's Grecian Valley: "The subtle varieties of the valley afford a

Stowe, the Grecian Valley. Photograph by Edwin Smith.

landscape that seems to answer our moods, that allows a unique and individual response by each visitor to its unobtrusive character. It expresses us and our changing moods, or such is the illusion that it encourages."[43]

I am not convinced that designers consciously sought to make gardens compatible with so-called Lockean epistemology; it is not clear what might establish such a claim. It is beyond question, however, that the passage from Whately expresses impatience with the demands emblematic gardens made upon their viewers. It is also the case that there was a convergence in the middle of the eighteenth century. Epistemologists, moralists, scientists, and aestheticians were all of them focusing in one way or another on individuals' responses to their surroundings. I cannot say why such an interest should have arisen at this moment, though it may have involved a reaction against authoritarian and rationalist strains in both politics and philosophy.

That Stowe was the most famous English eighteenth-century garden is evidenced by the flurry of guidebooks which were published to help visitors appreciate (read) it. Guidebooks were offered by the Buckingham bookseller Seeley beginning in 1744, and were revised and reissued for the next one hundred years.[44] Other descriptions and guides include Gilbert West's *Stowe: The Gardens of the Right Honourable Richard Viscount Cobham* (1732), William Gilpin's anonymous *A Dialogue on the Gardens at Stow* (1748), and George Bickham's *The Beauties of Stowe* (1750). The very fact that these guides were so popular says something about the way eighteenth-century viewers construed the task of visiting a garden: they sought help, a book or lexicon which would unpack the garden's meaning.

5. STOURHEAD

I would like to briefly describe two more mid-eighteenth-century gardens which further support the claim that a garden can be like a poem. Stourhead, in Wiltshire, is one of the most beautiful of all landscape gardens. It differs from Stowe in that it was designed by its owner, the banker Henry Hoare, rather than by a troop of hired garden designers. It therefore exhibits more stylistic unity than does Stowe, and it expresses a more personal content. (In this respect, it recalls Pope's estate at Twickenham.)

Stourhead is laid out as a circuit. A path descends from the house and circles a lake, passing by temples, a grotto, a hermitage, a Palladian bridge, a rusticated cottage, a medieval cross, and more. Inscriptions give some clue to the iconographic program, which Kenneth Woodbridge has argued is based on Virgil's *Aeneid*. The words "Procul, o procul este profani" (Begone, you who are uninitiated! Begone!) are carved over the door of the first temple passed, the Temple of Flora. These words are uttered by the Cumean sibyl as Aeneas is about to descend into the underworld and be told of the founding of Rome.[45] Perfectly paralleling Aeneas's experience, the path descends to a grotto containing statues of a sleeping nymph and a bearded river god. Inscriptions provide a further link to Virgil's epic. A quotation from book 1 over the grotto's entrance refers to a cave where Aeneas took refuge.[46] Paulson points out that the river god alludes to Aeneas's encounter with

The grotto at Stourhead, painted by F. Nicholson. Reproduced by permission of the British Museum.

Father Tiber, who told him "Here is your home assured."[47] Here as at Stowe the very topography of the garden contributes to the iconography, for the steep path out of the grotto marks Aeneas's difficult journey back to the upper regions.

Further layers of meaning enrich the Stourhead circuit. Woodbridge writes that "Stourhead is dedicated to the pagan deities of rivers and springs; and to heroes—Aeneas, Hercules, and King Alfred."[48] A statue of Hercules stood in the Pantheon (which was originally known as the Temple of Hercules), while a crenellated Gothic tower dedicated to King Alfred was placed two miles northwest of the Stourhead House.[49] In his descrip-

Stourhead, the Temple of Apollo atop the hill, seen from the portico of the Temple of Flora. Photograph by Edwin Smith.

tion of Stourhead, Ronald Paulson notes that "The basic elements, besides the long journey through the wilderness, are temples of tillage and harvest, of fame, and of wisdom, in that ascending order."[50] He suggests that the ultimate destination of the circuit around the lake is the Temple of Apollo, which functions as the Temple of Wisdom. Finally, Max F. Schultz, in a fascinating paper "The Circuit Walk of the 18th-Century Landscape Garden and the Pilgrim's Circuitous Progress"[51] points out the multiple Christian and pagan associations which attach to any circuit walk like that at Stourhead. The circular path round a garden inevitably recalls certain archetypes—patterns of ritual repetition and eternal return—which characterize not only Aeneas's journey but also more primitive fertility cycles and later Christian parables of the pilgrim's progress, which in turn model the soul's journey through life. Schultz speculates that "it would have been extraordinary if the religious associations of the circuit walk had not occurred to visitors."[52]

The final gloss added by readers of Stourhead is a personal one. Henry Hoare's garden refers not only to well-known literary and religious figures; it also tells us something about Henry himself. That is, Stourhead is a highly personal poem as well as an allusive one. Again quoting first Paulson, then Woodbridge: "[Henry Hoare] makes his garden almost literally a poem, creating a series of emblems whose statement at its most general is about the course of man's life on earth and ultimately about his choice between a life of duty and a life of retirement and contemplation."[53] "Henry, in his garden, celebrated the founding of Rome, just as he, like Aeneas, was establishing a family in a place."[54]

6. WEST WYCOMBE

To end my description of emblematic or poetic gardens on a lighter note, I would like to close with an account of a ribald garden, Sir Francis Dashwood's estate West Wycombe. Sir Francis was a cultivated man, one of the founders of the Society of Dilettanti, a member of parliament for twenty-two years, and chancellor of the exchequer under Lord Bute. He had, however, a darker side. His youthful escapades on the grand tour were notorious. In Russia he masqueraded as the deceased Charles XII of Sweden in order to woo Tsarevna Anne; in Italy he was expelled from the dominions of the church.[55] Upon returning to England, he and a group of fellow rakes founded a club which met in an old Cistercian abbey in Medmenham. The group, known variously as the Knights of St. Francis of Wycombe, the Mad Monks of Medmenham, and, later, the Hell-Fire Club, reputedly engaged in obscene parodies of religious rites and in the deflowering of local virgins. The club's motto was "Love and Friendship," and the Rabelaisian inscription "Fay Ce Qu Voudras" was carved above the abbey door.

When public interest in the group's activities made their meetings at the abbey untenable, Dashwood decided to create a setting at his own home, West Wycombe. A set of caves was dug beneath the parish church, which sits on chalky hills overlooking the house. Some say the caves themselves were designed to mimic the female anatomy.[56] In any case, Dashwood designed other parts of his West Wycombe estate in keeping with his club's endeavors. His was clearly an X-rated garden.

Scholarly studies of this aspect of West Wycombe are hard to come by. But the fol-

West Wycombe, the Venus Temple. Photograph by David Conway.

lowing features are acknowledged in various popular accounts of the gardens. First, there was a central lake shaped like a swan, possibly intended to recall Leda and her fate. A number of islands dotted the lake. On one of them, reachable only by boat, stood a Temple of Music designed by Nicholas Revett. Another of the garden features in keeping with the overall theme was the temple of Venus, which stood on a belly-like mound. An anatomically shaped Venus chamber was dug into the mound. Dashwood's friend John Wilkes said of the temple that "the entrance to it is the same entrance by which we all come into the world and the door is what some idle wits have called the Door of Life."[57] In Dashwood's time the temple mound was adorned with forty-two erotic statues.[58] Lord Bute,

A View of the Walton Bridge Venus's Temple, &c in the Garden of Sr. Francis Dashwood Bart at West Wycomb in the County of Bucks
Veüe du Pont, du Temple de Venus, &c dans le Jardin du Chevalier Fr. Dashwood à West Wycomb dans le Comté de Bucks.

West Wycombe, the Walton bridge and Venus Temple, engraving by William Woollet after William Hannan. Reproduced by permission of the Yale Center for British Art, Paul Mellon Collection.

who particularly admired this temple, advised Dashwood to "lay out 500 pounds to erect a Paphian column to stand by the entrance."[59] Finally, in his *History of Gardens,* Christopher Thacker quotes a volume of *Victoria County History* to the effect that Dashwood's lake and gardens were "laid out by a curious arrangement of streams, bushes and plantation to represent the female form."[60] Donald Mannix in his book *The Hell Fire Club* is much more explicit. He tells how two mounds each topped with a circle of red flowering plants were lined up at a certain distance from a triangle of dark shrubbery. Sir Francis reputedly took a local priest up into a nearby tower, asked him "What do you think of my gardens?" then arranged to have three fountains turned on. Two of them spouted a milky

A View of the Cascade &c. in the Garden of Sr. Francis Dashwood Bart. & of the Parish Church &c at West Wycomb in the County of Bucks.

West Wycombe, the cascade, engraving by William Woollet after William Hannan. No recumbent female forms are apparent. Reproduced by permission of the Yale Center for British Art, Paul Mellon Collection.

white fluid from the top of each red-flowered mound while the third gushed from the area of the shrubbery.[61]

While Lord Cobham's gardens at Stowe generated a spate of guidebooks to help visitors read the gardens, no such industry was spawned by Sir Francis's creations. Arthur Young wrote of the park in 1767 that "The situation is very agreeable on an eminence rising from a most elegant river which meanders through the park and gardens, with the happiest effect,"[62] while Brayley and Britton's tour book *The Beauties of England and Wales* (1801) speaks of "the variety of fascinating scenery, which results from the harmonious intermixture and disposition of its woods and water." The authors add that "The character of the place is animated and beautiful; and the late removal of various insignificant and unmeaning buildings, has restored the appearance of the ground to its genuine simplicity and nature."[63]

As I said at the outset, I have not been able to find scholarly confirmation for the more extravagant claims made about Sir Francis's garden at West Wycombe. William Hannan painted four scenes of the estate during Dashwood's time. William Woolett's engravings of Hannan's landscapes show no traces of recumbant female forms hidden in the undulating lawns. (But let me note in passing that there is such a female form in a contemporary garden, the Turfwoman in James Pierce's Pratt Farm in Clinton, Maine.) Nevertheless, rumors about Sir Francis's personal excesses and about the erotic aspects of his garden have persisted from his time on. I take this, in and of itself, to be sufficient confirmation for my claim. The mere fact that people for generations have continued to *think* that Dashwood created an erotic garden as a site for debauched adventures shows they believe that a garden can have a sexually explicit design or program. Thus even the persistence of ungrounded rumors about the iconography of West Wycombe attests to the rich symbolic powers we willingly attribute to gardens.

7. INTENTION

I have described four eighteenth-century gardens, each of which resembles a poem. Twickenham, Stowe, Stourhead, and West Wycombe are learned and allusive. They present complex iconographical programs for their viewers to read, discourses about literature, politics, morality, and religion. In the following sections, I would like to give a more general argument for the similarity of gardens and poems. Rather than presenting further examples of gardens which must be read, I shall turn to some of the controversies now current in the field of literary criticism and show that these apply to gardens as well.

In his introduction to the anthology *Against Theory,* W. J. T. Mitchell lists over ten varieties of theory (structuralism, semiotics, hermeneutics, deconstruction, speech-act theory, reception theory, psycholanalytic theory, feminism, Marxism, and various philosophical approaches such as antifoundationalism),[64] while Adena Rosmarin, in the same volume, lists six possible sorts of poetics (affective, intentional, semiological, ideological, formalist, psychoanalytic, and so on).[65] Each of these positions supports a different account of the nature of a text and different accounts of the enterprises of reading, interpretation, and evaluation. If gardens, too, can constitute texts, then gardens can partake in the debates now raging about theory. In what follows, I shall consider the application to gardens of three topics: (1) artistic intention, (2) multiple interpretation, and (3) style.

In their famous article "The Intentional Fallacy" (1954), Monroe Beardsley and William Wimsatt argued that authorial intention is both unavailable and inappropriate for critical practice.[66] This New Critical tenet has since then been abandoned. In fact, Steven Knapp and Walter Benn Michaels have recently argued in their controversial article "Against Theory" that meaning and intention are inseparable. Their goal is not to revive the sort of intentionalism that Beardsley and Wimsatt attacked, but rather to use this example in an argument that would deflate all literary theory. In any case, there are certainly interpretive claims which turn on evidence about authorial intent. And such claims arise with gardens as well as with poems.

Here is one example. Resemblances are often cited between particular gardens and particular landscape paintings. For instance, a number of writers have noted the similarity between a certain vista at Stourhead and Claude Lorrain's painting *Coast View of Delos with Aeneas.* Both feature similar structures similarly disposed. Thus Kenneth Woodbridge writes that the painting "has a Doric portico in the foreground with the Pantheon facing it, and a bridge to the left, in the same relative positions in which these features are seen on entering the gardens at Stourhead."[67] But what, if anything, follows from this? The similarity between garden and painting is compatible with a number of different situations. (1) Henry Hoare designed Stourhead as a copy of the painting. (2) The garden merely alludes to the painting. (3) In designing Stourhead, Henry Hoare was unknowingly influenced by the painting. (4) The garden and painting are linked by a longer chain of influence. (5) The resemblance is entirely accidental.

Which of these five suggestions is correct depends in part on facts about the garden's creation. If Henry Hoare never saw or knew of *Coast View of Delos with Aeneas,* then either (4) or (5) is the case. If Henry knew the painting but sincerely disavowed any direct connection, then (3) or (4) is the correct explanation. And, the choice between (1) and (2) turns on Henry's actual intentions in designing that segment of the garden. Evidence of those intentions may not exist now, and Stourhead's interpreters will have to mount more roundabout arguments to justify one or another account of that vista.

The example I have just sketched is not an idle riddle but an actual problem of garden interpretation. The complexities of such cases are immense. In his book *Influence in Art and Literature,*[68] Goran Hermeren lists thirteen different requirements for genuine artistic influence and six different sorts of reasons that can be offered to support the claim that one work influenced another! I shall return to the question of resemblance between a garden and a painting in chapter 4 and call into question the very notion that a garden might copy a painting. And, I shall say more about particular interpretations of Stourhead later in this chapter. For now, however, consider another problem about intention, this one concerning gardens and poems. How are we to interpret the following poem which occurs on the back of Stowe's Temple of British Worthies?

> To the memory of Signor Fido
> an *Italian* of good Extraction;
>   who came into England
> not to bite us, like most of his Countrymen,
>   but to gain an honest Livelihood.
> He hunted not after Fame,
>   yet acquired it,
> regardless of the Praise of Friends
>   but most sensible of their Love.
> Tho' he lived amongst the Great
> he neither learnt nor flatter'd any Vice.
>   He was no Bigot,
> Tho' he doubted of none of the 39 Articles.
>   And, if to follow Nature,
> and to respect the Laws of Society,
>   be Philosophy,
> he was a perfect Philosopher;
>   a faithful Friend,
> an agreeable companion,
>   a loving Husband,
> distinguish'd by a numerous Offspring,
> all which he lived to see take good Courses.
>   In his old Age he retired
> to the House of a Clergyman in the Country,
>   where he finished his earthly Race,
> And died an Honour and an Example to the whole
> Species.[69]

Hunt explains that these lines addressed to Signor Fido in fact commemorate one of Lord Cobham's greyhounds. The lines therefore contribute to the satiric tone of the entire ensemble, but their interpretation remains problematic. Were viewers really meant to circle around behind the temple and read the poem to Fido, or was it merely a hidden, private joke? If the poem was meant to be seen and added in the total effect of the Elysian Fields, then doesn't a problem of decorum arise? The serious political points made by the figures and inscriptions of the Temple of British Worthies seem in danger of being undercut by the broad satire describing a dog's moral and intellectual virtues in human terms. In sum, our understanding of Stowe's Elysian Fields depends in part on how we settle certain questions about intent—on whether we assume we are meant to see the poem about Signor Fido, and whether we assume we are meant to read it as an integral part of the Elysian Fields, one which contributes to the meaning of the whole. As in the previous example about Claudean influence at Stourhead, it is possible *in principle* to settle such questions about intent, but the requisite evidence might be lacking in particular cases.

8. MULTIPLE INTERPRETATION

The second interpretive issue I would like to raise is that of multiple interpretations. It has become a commonplace in recent critical theory that texts do not have a fixed, determinate meaning. Deconstructionists maintain that every reading creates a new text, and that intertextuality links each text to every other in web of signification. Stanley Fish's account undercuts this radical permissiveness by relativizing interpretation to interpretive communities. Within each community, shared beliefs, assumptions, norms, and values guarantee that a certain interpretive strategy prevails. But since Fish places no limit on the number of interpretive communities that can coexist, texts remain polysemous in principle. I shall argue that the same is true of gardens. A given garden can sustain conflicting, incompatible interpretations, and over time we reread (reinterpret) gardens in incompatible ways. I shall make my point by considering several interpretations of Henry Hoare's garden at Stourhead.

Recall Stourhead's circuit walk. The account of it presented above was drawn from the writings of Kenneth Woodbridge and Ronald Paulson. Both authors argue that the walk around the lake mirrors Aeneas's adventures in book 6 of the *Aeneid.* But others disagree. For example, Kimerly Rorshach, in her catalog for an exhibition at the Yale University Center for British Art, endorses the Woodbridge/Paulson view that "the lake at Stourhead represents Lake Avernus, the lake outside Naples near which was the legendary entrance to the underworld,"[70] then notes that "This interpretation has been challenged by [James] Turner, who believes that the lake at Stourhead is meant to evoke the sea described in Book I of *The Aeneid.*"[71] It may seem that not that much turns on this particular dispute, since both parties agree that the iconography of Stourhead's circuit walk is meant to represent Aeneas's journey. Yet Turner rails against his fellow exegetes, declaring that Woodbridge and Paulson "have confused the garden's chronological development, misrepresented its allusions, and underestimated its unity."[72]

Turner's disagreement is not just about the identification of the central body of water. Although he follows Woodbridge and Paulson and keys the garden's overall iconographic program to the *Aeneid,* Turner maintains that they read the circuit in such a way that many of its features are neglected. In particular, he claims their interpretation neglects the many nonclassical elements at Stourhead: Stourton church, the Bristol cross, Peter's pump, Alfred's tower, which crowns the western horizon, and Stourton village itself, which forms part of the eastern vista. Turner argues that from the very start of the circuit, Stourhead presents visitors with a counterpoint in styles: "[At] the first viewpoint, the Temple of Apollo reared up unexpectedly in front and Stourton Church appeared almost immediately to the left, far below, giving the visitor a curious feeling of disembodied height. The Gothic and the Classical are dramatically juxtaposed. (71) . . . From the Pantheon a composite scene is revealed—the Temple of Ceres close to the English village with its Gothic cross, the Temple of Apollo, the Hermitage, ruin, and cascade. The counterpart of Gothic and Classical is thus maintained, and continues throughout the journey."[73]

Turner identifies two structures at Stourhead, one physical, the other textual.[74] The latter is based on five inscriptions visitors encounter in walking around the garden. Turner argues that the textual structure supports his reading of the garden. He notes that the inscription on which Woodbridge and Paulson place so much weight—the phrase from book 6 of the *Aeneid* inscribed over the Temple of Flora—was never mentioned in Henry Hoare's time. Moreover, he argues that the route around the garden was changed by Henry's grandson, and that originally the first inscription visitors would have encountered is the passage from book 1 of the *Aeneid* carved over the entrance to the grotto.[75] As the final piece of evidence for his interpretation, Turner argues that the feature referred to in Henry's letter quoting from the *Aeneid*, book 6, was not the grotto but an underpass at the southwest corner of the garden. Turner explains:

> An allusion to the sixth book of the *Aeneid* may be intended at Stourhead, but it is as faint and nonchalant as Hoare's "facilis descensus Averno," an amusing *ad hoc* parallel between the Zeals road underpass (a minor feature of the garden) and the descent to Hades. To take the [Temple of Flora] description as a key, and to interpret the lake's circuit as a sibylline voyage is to distort the garden's sequence and emphasis; to assert that the allusions of Stourhead are "almost exclusively to Book VI" is patently wrong. A far more cogent and plausible program is provided by the *first* book of the *Aeneid,* the immediate context of the first inscription.[76]

Turner's quarrel with Woodbridge and Paulson, then, turns on three crucial claims: (1) that their interpretation fails to take into account many of the garden's features, (2)

A view of Stourhead, painted by Coplestone Warre Bamfylde (engraved by Francis Vivares), showing some of the garden's nonclassical elements (the Bristol cross, the parish church). Reproduced by permission of the Yale Center for British Art, Paul Mellon Collection.

that they accord the inscription from book 6 a wrongful prominence because they misidentify the original route of the garden circuit, and (3) that the letter from Henry Hoare alluding to the descent to the underworld does not describe the Stourhead grotto, but a quite different underground passage. Turner completes his argument by showing how the garden can be read in the context of book 1 of the *Aeneid*.

The inscription which Turner believes is crucial for our understanding of Stourhead is the phrase "Intus aquae dulces, vivoque sedilia saxo, nympharum domus" [Inside are sweet waters and seats of living rock—a house of nymphs] carved over the entrance to the grotto. Turner suggests that the Stourhead landscape corresponds topographically to the calm harbor described in book 1 of the *Aeneid*,[77] and he relates the overall message of the garden to the literary tradition of rural retirement. If storms represent political strife, then a calm harbor—and by extension the entire Stourhead landscape—stands for shelter, respite, and moral integrity.[78] Furthermore, the *Aeneid* opens with a storm at sea; Neptune then appears in a horse-drawn chariot and calms the waves. Turner deduces from drawings and contemporary reports that a statue of "Neptune and his 4 Naggs" graced the lake in front of the Temple of Flora.[79] The statue formed part of the scene visible from the viewing hole of the grotto. Turner concludes that "The controlling text in [the circuit at Stourhead] is the first one to be encountered, the lines from the first book of the *Aeneid*."[80]

In the closing section of his paper, Turner shows how one final nonclassical element, Alfred's tower, can be integrated into Stourhead's iconographical program. The inscription on the tower commemorates Alfred as a giver of peace and of law. Turner writes,

> Alfred, at the far western point of the garden's axis, acts historically as Neptune does mythically: he quells violence, "gives peace and rest to Earth," and protects the good land. The twin guardians of the estate are representatives of two elements that had already been embodied in the Elysian Fields at Stowe, Ancient Virtue and the British Worthies. The interweaving of the Gothic and Classical modes is thus brought to a significant conclusion.[81]

I cannot ajudicate all of Turner's differences with Woodbridge and Paulson. In particular, I am not in a position to decide their claims about the Stourhead circuit in Henry Hoare's time and which of the monuments and inscriptions would be encountered first. It is a strength of Turner's account that it encompasses all of the garden's features, not just those classical structures easily tied to episodes from the *Aeneid*. On the other hand, some of the charm of the earlier interpretations is lost, since, on Turner's view, the garden no longer has a narrative structure, and visitors' progress along the path no longer corresponds to Aeneas's progress in Virgil's epic.

Imagine a "metric" imposed on competing interpretations of a given work of art. It ranges them according to overlap and inclusion, on the one hand, and incompatibility and contradiction, on the other. Though Turner and Woodbridge/Paulson offer competing accounts of Stourhead's iconography, their interpretations don't seem all that "distant," since all three make reference to the *Aeneid*. I would like to turn to two other accounts of Stourhead which are quite different from those already considered. The first proposes a second reading which coexists with the Virgilian one; the second denies the Virgilian theme altogether.

Recall Max Schulz's claim that the walk around the Stourhead circuit has Christian as well as classical significance. While not denying that the sequence from temple to grotto to temple parallels Aeneas's journey from Troy, his descent into the underworld, and the founding of Rome, Schulz maintains that Aeneas's adventures were seen as prefiguring the life of Christ, and so Stourhead also represents the Christian cycle of sin and redemption, the story of paradise lost and regained. On this view, any garden is automatically associated with that first garden, Eden, and any circular path recalls the Christian paradigm—"the circuitous pilgrimage of the soul back to its spiritual home."[82] Thus Schulz claims that visitors attending to Stourhead's Virgilian associations, "to be found in Book VI of *Aeneid*, . . . would know they had not only duplicated symbolically Aeneas's journey from Troy by way of Delos sacred to Apollo, his descent into Hades, and his founding of Rome, but had encapsulated in that walk the archetypal patterns of life and death informing Aeneas's journey."[83]

Schulz traces these archetypal patterns to a variety of sources—Judaic, Neoplatonic, and Christian—and he argues that they evolved into a romantic topos of paradise given, lost, and regained.[84] It does indeed seem natural to associate a garden with Eden. Earlier I quoted Schulz's claim that "it would have been extraordinary if the religious associations of the walk had not occurred to visitors."[85] Elsewhere he remarks that "it represented no extreme exercise of mind to experience the eighteenth-century landscape garden as a new scene of human bliss, where Eden could be ritualistically renewed, and in that symbolic action the original earthly paradise rediscovered as prelude to the final celestial paradise."[86]

What seems troubling about Schulz's account is that it appears so little tied to Stourhead's actual features and topography. On his view, any scenic garden circuit is equally a candidate for the Christian interpretation just presented and the archetypal patterns it overlays. Perhaps the Stourhead circuit could be identified more closely with details of the soul's or pilgrim's progress. But at least one interpreter of Stourhead denies Schulz's reading because he denies that the *Aeneid* had the Christian significance Schulz claims for it in the eighteenth century. In his article "The Iconography of Stourhead," Malcolm Kelsall denies the claim, quoted from Paulson, that the *Aeneid* "was generally interpreted by the Christian exegetes as a parable of the Christian soul's journey through life, echoed in the *Tabula celetis* and other classical texts and in the metaphors of Puritan devotional literature."[87]

Kelsall finds further fault with the Woodbridge/Paulson reading of Stourhead. He notes that "concentration upon a supposed sequence of Virgilian allusions in a circuit walk has lead to the suppression of the clear visual counterpoint between the classical vistas within the garden and the Christian and Gothic images without."[88] Yet Kelsall rejects Turner's method of integrating Stourhead's classical and Gothic references, and he criticizes Schulz and others for failing to read the *Aeneid* as its eighteenth-century readers did, that is, as a political poem rather than as a piece of Christian exegesis.[89]

Insisting that Stourhead "lacks . . . any clear reference, visual or verbal, to the founding of Rome,"[90] Kelsall also denies any relation between the garden landscape and Claude's *Coast View of Delos with Aeneas.* Claiming that "such recondite allusion would be unusual in eighteenth-century gardens,"[91] he proposes that the obvious allusion in the Stourhead vista that resembles Claude's painting is to the Pantheon, "a temple built . . . by Augustus's marshal Agrippa, and now seen, as if by magic, within the green world of the English countryside. . . . Everyone would perceive the reference to the Augustan temple. The primary association, therefore, is with the natural religion of the ancients."[93]

Kelsall identifies natural religion as one of the garden's central motifs;[93] he deems chastity the other. Unlike others who take the inscription "Procul, o procul este profani" to refer to book 6 of the *Aeneid,* Kelsall interprets these lines in relation to natural religion: "The profane are those who see nature in terms of sensuality or libertinism."[94] To reinforce this reading, he points out that inscriptions identify the river god in the grotto not as Father Tiber from *Aeneid* 8 but as Daphne's father Peneus from *Metamorphoses* 1.[95] Viewers are thus invited to recall a tale which underlines the garden's theme of chastity, Apollo's attempted rape of Daphne and her transformation into a laurel tree.

Like Turner, Kelsall emphasizes Stourhead's integration of classical and nonclassical elements, but he gives this a religious rather than a political reading. Kelsall makes much of the view *out* from the approach to the Pantheon, "the counterpart of the original Claudean vista which struck the eye coming in."[96] This view in fact focuses on St. Peter's Church—"the Church of the true God of the Christian revealed religion."[97] Kelsall concludes that the moral of the entire garden is Christian humanism. The dialectic evidenced throughout the circuit contrasts classic and Gothic, Rome and Britain, natural and revealed religion. The dialectic continues, Kelsall claims, with Alfred's tower set apart on a hill in order to distinguish between ancient and modern Augustanism.[98] "The tower counterpoints the Apolline temple just as the church and market cross are set in juxtaposition to the Pantheon. They too are acknowledgements of 'Divine Providence'."[99]

Since I know little about eighteenth-century construals of Virgil's *Aeneid,* I cannot weigh the merits of Kelsall's arguments against those of Woodbridge, Paulson, and Turner. But what I want to emphasize in this section, apart from the intrinsic interest of these competing accounts, is the interpretive demands placed on Stourhead's viewers. Arcane facts must be known in order to read this garden. And the competing accounts must be judged like scientific theories, compared with respect to inclusiveness, simplicity, adequacy, coherence, and so on. All this in order to understand a garden!

The interpretations of Stourhead canvassed so far all have one thing in common. Each tries to uncover the meaning intended by the garden's designer. Yet not all critical theories accord such power and autonomy to the creators of works of art. Marxist, psychoanalytic, and feminist interpretations, for example, often uncover significance of which the artist was unaware.

Two writers who offer such approaches to landscape are James Turner and Carole Fabricant. In his paper "The Sexual Politics of Landscape: Images of Venus in Eighteenth-Century English Poetry and Landscape Gardening,"[100] Turner notes two traits that have been associated with Venus from the Renaissance on—sexuality and modesty. These two traits are often combined in one and the same image: Venus's beauty invites, yet her posture and her surroundings (say, a shady bower) fend off, the viewer. Turner argues that this attitude toward sexuality and possession was extended to landscape when the serpentine line championed by Hogarth was utilized as a principle of landscape design. "The Venus de Medici played a crucial role in establishing this mutuality of landscape and sexual gesture. . . . Her form and posture reconciled two contrary motions, just as her gesture combined concealment and display, modesty and availability."[101] Writing of Twickenham and Rousham, two gardens each of which housed a statue of Venus de Medici in what Turner describes as "tubular structures formed by sinuous expansion and contraction of woods,"[102] he says "Both places embody a dialectic of privacy and sociability, self-concealment and self-display; landscape and owners both 'assemble' and 'retire' in Walpole's words. This contrary motion is both social and sexual."[103] And later, discussing Pope's *Epistle to Burlington,* Turner speaks of the poet's "aesthetic of sexualized topography."[104] Turner thus sees a hidden sexual agenda in all of the landscape gardens in the first half of the eighteenth century. He reads the smooth and undulating designs at Twickenham, Rousham, and the Leasowes as ciphers for sexuality and desire.

In her paper "Binding and Dressing Nature's Loose Tresses: The Ideology of Augustan Landscape Design,"[105] Carole Fabricant gives a feminist reading of the eighteenth-century garden aesthetic which is compatible with many of Turner's claims. Fabricant sees a convergence among aesthetic, economic, and sexual forms of possession.[106] She argues that nature was viewed as a wife or mistress. Like a woman, nature was a source of pleasure; like a woman, she was to be used and improved; and, like a woman, she was to be available to her master yet chastely screened from the view of others.

Analyzing Addison's *Spectator* essays, Fabricant points out that women "are continually judged for their ability to gratify the eye and the senses. Moreover, women, like landscapes, are converted into paintings, into framed—hence ownable and 'possessable'—objects designed specifically for male scrutiny."[107] Turning to Thomson's poem *The Seasons,* Fabricant points out that "Nature is continually described here in terms of a total visual (as well as implicitly sexual) yielding of herself."[108] Fabricant argues that an owner's relation to the gardens of his estate was similarly sexualized: "The male owner's 'penetration' into the 'inner spaces' of his garden was a journey into and through a variety of enclosures and structures deliberately designed as parts of a feminine landscape: e.g., the Vale of Venus at Rousham, the Temple of Flora at Stourhead, and the Lady's Temple, the Temple of Venus, and the Queen's Valley at Stowe."[109] Thus Fabricant maintains that the iconographic program which Sir Francis Dashwood explicitly incorporated into his garden at West Wycombe was present implicitly in many other eighteenth-century landscape gardens.

Fabricant's account of landscape aesthetics thus finds sexism and patriarchy rampant even in those gardens not consciously designed to be erotic. We might ask whether gardens designed by eighteenth-century women would be open to similar charges. Unfortunately, I don't know of any major landscapes created by women in that era.[110] If eighteenth-century women were not, in general, allowed to engage in garden design on any large scale, this very fact might confirm Fabricant's claim that the role of landscape improver was identified with pervasive patriarchal and sexist attitudes.[111]

Fabricant's reappraisal extends even to the quotation from Walpole which I have taken as my organizing theme, the claim that painting, poetry, and landscape are the three sisters, for she notes "It need hardly be pointed out that these 'sisters' remained under the constant guidance and supervision of their loving but strong-willed 'fathers'—of men like Brown."[112] While these articles by Turner and Fabricant do not present additional interpretations of the Stourhead circuit to compete with those already described, they introduce considerations that the garden's interpreters must either challenge or incorporate. Thus with gardens, as with poetry, a new and radical constituency is forcing a reevaluation of critical canons and critical procedures.

9. STYLE

The last issue I would like to take up in this chapter is that of style. In his essay "The Status of Style," reprinted in *Ways of Worldmaking,* Nelson Goodman criticizes hasty accounts of style based on a facile distinction between form and content. He points out that "style comprises certain characteristic features both of what is said and of how it is said, both of subject and of wording, both of content and of form."[113] He elaborates: "What is said, how it is said, what is expressed, and how it is expressed are all intimately interrelated and involved in style."[114] Exemplification is added to the mix as well, and Goodman eventually concludes that "Basically, . . . style consists of those features of the symbolic functioning of a work that are characteristic of author, period, place, or school."[115]

Richard Wollheim discriminates more finely among such features when he distinguishes general from individual style.[116] General style, he suggests, comes in three varieties: (1) universal style (classicism, the geometrical style, naturalism), (2) historical or period style (neoclassicism, art nouveau, social realism), and (3) school style (the style of Giotto, Verona, or the court of Rudolf II).[117] Individual style is "what we characteristically refer to when we use the phrase 'the style of a'—where a stands in for the name of a painter—to refer to something in the work of a."[118]

Wollheim's goal is to defend a generative conception of style in which individual style has psychological reality.[119] On this view, accurate individual style descriptions of an artist's work pick out features generated by his interests, preferences, choices, procedures, and skills,[120] what Wollheim calls his mental store.[121] General style, by contrast, is identified "taxonomically."[122] That is, while general style descriptions refer to interesting or distinctive features apparent in a work, there is no presumption that these features are tied in an essential way to the artist's creative process. It follows from these definitions that general style can be learned, but individual style must be formed.[123]

Wollheim warns that the claims he makes pertain to the art of painting and cannot be extended to other arts without distortion.[124] Nevertheless, Jenefer Robinson has extended Wollheim's distinction between general and individual style to the literary arts.[125] Consider a further extension to the art of gardening.

Gardens which, like those of eighteenth-century England, aspire to be high art can sustain a distinction between general and individual style. But the distinction remains problematic, and general style terms from the other arts do not transfer readily to gardens. Consider one example Wollheim offered of historical style in painting, that of neoclassicism. Neoclassical paintings like those of Ingres and David emulate the classical world in their choice of subject matter and moral outlook as well as through such formal and expressive components as balance, restraint, rationality, and repose. While gardens like Stowe and Stourhead are equally indebted to the classical world, borrowing both architecture and iconography from antiquity, no one deems them neoclassical gardens. And since they are so eclectic, stylistic labels cannot be derived from their architectural elements alone. Recall the many comments about Stourhead's mix of classical and Gothic elements. The eighteenth century's enthusiasm for chinoiserie generated even randier mixes. Kew Gardens, for example, had a mosque, a Chinese pagoda, and a Roman triumphal arch alongside the more familiar classical temples and Palladian bridge. The relevant general style term remains "English landscape garden," or perhaps one of the neologisms Hunt and Paulson propose: poetic garden or emblematic garden.

In a brief article "The Nomenclature of Style in Garden History,"[126] Richard Woodbridge discusses some other art-historical terms that have been applied to gardens. These include "Mannerist," "Baroque," "Rococo," and "Picturesque." Roy Strong, for example, in *The Renaissance Garden in England,* classes as Mannerist certain sixteenth-century Italian gardens as well as various seventeenth-century English gardens which they influenced.[127] These gardens are distinguished by terracing, grottos, geometric parterres, ambitious iconographic programs, elaborate waterworks, and, most distinctive of all, automata like those described by Hero of Alexandria in his work *Pneumatica*—for instance, statues that move and birds that sing, all due to water pressure. This general style classification is, therefore, based on external features as Wollheim demands. Woodbridge notes, however, that such style classifications are useful to "suitably programmed minds,"[128] and that the terms must always be either stretched or restricted, sharpened or extended, when applied to new arts.

One further difficulty in singling out general style terms that apply to gardens is the fact that poetry and painting do, while gardening does not, support the notion of genre in addition to that of style. As Jenefer Robinson points out, poems within a given genre can be marked by different period styles. Thus she contrasts the Renaissance with the Augustan pastoral.[129] We can think of many genres in eighteenth-century poetry (the mock epic, the epistle, the pastoral, the ode) and painting (the history painting, the conversation piece, the allegorical portrait). Comparable garden genres are hard to think of. Following Schultz's essay, discussed above, we might propose the circuit garden as one garden genre. The water garden is another, the terraced garden perhaps a third, though neither was common in eighteenth-century England. It is tempting in this context to propose the poetic garden as a garden genre rather than a (general) garden style. Since gardens with iconographic programs that had to be read were indeed created in Renaissance Italy and in seventeenth-century France, among other places, we might hope to identify this genre, the poetic garden, across different period and national styles. But rather than the Renaissance poetic garden and the French poetic garden, garden historians write of the Italian Mannerist garden and the French formal garden.

These difficulties might simply reflect the nascent stage of garden history and criticism, as opposed to the study of literature and painting, but I suspect there are further factors which account for gardens' recalcitrance in the face of critical taxonomies. It may be that an art form, in order to sustain the distinction between style and genre, has to sustain the notion of content more robustly than does the garden. Robinson suggests that a genre "usually specifies both a certain sort of subject matter and a certain universal style category, for example, tragedy, comedy, epic, lyric, pastoral, and elegy."[130] All the gardens discussed in this chapter had subjects in a literary sense, but the same is not true of those eighteenth-century gardens assimilated to painting rather than to poetry. Thus only a few gardens function symbolically in such a way that a genre designation could take hold. The variations that we tend to notice among gardens exist not because they tell different types of stories, but because they present different sorts of scenes and express different sorts of moods.

Note that the candidate garden genres I proposed—circuit garden, water garden, terraced garden—all classify gardens according to structural features rather than subject matter or content. In fact, most gardens are compared and differentiated on the basis of the sorts of outward characteristics (climate, topography, setting, architectural elements, use of water, predominant plant types, etc.) that contribute to style descriptions rather than to genre categories. Moreover, the general style descriptions applied to gardens tend to classify them according to nationality—the English garden, the French garden, the Italian garden, and so on. There is a reason for this. Gardeners, unlike poets and painters, develop a site, and this involves severe restrictions. Climate, topography, soil type, available water, even such social factors as patterns of land ownership and use, affect garden design. Together, these constraints limit the extent to which, say, an English garden can resemble a French, Moorish, or Japanese garden, and they make it difficult for garden styles to travel across cultures. There is likely to be more similarity among the different period styles of the gardens of a given culture—e.g., in Strong's division of Italian gardens into three periods: Humanist, High Renaissance, and Mannerist (13–14)—than similarity across cultures that would permit us to identify a single garden genre common to Italy, France, and England.

Granted, certain garden styles were in vogue throughout Europe at various times. Thus Patrick Goode writes in the *Oxford Companion to Gardens* that Bernardo Buontalenti's sixteenth-century gardens at Pratolino, near Florence, were destroyed in 1819 to make a *giardino inglese*.[131] The nineteenth-century vogue for the "English garden," like the eighteenth-century vogue for Chinoiserie, involved borrowing certain obvious stylistic features—naturalized plantings and ponds, on the one hand, pagodas and arched wooden bridges, on the other—rather than adapting the unfamiliar art form to the native situation and arriving at a new stylistic synthesis. In sum, gardens can sustain the notion of (general) style, though style terms from the arts of painting and poetry do not switch over smoothly to apply to gardens, nor does the concept of genre play as important a role as with gardening's two sisters.

Turning to individual style, we see that gardens again present special problems. To identify the style of a given artist, a number of his works must be compared in order to distinguish characteristic traits from adventitious ones. Yet very few eighteenth-century gardens survive, and those that do were often worked successively by a number of garden designers. In fact, discussions of early eighteenth-century gardens are often taken up with disputes about just who had a hand in them. The careers of Charles Bridgeman, Stephen Switzer, and William Kent are hard to track. Moreover, many amateurs had a hand in designing their own and one another's estates. The circle comprising Pope and his friends—Vanbrugh, Lord Cobham, the Earl of Bathurst, Ralph Allen, and so on—contained many amateur gardeners. Perhaps we can never get clear on their tangled contributions to various estates.

Think how different our concept of literary style would be if poems were more like gardens. Suppose poets tended to rewrite their predecessors' compositions rather than create original works, or at the very least felt free to append new verses in a different style to other poets' poems. Suppose, too, that poems tended to alter once written. That is, suppose that poems, once penned, were not fixed, but rather the words on the page gradually changed and new words often appeared. If poetry resembled gardening in these respects, then we would be much less able to track a poet's individual style. A change comes with the advent of Capability Brown; here we have a gardenist who developed a distinctive style, so much so, in fact, that he was maligned as unimaginative, but also widely imitated. I shall discuss his career and the responses his gardens evoked in chapter 6. Humphry Repton, whose gardens were associated with Brown's and subsumed under the label "picturesque," may not have created designs as immediately recognizable as Brown's. But his famous Red Books—volumes he prepared while consulting about each estate, each containing drawings of the estate as it looked at the start and transparent over-leaves showing proposed improvements—give him a signature of sorts as well.

THE SISTER ARTS II

Gardens and Painting

I. INTRODUCTION

Painshill Park near Cobham, Surrey, a garden created by Charles Hamilton between 1738 and 1773, resembles Stourhead in a number of respects. Both are gardens in the Claudean mode, with a central lake surrounded by rolling hills, varied trees, and a number of garden structures. To create Painshill, Hamilton transformed three hundred acres of inhospitable moorland through intensive excavation, earth moving, and planting.[1] The garden was laid out as a hilly four-mile circuit. Water raised from the river Mole supplied the central lake in which Hamilton built a number of islands. Painshill contained temples, monuments, and follies in various architectural styles: a Gothic temple, a Gothic tower, a ruined abbey, a Turkish tent, a mausoleum in the form of a Roman triumphal arch, a Grecian temple designed by Robert Adam, a rusticated hermitage, an elaborate grotto, and a variety of Palladian and Chinese bridges. The garden also contained a wide variety of botanical specimens. It was especially known for its cedars and for its many species of conifers from North America. Eighteenth-century visitors to Painshill were guided around the garden in a prescribed circuit, encountering a carefully ordered sequence of monuments, scenes, and vistas.

Painshill, the Gothic Temple. Photograph by David Conway.

Not only were Painshill and Stourhead similar in layout and appearance, they were both designed by gentleman-owners, Charles Hamilton and Henry Hoare, who were themselves well acquainted, having matriculated together at Westminster School. Hamilton advised Hoare about the design and planting of Stourhead (85–86), and in 1766, when he was beset by financial troubles, Hamilton obtained a loan of six thousand pounds from Hoare, an affluent banker. Unfortunately, this was not sufficient to offset his other outstanding debts, and Painshill was sold at auction in 1773.[2]

Despite similarities in appearance and origin, Painshill and Stourhead function very differently. While Stourhead is a poetic garden whose complex iconography sustains the interpretive debates surveyed earlier, Painshill was instead a painterly garden.[3] One commentator, Michael Symes, writes:

Painshill, the view from the Gothic Temple showing the lake below. Photograph by David Conway.

Hamilton composed the pleasure gardens as a series of pictures which altered continually, with surprises and illusions. The lake was made to seem bigger than it was by its shaping and by the arrangement of islands so that the water could not be seen all at once. There were certain set scenes in the gardens, usually centered round a temple or other folly. The paths were skillfully contrived to give the visitor different perspectives and angles from which to view the lake and other parts of the grounds, and the plantings played their part in concealing a view until it appeared to its best advantage.[4]

Thus Painshill offered visitors a series of engaging visual scenes with contrasting emotional tones and carefully composed visual surprises, but it did not have a complex meaning that visitors were to puzzle out.

Certainly, the fact that Stourhead does, while Painshill does not, convey an intricate iconography is not apparent from the "look" of the gardens alone. Some of Painshill's monuments did in fact have carvings and inscriptions. The pediment of the Temple of Bacchus contained a sculpture (in papier-mâché) of Silenus, drunk, riding an ass and surrounded by satyrs and bacchantes. The temple itself also housed Hamilton's prized marble, a statue of Bacchus over seven feel tall (67). Together these sculptures may well have referred to one of Hamilton's attempted money-making enterprises, bottling champagne from the vineyards on the southeast slopes of his estate.[5]

Despite these clear-cut references to drunkenness and wine, further facts suggest that the temples and monuments at Painshill did not express a set iconographical program. First, the other statues adorning the Temple of Bacchus—copies of the Apollo del Belvedere, the Venus de Medici, Mercury, and the Venus Marina flanking the entrance, and busts of twelve Roman emperors[6] disposed around Bacchus in the interior—would not have contributed to or sustained the bacchanalian theme. Moreover, Hamilton used other follies on his estate in a similar fashion—to house the collection of antiquities he acquired on the grand tour. The mausoleum contained funeral urns, a sarcophagus, and Roman and Greek artifacts (63), while the Gothic tower contained additional marbles.[7] It is unlikely that garden temples serving as repositories for an extensive and randomly assembled collection of sculpture would convey a message via that collection, that is, that they would embody an iconographic program referring to each of the gods and personages represented.

One might object that this argument fails because we can imagine *some* program or other embracing all these varied characters—Brutus, Bacchus, Lucius Verus, Caligula, Flora, Minerva, and more. But a third consideration weighs against Painshill's conveying a fixed poetic or emblematic meaning. This is the fact that none of the writers who left accounts of eighteenth-century visits to Painshill—John Parnell, Horace Walpole, Richard Pococke, Thomas Whately, William Gilpin, William Robertson—makes any mention of an iconographical program sustained by the garden. More important, Hamilton himself does not mention any such program in his writings. This must be considered definitive. Recall Danto's doppelganger examples cited earlier. Two gardens might have the same appearance yet express quite different meanings; alternatively, two gardens might have the same appearance yet only one express any meaningful or denotative content (and this is in fact the relation I believe holds between Stourhead and Painshill). The fact of the matter in such cases would be determined by the designers' intentions. Thus Hamilton's silence on these matters provides crucial support for the claim that Painshill is a painterly rather than a poetic garden.

Painshill, the Mausoleum. Photograph by David Conway.

Let me conclude with two additional points which support a connection between Painshill and painting. First of all, while in Rome on the grand tour in 1725–27 and again in 1731–34, Hamilton himself took up the art of painting.[8] He may well have sketched some of the Roman scenes discussed in chapter 2. He also acquired a large collection of paintings at this time, many of them landscapes by Italian masters.[9] Thus Hamilton would have possessed both the knowledge and the skill to create a painterly garden. (I shall take up in chapter 5 the question of whether and to what extent the principles of painting are appropriate guides to garden design. This question was hotly debated by Humphry Repton and Sir Uvedale Price in their writings on the picturesque.) And second, a number of eighteenth-century visitors to Painshill did stress its painterly aspects, its presentation of carefully framed scenes, "landskips," and vistas. For example, Richard Pococke said that "The whole circuit is four miles, and there are a great variety of prospects from the different parts of it."[10] John Parnell described some of these in detail in 1763.[11] Thomas Whately declares that Painshill "little benefited by external circumstances, but the scenes within itself are both grand and beautiful, and the disposition of the gardens affords frequent opportunities of seeing the park, in a variety of advantageous situations." Overall he maintains that "a boldness of design, and a happiness of execution, attend the wonderful efforts which art has there made to rival nature."[12] Finally, William Robertson, an architect who visited Painshill in 1795—after Hamilton had sold the estate but while his overall design as well as his collections (his marbles and so on) were still intact—wrote that "Mr. Hamilton studied painting for the express purpose of improving this place and such was his passion for planting and ornamenting that he expended the greater part of a fine property on this place."[13]

I have been contrasting Stourhead and Painshill to introduce the notion of a painterly garden and to motivate the second of the sister arts comparisons, that between gardening and painting. Because both gardens and paintings are visual arts, and because the label "landscape" applies to each, the comparison between them seems more apt and more persuasive than that between gardens and poems. Many eighteenth-century gardeners, connoisseurs, critics, and historians noted the kinship between these first two arts. For example, Pope declared "All gardening is landscape painting";[14] Addison wrote that "a man might make a pretty landskip of his possessions";[15] and Vanbrugh, when consulted about the gardens at Blenheim, said "you must send for a landscape painter."[16] Thomas Whately took the comparison between gardens and paintings as a given, a commonplace to be subjected to rhetorical play in the opening lines of his book *Observations on Modern Gardening* (1770),[17] while Horace Walpole, writing in the same year, grounded his famous encomium of the garden designer William Kent in the claim that he was "painter enough to taste the charms of landscape."[18] A later writer, Christopher Hussey, says of Kent "it was he who first conceived the approximation of gardens to painted landscape, with lakes, vistas, temples, and woods worked into a composed whole."[19]

Despite the plausibility and appeal of the comparison between gardens and paintings, the topic is a vexed one. There are a number of different relations which might hold between these two arts. A painting can portray (imitate, represent, be "of") a given garden. Recall the paintings of his estate at Chiswick that Richard Boyle, Lord Burlington, commissioned from the Flemish artist Pieter Andreas Rysbrack in 1728.[20] A painting can also allude to, evoke, recall, or remind us of a particular garden. Each of these relations ordinarily proceeds via some degree of resemblance between painting and garden, although a painting and a garden can resemble other in various respects without any of these relations holding. Finally, a painting can "create" a garden by depicting an entirely fictional garden scene, one which does not exist in the real world.[21] Turning to relations in the other direction—those in which gardens are modeled on or influenced by paintings—a similar array of possibilities exists. That is, a garden can recreate or copy a landscape painting; a garden can allude to, evoke, recall, or remind us of a painting; and lastly, a garden can *function* as a landscape painting if it represents some other piece of land, either real or ideal.

The authors of the statements quoted above did not separate out these various possibilities, so just what sort of comparison their remarks endorse is not always clear. Here I shall concentrate on three relations which might be thought to link gardens and paintings: imitation, allusion, and representation.

2. IMITATION AND ALLUSION

It was claimed of a number of eighteenth-century English gardens that they imitated (more precisely, that certain portions of them imitated) particular landscape paintings. For example, Ronald Paulson in his book *Emblem and Expression* writes of Castle Howard in Yorkshire that statues ranged along the grounds caught and guided the visitor's eye and that the temple which comes into view "emerges in fact as part of a picture, a three-dimensional version of a landscape painting by Claude Lorrain."[22] Hunt and Willis elaborate this claim: "At Castle Howard, Vanbrugh certainly invoked three of the most famous ingredients of such a Claude as the *Pastoral Landscape with the Ponte Molle,* a square and a round building (the Temple of the Four Winds and the Mausoleum, built later by Hawksmoor and Daniel Garrett) and a Palladian bridge."[23]

Stourhead is another garden whose affinity to Claudean landscapes was noted. And since some of Claude's paintings illustrated episodes from the *Aeneid,* there is an iconographic link as well. Kenneth Woodbridge writes, "There is a picture by Claude Lorrain in the National Gallery called *Coast View of Delos with Aeneas* which shows the Pantheon, bridge and Doric portico bearing a curious resemblance to the way in which similar buildings are related to the garden at Stourhead. It represents an episode in Aeneas' journey, before his arrival in Italy. . . . Had Henry Hoare at some time seen *Coast View of Delos with Aeneas?* He had a copy of a similar painting . . . but he was never able to possess an original. Like Aeneas, he was establishing his family in a place."[24]

In addition to the suggestion that part of the Stourhead landscape was modeled on the paintings of Claude Lorraine, a letter which Henry Hoare wrote to his daughter Susanna in 1762 introduces a second comparison. Describing a stone bridge that had just been

A view of Castle Howard showing the features reminiscent of a composition by Claude Lorrain.
Reproduced by permission of the Harry Smith Horticultural Photographic Collection.

added to the Stourhead landscape, he says "I took it from Palladio's bridge at Vicenza, 5 arches; and when you stand at the Pantheon the water will be seen thro the arches and it will look as if the river came down through the village and that this was the village bridge for publick use. The view of the bridge, village and church altogether will be a charming Gaspd picture at the end of the water."[25] The reference is to the painter Gaspard Dughet, also known as Gaspard Poussin, whose landscape scenes had become very popular.

Dorothy Stroud lists both Stourhead and Painshill as "landscapes inspired by the paintings of Claude Lorrain and the Poussins."[26] Thomas Whately, Horace Walpole, and Uvedale Price all visited Painshill and described the gardens. Christopher Thacker reports that these writers "said that Hamilton had studied Italian painters in designing his garden, and that the spirit of Salvator Rosa was evoked with particular success."[27] Walpole called the wooded area near the head of the central lake Alpine. H. F. Clark makes a stronger claim, not just that a spirit was evoked but that "[a] slice of the Alps, closely modeled on the drawings of Salvator Rosa, was made at the head of the lake." The painter Gaspard Poussin inspired another of Hamilton's projects. H. F. Clark explains that Hamilton "made for his friend the Marquis of Lansdowne at Bowood a cascade from a picture by Gasper Poussin."[28] Dennis Wood, writing in the *Oxford Companion,* concurs with this claim: "The cascade at the entrance to the lake was added in 1785 by Charles Hamilton of Painshill in imitation of a painting by Gasper Poussin."[29]

One last amusing example of a garden influenced by or modeled on a painting is reported by Christopher Hussey in his book *The Picturesque.* He claims that William Kent planted dead trees in Kensington Gardens to heighten the similarity to Salvator's rugged, romantic landscapes.[30] Horace Walpole, in *The History of the Modern Taste in Gardening,* writes that "Kent, like other reformers, knew not how to stop at the just limits. He had followed nature, and imitated her so happily, that he began to think that all her works were equally proper for imitation. In Kensington-garden, he planted dead trees, to give a greater air of truth to the scene."[31]

Note the considerable variety in the quotations presented above. Writers speak of gardens imitating paintings (Wood), inspired by paintings (Stroud), being modeled on paintings (Clark), evoking paintings (Thacker), and creating three-dimensional versions of paintings (Paulson). And some simply note a striking coincidence between certain features and their disposition in particular paintings and particular landscape gardens (Woodbridge). I would like to examine what seems the strongest of these claims, the possibility that a garden might imitate or copy a landscape painting. In the discussion that follows, I shall use the terms "copy" and "imitate" interchangeably.

Let me begin with some general remarks about copies. The paradigm of an imitation or copy in our culture today probably comes from the Xerox machine. A xerox copy of a manuscript page is another page so like the original as to be almost indistinguishable from it.

The example of a xerox copy is misleading in two ways: an automatic mechanism is involved, and the original and copied pages are virtually identical. In fact, however, resemblance is neither necessary nor sufficient for one item to be a copy of another. Staples coming off the assembly line of a Tiny Tot stapler factory will resemble one another to as high

The cascade at Bowood, designed by Charles Hamilton. Reproduced by permission of the Harry Smith Horticultural Photographic Collection.

a degree as the xeroxed pages just discussed. But none of the staples is a copy of any other (though each may be a copy of a prototype used to design the production line). This shows that resemblance is not sufficient for the "copy of" relation.[32] Nor is any given degree of resemblance necessary for this relation. On those occasions when the Xerox machine malfunctions and the copy emerges all streaked and smudged, the page produced is still a copy, though perhaps an unacceptable one.

These cases remind us that the relation "copy of" involves a balance between two factors, resemblance and intention. A copy is generated when someone intends to produce an item which resembles another to a sufficiently high degree. The copy must be produced in such a way that a causal chain goes back to the original. This causal chain can involve a mechanical process, as in the case of a Xerox machine. In the case of handmade copies— for example, a medieval monk copying an illuminated manuscript—the causal chain includes the copyist's intentions and perceptions. These could be spelled out in more detail: the copy results from the copyist's intention to produce a likeness of an object which he perceives as he does because of his perceptual skills, the viewing conditions, his background knowledge, his interests and emotions, and so on. This requirement brings about a sort of defeasibility. If the copyist hasn't seen the original or doesn't intend to produce a likeness, then his creation is not a copy no matter how much it resembles that original. (We might leave room here for unconscious copying to cover cases where an artist is unknowingly influenced and ends up producing a work which closely resembles another he or she has seen. But even here resemblance alone would not establish the copy relationship. Proof of the artist's access to or knowledge of the copied item would also be required.)

Are there perfect copies? If we deem a xeroxed page a perfect copy because no observer can tell it from the original, then we are endorsing an epistemic conception of copy, one relativized, moreover, to a given group of perceivers. One might instead seek an ontological conception according to which a perfect copy is not just indistinguishable from its original but is a perfect replica, sharing all the original's nonspatiotemporal properties. Some of the views Nelson Goodman defends in *Languages of Art* point to shortcomings of this second approach. Goodman maintains that resemblance is a relative notion, that two objects resemble each other in certain specifiable respects. Furthermore, every object has countless aspects, many of them incompatible.[33] It follows that no object can copy (i.e., be a copy of) some other object in every way. In fact, Goodman goes further. In *Languages of Art* and in the paper "The Ways the World Is," he denies that there is any definitive way that any object is. I suspect Goodman would say of the notion of a perfect copy just what he says about the copy theory of representation, that it is "stopped at the start by inability to specify what is to be copied."[34]

I have been drawing on Goodman's views to challenge the ontological conception of perfect copy. Unfortunately, those views threaten to scuttle the concept "copy" altogether by denying us the notion of an original against which copies can be matched. Rather than endorse Goodman's dissolution of an objective world into countless competing versions, let us dispense with the notion of a perfect copy and gloss "copy of" as a relation which admits varying degrees of success. If B is a copy of A, then A played an appropriate causal role in B's creation. Whether B is generated through a mechanical process or through some person's talents and skills, the overall intention which guides the endeavor is the desire to produce a likeness. The success of the copy is determined by the judgments of people (1) with properly functioning perceptual faculties (2) who have had some experience with things of type A. Clauses (1) and (2) are intended to prevent the rejection of any purported copy on the grounds that some people can always be found who see no resemblance between it and the original. While there will no doubt be cases where copy and original are indistinguishable—for example, the two xeroxes described above, or an excellent forgery that has fooled all the experts who have examined it to date—it will often be true that one item is a copy of another though many or even most people can tell them apart.

One important trait to notice about the loose sense of copy I am proposing here is that copies can inhabit different media than their originals. Consider a pencil copy of a Dürer engraving, a wax copy of a Ghiberti bronze, a black-and-white copy of a brightly colored ad. These examples remind us that copies, unlike replicas and models, do not have to capture all the distinctive properties of their originals.[35]

Let us return now to gardens and consider how the copy relation might be exercised between two quite different media, gardens and paintings. Since my interest here is in gardens' capacities or powers, my concern is whether gardens can imitate or copy particular landscape paintings.[36] Suppose then that a garden designer in eighteenth-century England attempted to imitate the section of Claude's *Coast View of Delos with Aeneas* mentioned by Woodbridge and others, the round and square temples and Palladian bridge which occupy the foreground and right middle distance. Similar structures could be placed in similar positions in an English garden, but many details of the painting would be missing: the two feathery trees (one a palm?) in the very center of the scene, the crenellated tower in the distance beyond the Pantheon, the rustic retaining walls behind the Doric temple. Moreover, the vistas that opened up between the structures would reveal not the harbor at Delos but the coast of Cornwall or the moors of Yorkshire, in short, some stretch of English countryside. (This objection in part rehearses the argument made by Mara Miller about the impossibility of copying or relocating a given garden.)

Coast View of Delos with Aeneas, by Claude Lorrain. Reproduced by permission of the National Gallery.

Any attempt to copy a painting using a garden as one's medium must come to grips with the painter's ability to portray a scene which extends indefinitely into space. The vistas and horizons of panoramic scenes could not ordinarily be reproduced in a garden unless they were quite indeterminate, or unless the garden happened to be situated on the actual site depicted by the painting—for example, a garden in Greece, overlooking the harbor at Delos, designed in imitation of Claude's *Coast View of Delos.* And even a garden so fortuitously sited would be unlike the painting in many respects. Certain details would inevitably be lost with the change in media, the switch from watercolor or oils to soil, water, masonry, and plants. Thus a garden might not be able to reproduce the colors, brightness, and illumination of the painting it copies. For example, how could one recreate in a garden the "Old Master" cast of many eighteenth-century landscape paintings? (Tourists of the time imposed these subdued tonalities on the natural landscape by viewing it through a Claude glass.) And finally, a garden is subject to daily and seasonal changes. A garden designed to imitate the early morning autumn light depicted in a particular painting would fail to resemble its model at dusk, in summer, during rain, and so on.

One might object that all these quibbles are beside the point. Since we have rejected the (ontological) notion of a perfect copy, no list of disanalogies between landscape paintings and gardens designed in imitation of them will count against the copy relation. But this raises a further problem. The relations "copy of" and "allusion to" occupy parts of a continuum. Since no copy shares all the traits of the original, how are to we distinguish among the following (confining examples to the art of painting): a good copy of a given landscape painting, a poor copy of that same painting, a painting which copies some portion of the original, a painting which alludes to the original, a painting which merely resembles the original in a number of respects? (Of course, similar examples can be constructed involving a garden and a painting. A garden might copy an entire painting, either well or poorly, copy a portion of that painting, allude to the painting, or merely resemble it in a number of respects.)

In order to sort out these cases, we must distinguish copying from alluding to. To copy something is to create a likeness of it. To allude to something is to refer to it indirectly, to make others think of it though it is neither named nor reproduced. While allusion is often considered a literary device, it pertains to the visual arts as well. Thus paintings can allude to other paintings as well as copy them. This is most often done by reproducing distinctive features of the target painting (the painting being referred to).[37] For example, Manet's *Déjeuner sur l'herbe* alludes to Raphael's *The Judgment of Paris* by reproducing the postures of the three right-hand figures, the naked nymph and reclining river gods. Lichtenstein's series of *Cathedral* prints allude to Monet's paintings of Rouen cathedral by reproducing both their subject matter (the facade of a cathedral) and their structure (a series of views of the same subject). Lichtenstein's varicolored cathedrals do not, however, capture the appearance of an edifice in different sorts of light and weather. Instead, the series' "mass production" undercuts the impressionist zeal to capture momentary atmospheric effects. Lichtenstein remarked in an interview that "The *Cathedrals* are meant to be manufactured Monets. . . . It's an industrial way of making Impressionism—or something like it—by a machine-like technique."[38]

I support an intentionalist account of allusion, in keeping with the intentionalist account of meaning offered in chapter 3. Of course, circularity must be avoided. It is not helpful to propose that resemblance plus the intention to copy constitutes the relation "copy of," while resemblance plus the intention to allude constitutes the relation "allusion to." Rather, the parameters of such resemblance must be indicated and the accompanying intentions must be spelled out in such a way as to eliminate reference to copying and allusion. Let us say that one painting alludes to another when (1) the artist intends to make others think of the target painting, and (2) does so by referring to it indirectly. Clause (2) as it stands is unacceptably vague. While I don't think that we can formulate necessary and sufficient conditions for allusion, talk of indirect reference can be spelled out in Gricean terms, that is, in terms of the reflected and iterated intentions of both maker and viewer.[39] The artist reproduces certain salient aspects of the target painting—subject matter, theme, composition, coloring, style, and so on—intending that the audience will recognize their source and will think of the target painting as a result of recognizing his intention that they do so.[40]

This account of allusion allows for allusion between different arts, since it simply requires that one art work reproduce or transform salient aspects of another. With this generous understanding of the mechanics of allusion, allusion can operate not only from one literary work to another, but also within and between the other arts (from painting to painting, from painting to poetry, from poetry to music, and so on) and, of course, from garden to painting. Clearly, those cases linking different arts will not achieve the same standards of likeness as those which stay within a given art. Peter Kivy, for example, in his book *Sound and Semblance,* demonstrates the extraordinary range of musical representation. He shows that music can represent not only other sounds—bird songs, laughter, rushing water—but also such abstract concepts as God's patience and the brightness of first light at the creation.[41] The latter two examples do not turn on any simple sort of resemblance between musical sound and representational content. When we deal with such cross-modal cases—including those involving gardens—the question of whether we are dealing with allusion, copying of a portion, or poor copying of the whole, will have to be decided contextually, in terms of what sorts of similarities the artist could have created.

This said, we can in principle distinguish gardens that imitate paintings from gardens that refer to paintings in other ways. This latter category includes gardens that allude to paintings or evoke them, gardens that bring them to mind. These various relations must be sorted out by reference to the garden designer's intentions. If the designer intended the garden to be a replica or likeness of a particular painting (or a portion of the painting), then the garden is a copy. If the designer intended to have visitors think of the painting as they viewed the garden, then the garden alludes. Note that these two possibilities are logically independent. One might want to make a garden that looked just like a given painting, but not care whether viewers thought of the work or its artist. Or, one might want viewers to think of a particular painting but not care about creating a simulacrum. The two possibilities might also coincide. That is, one might want to make viewers think of a particular painting and also create a garden that resembles it. Finally, if viewers of a garden do tend to think of a particular painting, but this association was not intended by the garden designer, I shall say that the garden brings the painting to mind, where this phrase is meant to flag the absence of any intention on the designer's part to influence his audience in this way.

There will always be a fact of the matter when we try to sort out such cases. The designer either did or did not have the relevant intentions. However, those intentions may not be retrievable now. There may just be no extant evidence about the particular intentions of eighteenth-century garden designers. And if we grant the existence of unconscious intentions and desires, it may not even have been possible for their contemporaries to determine whether a given work alludes to another. But in principle, such cases are decidable. That is, we can specify the kind of evidence that would be decisive, were it to be found: archival records, journal entries, recalled conversations, in which the designers indicate what relation they wish their creation to bear to the painting in questions. (For an example of what would count as confirming evidence, recall the letter quoted above from Henry Hoare to his daughter in which he called a view with a newly built Palladian bridge "a charming Gaspd picture.") Of course, granting that such evidence is available in principle does little to produce it in fact.

Given these qualifications, it remains possible for a garden to copy a given landscape painting. This task could be accomplished in two ways. The garden could present something like a two-dimensional version of the painted scene, copying it out, for example, in a knot garden of evergreens, boxwood, or herbs. Roy Strong notes that some English Renaissance gardens featured complex motifs depicted in this manner. For instance, the garden at one of the Oxford colleges contained knots laid out in the form of the royal and college arms and a sundial.[42] Imagine a similar endeavor instead tracing the outlines of Claude's *Coast View of Delos* or Poussin's *Landscape with a Snake*. More elaborate arrangements like the seventeenth-century French parterres de broderie might model a given painting with flowers, plants, and colored gravel. This would permit the introduction of color and shading. One final twist on this arrangement would be a garden whose representational content altered as a changing succession of plants bloomed over the course of a season. For example, the figures depicted in the garden copy of *Coast View of Delos* could age as yellow tulips and bronze lilies forming their hair gave way to white peonies; the seas could become more ominous and textured as spiky delphiniums supplanted campanula; and the entire scene could exhibit meteorological changes as skies of dark purple iris give way to tansy and multihued asters—sunshine and a rainbow.[43]

Either of the two-dimensional methods just described would generate an awkward, bizarre rendition of the painting in question—surely a horticultural version of paintings on velvet. I don't know of any eighteenth-century gardens that attempted to copy paintings in this manner, yet it is clearly a possibility, a resource to be counted among the powers of gardens. Obviously the more satisfactory way for a garden to imitate a landscape painting is to reproduce the painted scene in three dimensions. There are of course "painting-on-velvet" versions of this enterprise. At present, a group in Columbus, Ohio, is designing a park which will contain a three-dimensional topiary version of Georges Seurat's famous painting *La Grande Jatte!* But clearly there is another way to create a three-dimensional version of a given landscape painting—namely, to recreate as many of the painting's salient features as possible—topography, architecture, water, plantings, colors, etc.—in a natural setting. The resulting garden would then contain a three-dimensional copy of a two-dimensional painting.

I would like to describe briefly a contemporary garden that exemplifies some of the referential relationships I have been discussing. Beginning in 1967, the writer and concrete poet Ian Hamilton Finlay created a garden called Stonypath in the southern uplands of Scotland. Small in scale and replete with traditional garden features—ponds, pools, temples, bridges, columns, sundials, monuments, inscriptions—Stonypath has been compared to two gardens designed by eighteenth-century poets, Alexander Pope's Twickenham and William Shenstone's The Leasowes.[44] But Finlay's creation is also extraordinarily self-conscious and political. In an article in *Art in America* Claude Gintz declares Stonypath a "poetic-philosophic garden" which Finlay uses "as a base from which to launch a symbolic counterattack against modern culture."[45] I shall discuss Stonypath in greater detail in chapter 7. Here I shall concentrate on one way in which this garden complicates and deepens the ties between gardens and painting. Certain sections of Stonypath are garden segments that variously imitate and allude to famous landscape paintings.

The representational relationships in question were created in the garden, then documented in photographs (by David Paterson) which were exhibited in a 1980 exhibition titled Nature Over Again after Poussin.[46] The title is itself a play on the words of Paul Cézanne, who described his singular method of representing shape and volume as "redoing Poussin after Nature." The comparison is apt since both Cézanne and his seventeenth-century predecessor were known for their intellectual and geometrizing styles of paint-

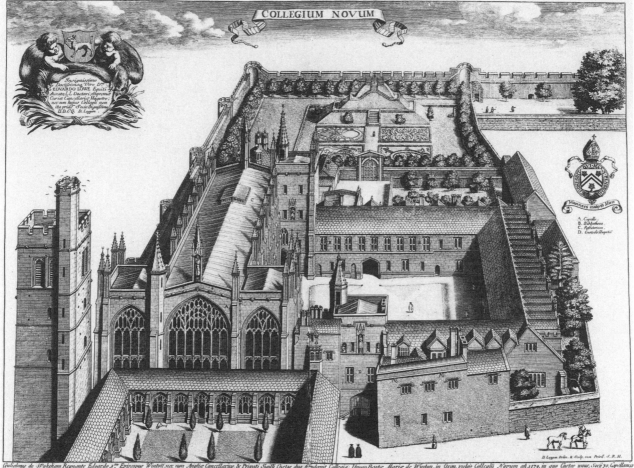

This knot garden at New College, Oxford shown here in a seventeenth-century engraving, which depicts a sundial, heraldic emblems, and more. Photograph courtesy of New College, Oxford.

ing.[47] The images in Finlay's exhibition were created as follows: a section of the garden was planted to evoke or reproduce the work of a particular landscape painter. Then that painter's characteristic signature—for example, Dürer's "AD" with the capital A framing or housing the smaller D within its lower half, or Nicholas Poussin's "NP" with the right-hand vertical of the N also forming the stem of the P, or Claude Lorrain's all upper-case

"CLAUDI"—was carved on a stone. The carved stone was placed in the foreground of the created scene, and the entire ensemble was then photographed by Finlay's collaborator.

One item in the Nature Over Again after Poussin exhibit represented Dürer's watercolor *Das grosse Rasenstück* ("The Great Piece of Turf"). Stephen Bann writes of this section of the garden that

> the reference is precisely to the celebrated water-colour by Dürer, which is not only recreated through a careful planting of reeds, irises and other vegetation but also "signed" by the insertion of a stone block bearing Dürer's monogram. An interesting effect is obtained by this "signature," which is indeed not lost but accentuated when the garden feature is captured in a photograph. It is as if Dürer's vision were inscribed on the world itself—which includes of course our consciousness of landscape—in the same way as his monogram is perpetuated in the block of stone.[48]

Another author, Claude Gintz, describes the mechanics of this scene as follows:

> Finlay asks visitors to regard various corners of nature as so many traces of their own culture. For example, beside the "Temple Pool" he has placed a stone slab engraved with the familiar initials "AD," thereby presenting the landscape itself as a representation of Dürer's watercolor *The Great Piece of Turf.* (Elsewhere on the grounds, we encounter, engraved in stone, the signatures of Poussin, Claude, Friedrich and Corot.) By inverting Cézanne's famous dictum "Poussin over again after nature," Finlay believes he can escape the modernist reductivist impasse.[49]

In addition to Dürer and the artists just named, Finlay's exhibit included garden/photo representations of the work of landscape painters Albrecht Altdorfer, Gaspard Dughet, Jean Honoré Fragonard, Giovanni Francesco Guercino, Salvator Rosa, Jacob Ruisdael, and Antoine Watteau.[50]

The Dürer vista by Stonypath's Temple Pool clearly represents a particular painting by that artist. It does so by copying or reproducing the scene Dürer has depicted in *Das grosse Rasenstück.* Commentators do not mention other individual paintings in their discussions of Stonypath and/or Nature Over Again after Poussin. Therefore, with the other eleven artists just mentioned, it is not clear whether Finlay has, in and through his garden, represented particular landscape paintings, alluded to each artist's entire oeuvre, or simply evoked the style of each painter without recreating or referring to a given work. Some remarks by Stephen Bann suggest the latter possibility: "The photographic plates, each taken in a specially adapted section of the garden, are used to secure identification with

Ian Hamilton Finlay's garden version of Dürer's painting *Das grosse Rasenstück*. Reproduced by permission of Ian Hamilton Finlay. Photograph courtesy of Reaktion Books.

traditional types of landscape, as represented by the great painters: Claude, Fragonard, Watteau, Salvator Rosa, etc. Finlay could scarcely have demonstrated more forcefully the way in which the garden has come to seem, for him, the epitome of culture as a whole."[51]

Bann's mention of *types* of landscape might be taken to mean that Finlay's landscape ensembles refer even more generally to subgenres of landscape—classical or ideal, sublime, rococo, and so on. However, the inscribed signatures in the foreground of each scene establish more specific references. I think we should interpret "types of landscape" here as referring to those recurring characteristics which allow us to identify both general and individual style. (I discussed Wollheim's distinction between general and individual style in chapter 3.) Nelson Goodman rightly insists that style descriptions are based on content as well as form. Finlay's garden scenes refer to the style and oeuvre of particular artists by reproducing crucial content: the sorts of landscape details they typically represented— stubbly furrowed fields (Corot), steep inclines, gnarled pines, and jagged fallen trees (Rosa), richly textured ground with low foliage and rustic stepping stones (Dughet)—as well as the emotions they typically evoked.[52] Together, the scenes, artifacts, photos, and labels Finlay assembled to create his 1980 exhibit have a density of reference rivaling that in Pope's allusive waterfront ensemble discussed in chapter 3. Many of the chains of reference here, however, are visual rather than verbal. They testify to the links between gardens and landscape paintings, to gardens' ability to imitate and allude to representations.

At the beginning of this section I quoted various claims about eighteenth-century gardens that were said to copy paintings by Claude Lorrain, Gaspard Poussin, and Salvator Rosa. I have also indicated the difficulties involved in definitively establishing such claims. Interestingly, few present-day commentators believe that such copying was an important or central feature of eighteenth-century English gardens. Consider the gardens designed by William Kent. While Horace Walpole, writing in 1770, called Kent "painter enough to taste the charms of landscape" and claimed that he "realised the compositions of the greatest masters in painting," recent writers offer alternative accounts of his designs at Claremont, Rousham, Stowe, and elsewhere. Thus Christopher Thacker's comment that "Kent's training led him to see gardens not only in terms of Claudean landscapes, but as compositions of a three-dimensional yet essentially painterly kind, where the visitor proceeds from one 'landscape picture' into another, and so onwards through the garden" clearly stops short of claiming that Kent copied particular landscape paintings.[53] Derek Clifford, in *A History of Garden Design,* suggests that "there is good reason for supposing that Italian gardens rather than Italian pictures were his model."[54] Edward Hyams, in *A History of Gardens and Gardening,* declares that Kent's object was not "to make, in his gardens, living copies of the paintings of Claude Lorrain, Salvator Rosa or Poussin, or of any other landscape painter."[55] Dorothy Stroud, in the *Oxford Companion to Gardens,* writes that the landscape designs which emerged from Kent's pen "suggest that both in the composition and the technique adopted he was strongly influenced by the masque designs of Inigo Jones."[56] Finally, Kenneth Woodbridge writes, "So deeply ingrained in the thinking about this period of garden history is the idea that Kent was inspired by the paintings of Claude Lorraine that comparisons have been stretched beyond the bounds of probability, while other sources such as direct experience of Italian gardens, the theater, and the extended vistas of André Le Nôtre have been ignored."[57]

Note the sorts of considerations that figure in these denials. Though Kent had been trained as a painter, and had seen (and probably owned) works by Claude, these authors cite other experiences and skills that may have equally influenced his garden designs—in particular, his visits to Italian gardens and his commissions to build stage scenery.

There are similar denials with regard to the later gardens mentioned above: Stowe, Castle Howard, and Painshill. For example, Hunt and Willis, in their introduction to *The Genius of the Place,* come to this measured conclusion:

> It is difficult sometimes to see how designers transferred these landscape paintings to the three-dimensional world of English estates. At Castle Howard, Vanbrugh certainly invoked three of the most famous ingredients of such a Claude as the "Pastoral Landscape with the Ponte Molle." . . . At Stourhead its creator's Virgilian theme for the garden lends support to the suggestion that the layout and character are modelled upon Claude's "Coast View of Delos with Aeneas." But with those exceptions and that of Painshill, where part of the lakeside is known to have been modelled on some Rosa sketches, it seems likely that the role of pictures as a pattern-book of designs has been exaggerated or misunderstood (p. 15).

Hunt and Willis describe even the three cases that they concede—Castle Howard, Stourhead, and Painshill—in terms that fall short of the copy relation: the first "invokes" a painting while the other two are "modeled upon" paintings. Michael Symes, while granting the truth of Thomas Gray's claim (from a 1754 letter) that "Mr. Hamilton formed many of the beautiful scenes in the grounds at Painshill from the pictures of Poussin and the Italian Masters," goes on to insist that "this does not necessarily mean that Hamilton copied specific paintings at Painshill. The likelihood is, rather, that Italian campagna paintings generally were one of a number of influences on him. He was a keen collector of Italian paintings . . . but he also knew the Italian countryside at firsthand from his two visits there."[58]

S. Lang argues that "The theory most prevalent, that the English landscape garden was modeled on paintings by Claude or Gaspard or Salvator Rosa, cannot be reconciled with an assumption of a slow development towards the fully fledged landscape garden."[59] Lang proposes the theater as the landscape garden's actual source.[60] Finally, Malcolm Kelsall writes of Stourhead and its eighteenth-century visitors:

> Any educated visitor of the age would appreciate that the garden is like a living picture and that the invitation is to walk back in time into idealized antiquity alive here, now, in England. No visitor of the time has left upon record remembrance of either of the Claude paintings which undoubtedly shaped Henry Hoare's visual imagination. Such recondite allusion would be unusual in eighteenth-century gardens.[61]

Let me sum up the tenor of this discussion. While it is possible for a garden to copy a painting, this relation is hard to document for eighteenth-century gardens. To establish the copy claim, one must demonstrate both resemblance between the two works and intention on the part of the garden designer. Coincidence must be ruled out, as must such other symbolic relations as allusion, evocation, and the like.

The conclusion just conceded—that a garden can, at least in principle, copy a painting—constitutes one among what I have been calling the powers of gardens. However, the conclusion does nothing to advance the central claim under investigation here, the claim that gardening, painting, and poetry are sister arts. The conclusion of chapter 3 regarding gardening and poetry was this, that a garden can *function like* a poem. To establish the sister-arts claim, we must mirror this conclusion for the case of painting and show that a garden can *function like* a (landscape) painting. And this in turn requires showing not that a garden can copy a painting, but that a garden can *represent* some other piece of land.

Can gardens do this? Can gardens represent other pieces of land, either real or ideal? Representation has been a focus of debate in recent years among philosophers, psychologists, and art historians. In order to see whether gardens can function like paintings, we must briefly examine this ongoing debate and clarify what is meant by pictorial representation.

3. REPRESENTATION

In his paper "How Do Pictures Represent?" (1972), the philosopher Max Black surveyed an assortment of theories purporting to explain pictorial representation.[62] The theories appealed to causal history, embodied information, producer's intention, illusion, resemblance, and "looking like," respectively. Black found each of them lacking. I suggest that work by scholars in three different disciplines—the psychologist James Gibson, the philosopher Nelson Goodman, and the art historian Ernst Gombrich—delimits the range of plausible answers to Black's question "How do pictures represent?" Their accounts of representation emphasize in different degrees the contributions of resemblance and convention. That is, Gibson's direct realism explains representation as a form of illusion; Goodman's semiotic theory defends something like a radical conventionalism;[63] and Gombrich's evolutionary view posits a process of schema and correction whereby inherited conventions are altered in light of facts about human vision. In what follows I shall critically discuss each of these theories. Determining where and why each succeeds or fails will help us construct an alternative account of pictorial representation.

Direct realism is the view that representations function by providing us with the exact same visual experiences as the scenes they represent. Thus direct realists posit a resemblance between pictures and their subject matter, one so striking as to create an illusion in us. Gibson championed direct realism early in his career. In a 1954 paper he argued that pictures represent particular scenes by delivering to the eyes a sheaf of light rays exactly like the sheaf that would be delivered by the scene itself.[64] Gibson's views about representation altered over the course of his career.[65] Nevertheless, I want to examine the extreme view he defended in 1954 for three reasons. First and foremost, it is a perennially tempting theory with great explanatory power. Although direct realism is in fact false, many of us have trouble giving up the conviction that, somehow or other, pictures represent by resembling their subjects. Thus it is important to set out the theory's failings convincingly and at length. Second, many theorists writing on representation endorse some version or other of the extreme view. For example, Irwin Rock, in his *Scientific American* volume *Perception,* writes that "pictures can be so realistic because artists have used the tricks of pictorial cues in creating images nearly identical to those yielded by the actual scene."[66] As we shall see, that qualification "nearly" is a very important one. And finally, examining the extreme view is important because in learning why it fails, we learn of many differences between perceiving literal landscapes and perceiving landscape paintings. This will not only help establish the "distance" between gardens and paintings; it will also point to some of the distinctive features of gardens, to be explored in chapter 6.

The plausibility of direct realism can be traced back to the system of linear perspective first discovered in the Renaissance. Many writers attribute the system to the Florentine artists Brunelleschi and Alberti. Leonardo was the first to formulate it fully.[67] Linear perspective is most easily explained by reference to someone looking out a window. Assume the viewer is observing a detailed scene and imagine that lines are drawn from each object in that scene back to the observer. These lines will form what Leonardo called the visual pyramid or the pyramid of sight, a three-dimensional figure with its apex where the lines converge. Strictly speaking, since we see with two eyes, two such pyramids are determined by every scene. For now, let us just consider the imaginary lines converging from the scene to the observer's right eye. This visual pyramid extends indefinitely into space. To obtain a representation of the view from the window drawn in correct linear perspective, we simply trace the pattern that would be formed when the visual pyramid is intersected by any perpendicular plane—the window itself, an artist's canvas or sketchpad, and so on. The resulting picture will be an accurate geometrical projection of that three-dimensional scene onto a two-dimensional surface. It ought to deliver to the eye an exactly similar bundle of light rays as would be delivered by the scene itself.

There are many problems with this first account of representation. Above all, it does not accord with the facts of human vision. One difficulty was already hinted at. The visual pyramid converges to a single station point yet we see with two eyes. This is a crucial fact about human vision. Because our eyes are separated by about six centimeters, objects subtend slightly different visual angles to each eye.[68] And this results in a slightly different retinal image formed in each eye. These disparities provide important depth cues.[69] But since the system of linear perspective is defined in terms of the light rays converging to a single point, it overlooks the fact of binocular vision. Representations created in accord with the system must be viewed under extremely artificial conditions in order to generate light rays similar to those coming from the original scene. Such representations—paintings, drawings, and so on—must be viewed with one eye, through a peephole. Clearly these conditions don't replicate our ordinary visual experience of the world.

Movement as well as binocular vision provides difficulties for the direct realist position under consideration. Our eyes are constantly moving; and we ourselves are often ambulatory as we experience the world. Yet the hypothetical visual pyramid is composed of light rays converging to a single *unmoving* eye. If the eye moves to focus on different elements of the scene, an entirely new visual pyramid is generated. Moreover, microsaccadic eye movements—the small, constant, and almost indiscernible movements of each eye—are necessary for continued vision. They guarantee that no retinal receptors become overtaxed. If such movement were somehow prevented, certain sets of neurons would be continuously stimulated. They would soon shut down, and we would see nothing at all. In this case, then, direct realism contravenes any possible visual experience.

Our own bodily movements provide further visual clues. As we stroll through or in front of a scene, or merely turn our heads in order to see different portions of it, the objects before us change their apparent relations and appear to move at different relative

speeds. Patterns of occlusion between foreground and background objects change, nearby stationary objects seem to move in a direction opposite to our own motion, and objects
that are actually in motion appear to move at different speeds depending on their distance
from us. None of these effects is present when we view a represented scene. The relations
among the objects depicted remain fixed. Thus once again direct realism is not true to our
ordinary visual experience. If we allow for more natural viewing conditions—binocular
vision, an ambulatory perceiver—the light rays from the representation no longer match
those from the scene itself and the two perceptual experiences are quite distinct.

Two more differences between a painting and the scene it portrays complete the critique of direct realism. First, the range of light and brightness that can be captured in paint
is much less than that present in the real world. For example, Pirenne notes that the general level of luminance may be much higher, on a sunny day, or much lower, in moonlight,
than a painting can reproduce.[70] Rock points out that the lightest and darkest regions of
an actual scene can differ in their reflectance by a factor of 100,000 while even a photograph can only sustain differences of about 30.[71] And second, few paintings indicate the
disparities between central and peripheral vision. We see most clearly through the fovea,
or central part of our eye (in part because the color-sensitive cones are concentrated in the
center of the retina). Our peripheral vision, by contrast, is less accurate and less distinct.
As Ralph Norman Haber explains, "Every momentary image is clear and sharp only in its
center and progressively more fuzzy the further it is from that center."[72] While many
paintings employ aerial perspective to signal the decline in sharpness of vision with distance, very few take into account the diminished acuity to either side of the central focus.

Overall, then, the direct realist claim comes to this: a painting will send to our eyes a
bundle of light rays exactly like that coming from the scene represented only if the painting is viewed through a peephole, with one unmoving eye, the scene itself does not contain an extreme range of brightness, and the painting reflects the differences between
foveal and peripheral vision.

The conditions just specified will almost never be realized. Why, then, does direct
realism remain such a tempting view? One fact which contributes greatly to its persua-
siveness is the existence of the retinal image. Whenever we look around us, light is refract-
ed by the lenses of our eyes and an inverted image of the scene before us is formed on each
retina (the curved surface at the back of the eye). The eye here functions just like a camera obscura. Thinkers knew about the retinal image in the early 1600s. Kepler described
its formation in his 1604 treatise on optics,[73] while Descartes discussed experiments using
eyes removed from the carcasses of oxen that allowed him to directly observe the retinal
images formed.[74] Since light travels in straight lines, the rules of geometrical optics which

determine the characteristics of the retinal image also govern the pyramid of sight and the construction of perspective representations. This fact, I think, inclines many of us to believe that representation must at base have something to do with the matching of images, and so we endorse direct realism.

Despite these facts, it is very misleading to seek parallels between the retinal image and a painting or drawing constructed according to the rules of linear perspective. This is so because we neither see nor depict our retinal images.[75] We do not see our retinal images, because they are in our eyes, not before our eyes. Nor is there any subpart of us that might do the seeing.[76] More important, we do not even see the world *in terms of* our retinal image. A phenomenon known as constancy scaling occurs in which we interpret the world not directly as our retinal images show it to be, but with various corrections in the direction of how we know the world to be. The constancies involve various perceived properties—size, shape, brightness, color. For instance, if two objects of the same size and shape are placed so that one is twice as far from our eyes as the other, the first will create an image exactly half the size of the second. However, we don't *see* the objects as having these relative sizes. We judge the more distant one to be larger than the size of the image alone would warrant. Shape constancy, too, involves making corrections in the direction of the real. In a famous experiment from the 1930s, the psychologist Robert Thouless showed that we judge distant circles tilted away from us to be more circular than their projected shapes should warrant. He called the effect revealed by his experiment "phenomenal regression to the real." The fact of constancy scaling alone makes it clear that an artist intent on producing a realistic representation of a given scene cannot be said to simply reproduce his or her retinal image.

I have been arguing that misconceptions about the retinal image contribute to the plausibility of direct realism. The fact that a painting constructed according to the rules of linear perspective will generate an image similar in many respects—"shape, size relations, depth information, lightness, and color"[77]—to that formed on our retina persuades us that direct realism is the correct account of representation. We can avoid this temptation by employing different metaphors, that is, by construing the retinal image as providing stimuli that are received or information that is processed rather than images that are viewed. Gibson does just this in his later writings. His theory of ecological optics switches from the claim of matching light rays to the claim of equivalent information. Once he makes this change, Gibson no longer privileges any one theory of pictorial representation.

Our critique of direct realism has shown that representation is not explained by either (1) resemblance between picture and subject or (2) resemblance between our experiences of each. Let me discuss two alternative theories, those of Goodman and Gombrich, more briefly. If pictorial representation cannot be explained in terms of an exact resemblance between pictures and the objects they represent, then perhaps a quite different explanation is the correct one: pictures may function like natural language, referring to and characterizing objects and scenes through the same mechanisms that descriptive paragraphs use.

Nelson Goodman offers such an account of pictures in his book *Languages of Art*. He argues forcefully that resemblance has nothing whatsoever to do with representation.[78] Instead, Goodman deems representation a semiotic or semantic relation. One thing represents another if it denotes it. Pictures differ from other representations (for example, charts, graphs, paragraphs) in that every aspect of them is aesthetically relevant and demands (and rewards) our attention. (This is spelled out much more carefully in terms of a notational system with the properties of unambiguity, semantic and syntactic disjointness, and semantic and syntactic finite differentiation. These properties guarantee a system that is both dense and relatively replete.)[79]

While Gibson's direct realist account explained representation in terms of illusion, Goodman's semiotic account explains representation in terms of something like convention. The central role that Goodman accords to habit and entrenchment is evident in the following passages where he characterizes realistic representation: "The touchstone of realism [lies] not in quantity of information but in how easily it issues. . . . Realism is relative determined by the system of representation standard for a given culture or person at a given time." And again, "How literal or realistic [a] picture is depends upon how standard the system is. If representation is a matter of choice and correctness a matter of information, realism is a matter of habit."[80] Thus for Goodman, what a realistic picture represents is not determined by resemblance or by any other intrinsic property of the picture. It derives instead from external factors, factors determining how easily information issues from the picture. This may be a matter of social practice—for example, what conventions are in place in a given society; it may also be influenced by facts about human vision.[81]

Goodman argues that a picture's degree of realism cannot be a matter of the amount of information it conveys because two pictures, one "painted in ordinary perspective and normal color," the other "just like the first except that the perspective is reversed and each color is replaced by its complementary" would convey exactly the same information."[82] But just how easily would we be able to extract information from the second picture? Philosophers disagree about whether we could come to "read" color-reversed pictures as naturally as we read those using the standard arrangement of colors. Richard Wollheim claims that we would always have to laboriously decode the reversed representations,[83] working out, say, that certain red expanses represent green grass while adjacent orange swaths represent blue waves. We would have to work even harder to become sensitive to nuance in the reversed system, able to distinguish the orangey red of the water (blue-green waves) from the purplish red of the young trees (new pale yellow-green growth) and the brownish red of the lawn (sun-dried brownish-green grasses).

Whether abilities such as these could be cultivated is an empirical, not a philosophical, question. Psychologists have demonstrated the adaptability of human vision. For example, in one well-known experiment, a scientist fitted himself with inverting lenses which turned all his visual images upside down (thereby righting his retinal images.) Within a few days he was able to maneuver among crowded pieces of furniture and to write without hesitation.[84] I suggest that the representations Goodman deems realistic are those that engage adaptable aspects of the human visual system. Other writers label as "iconic" pictures that seem to us natural, devoid of artifice and convention. On Goodman's view, iconic pictures are just those which trigger our most "natural" or deep-seated pictorial habits.

Kendall Walton expresses his dissatisfaction with Goodman's theory as follows: "Goodman offers no insight into the motivations underlying resemblance theories. . . . Why have they often seemed so self-evident as not even to require defense? Why do they persist in the face of obvious difficulties? How could common sense have gone so terribly wrong?"[85] Of course common sense often does just go terribly wrong, so Walton is not here offering us any convincing argument against Goodman's theory. But he does suggest that Goodman fails to acknowledge and address our conviction that representations are like their subjects, that we see their subjects in them. Moreover, from the "inside"—that is, from the point of view of a perceiver interpreting a picture—how are we to tell whether representations which seem to us realistic and iconic seem so because they match certain aspects of our interactions with the real world, or because they are based on conventions which we have mastered and which have become second nature?

I propose the following response to Goodman's view: while any established representational practice will be at least in part conventional, not just any conventions can take hold. For instance, while it is conventional in Western art to represent circles, squares, cubes, and spheres as we now do in accord with the rules of linear perspective, no usable convention could arise according to which we would use pyramids to represent circles, ellipses to represent squares, curvilinear line segments to represent cubes, and so on. Too much information would be lost. Thus while it true that our system of representation is to some degree conventional, much more needs to be said to explain which conventions can and do take hold, which are suitable to ground a shared representational practice.[86]

In his classic work from 1960, *Art and Illusion,* the art historian Ernst Gombrich argues for a view of representation midway between an illusionist and a conventionalist account. He rejects Ruskin's notion of an innocent eye, claiming that artists do not present the world to us exactly as it appears. Instead, Gombrich proposes a more complex interrelation between present methods of representation and the past history of art. He suggests that artists capture visual appearances by starting with schemas passed on to them by previous artists and then varying these in accord with their own vision, emotion, intent, skill, and style. To support this claim, Gombrich considers depictions of curious and exotic phenomena. The fact that many of the errors and anomalies in Dürer's 1515 woodcut of a rhinoceros recur in James Bruce's 1789 engraving of the same animal shows the dependence of the later image on the earlier one. Gombrich explains the necessity for such dependence: "All representations are grounded on schemata which the artist learns to use. But we may now see why he is so dependent on tradition. The injunction to 'copy appearances' is really meaningless unless the artist is first given something which is to be made like something else. Without making there is no matching."[87]

In addition to laying out this "experimental" or "empiricist" aspect of pictorial representation, Gombrich emphasizes the contribution of the audience. Since artists do not present and viewers do not perceive what is seen by an innocent eye, viewing pictures involves interpretation. Moreover, Gombrich insists that *any* representation is ambiguous, capable of realistically representing a number of different scenes. For instance, any represented object might be medium in size and not too far away, or immensely large and very distant. The same set of marks could depict either situation according to the system of linear perspective. Gombrich also describes certain abstract configurations—later known as Gombrich gates—whose ambiguity extends not only to their size and distance from the picture plane but also to their shape and spatial orientation. Another source of ambiguity is the opposition between an object's inherent color and hue, on the one hand, and the illumination it receives from its surroundings, on the other. One and the same picture might represent a bright pastel object in very dim light or an object with subdued, washed-out color in bright daylight.

Gombrich says this about our "contributions" to the representations we view. "Any picture, by its very nature, remains an appeal to the visual imagination; it must be supplemented in order to be understood. This is only another way of saying that no image can represent more than certain aspects of its prototype; if it did it would be a double, and not even Pygmalion could make one. Unless we know the conventions we have no means of guessing which aspect is presented to us."[88] I believe Gombrich is right about the inherent ambiguity of all images; hence we must assume interpretation on the part of the perceiver. We know from the arguments laid out above that this interpretation cannot be based on a strict resemblance between the image and what it represents. Nor can it be based solely on convention; the viewer's perceptual experience matters as well. To find a middle ground beween the illusionist and conventionalist accounts of representation, let me turn in closing to two more recent imagination-based theories proposed by Richard Wollheim and Kendall Walton. Both authors spell out more fully the imaginative and interpretive tasks performed by the viewers of works of art.

In his book *Painting as an Art* (1987), Richard Wollheim explains representation in terms of a more primitive perceptual ability, seeing-in. Wollheim defines seeing-in as a perceptual experience that occurs whenever we see fanciful figures in clouds, frosted windowpanes, inkblots, or stained walls like those described by Leonardo in his Notebooks.[89] The crucial phenomenological property of seeing-in is what Wollheim calls twofoldness: we are always simultaneously aware of both the marked surface *and* the figure seen in it.[90] For Wollheim representation arrives "when a standard of correctness and incorrectness is imposed upon the natural capacity of seeing-in."[91] This standard is given by the intentions of the image's artist or creator. Of course not everyone will be responsive to such intentions; Wollheim is concerned with the reactions of appropriately informed and sensitive viewers. Their perceptual experiences will be the appropriate ones. They will interpret pictures correctly by *looking* at them, not simply by appeal to background information or by correctly guessing what the artist had in mind.

Kendall Walton agrees with Wollheim that representations engage their viewers' imaginations. However, he believes that Wollheim's notion of seeing-in is murky and underdescribed. Walton bases his theory instead on the imaginative activity involved in children's games of make-believe. In a series of papers and in his recent book *Mimesis as Make-Believe,* he distinguishes make-believe from other sorts of imagining. The crucial characteristic of make-believe is its use of certain objects in the world as props. For example, children playing at making mud pies pretend that globs of mud are pies, that the stones in them are raisins, that a larger glob is a larger pie, that dividing up a glob is slicing a pie, and so on. The objects in the world—the globs of mud—mandate or prescribe certain imaginings which the children engage in collectively, often without any explicit rules or arrangements except for the initial invitation "Let's make mud pies." Walton argues that works of representational art function in a similar way; they serve as props for games of make-believe. Paintings, novels, sculptures, plays all prescribe certain imaginings in their viewers.

Walton admits that the games of make-believe we play with works of art differ significantly from those played by children. One important difference is the degree of explicitness involved in each. We never enter a museum and propose to our companions, "Let's pretend that globs of pigment are trees, mountains, and streams" as we view a landscape painting. Not only are the rules of the game of painting implicit, they can't be recovered or formulated. But this leads to normative questions about the games Walton posits. What range of games is it possible or appropriate to play with a given painting, poem, or play? A parallel question arises for Wollheim's theory: what range of intentions can be recognized and realized in a given painting? Answers to these questions will determine the scope and limits of our representational practice.

Walton himself gives some examples of inappropriate games. Regarding a children's game of pirates, he says "A tree makes a fine mast on a pirate ship. A tunnel or a watermelon would make a terrible one."[92] And, regarding Seurat's painting *La Grande Jatte,* he comments that making the painting "a prop in games in which fictionally hippos are wallowing in a mud hole . . . is to misuse the work."[93] Confining ourselves to the art of painting, the question "What games is it appropriate to play with this work?" is really a question about interpretive limits and so a question about what things can be seen in terms of others. That is, given that paintings don't represent by recreating a visual experience exactly the same as that created by their subject matter, what range of patterns, shapes, and marks can be used to represent a given subject? I call this problem the problem of assimilative vision.

Ironically, one way to see the nature of assimilative vision is to consider for a moment a *non*visual example, that of metaphor. Metaphors bring together two disparate items in an identity claim that, while literally false, is figuratively true, economical of expression, and enlightening. Stanley Cavell has analyzed Shakespeare's metaphor "Juliet is the sun" in dazzling fashion, showing how Romeo's words express his love for Juliet and her importance in his life. The metaphor works because various astronomical facts and relationships apply to and illuminate the relation between the lovers: that Juliet is the center of Romeo's universe, the start of every day, the source of light and warmth, the nourishment he needs to grow.[94]

Of course, not all comparisons are equally effective. Consider, for example, "Juliet is the door" or "Juliet is the floor." While the element of "surprise" here is high, neither metaphor enlightens us about Romeo's feelings for Juliet, and neither flatters his beloved. Although we cannot formulate general rules for creating successful metaphors, we can analyze particular examples and explain why bad metaphors fail.

I suggest that metaphors and pictorial representations are similar in the following respect. Both seem to rely on a sort of likeness or similarity whose parameters can't be explicitly spelled out. But, in each case, we can indicate the range of items which can be effectively assimilated, those which support what I shall call "assimilative vision." We can see one thing in terms of another, metaphorically or, in the case of pictures, literally, not when they have all or a certain percentage of their properties in common, but when an isomorphism holds between the two preserving important structures and relationships. Thus Romeo's trope conveys the quality of his love for Juliet because it indicates that her centrality and importance in his life parallels that of the sun in our solar system. Similarly, a picture or painting represents a given scene not when the properties of the one match that of the other, but when possessed properties can be retrieved from presented ones.

To see how this works in the abstract, consider the following notation adapted from Anthony Savile. An object with property * needn't be represented by a picture which itself possesses *, but it must be represented by a picture with some property # which is such that * can be seen in terms of # (the denoted property in terms of the displayed one). And, there are limits on such assimilative vision. Whether a representation is iconic—that is, whether it seems natural to us, as if we are identifying and interpreting it just as we would the thing itself that it represents—turns on our ability to come to see automatically the possessed properties in terms of the presented ones.

The examples from Wollheim and Goodman discussed above involving complementary colors and reversed perspective are cases where it is an open question whether or not assimilative vision will take place. Wollheim denies the term "representation" to any ensemble which must be analysed and decoded before it is understood. The reversed format pictures would count as representations on his view *if* they came to seem natural to us and if we could understand them—extract information from them—as readily as we do from more traditional pictures. Examples of representations that we couldn't come to read in this way would include the following: a representation in which each object in a given scene is represented by the object to its immediate right; a representation in which each object is represented by an object whose description or name begins with the same letter; a representation in which each salient property is mapped onto a property from a different sense modality. Note that the latter representations might appear quite natural, but even knowing the principles that generated them, one wouldn't then be able to interpret them fully and correctly by merely looking. Thus whether or not a representation is iconic turns not on its appearance but on its principles of generation. Two identical representations might depict entirely different scenes, one iconically, the other not.

My theory of representation is based on the rejection of two extreme views and is in a middle ground between them. Representation is not based on resemblance between picture and subject, nor on a set of arbitrary conventions. Rather, pictorial representations function by presenting any from a range of images that engage our assimilative vision and allow us to retrieve possessed properties from presented ones. The presented properties—those displayed in the representation—must stand in relations isomorphic to those characterizing the subject matter. Only such an arrangement allows us to gain knowledge of the subject matter by viewing the representation. The range of properties that can fulfill this role is changeable; it is affected by the past history of art and the present facts of human vision. The notions of isomorphism and retrievability are broader than that of resemblance, and unlike the concept of convention, they are linked in various ways to our perceptual capacities and skills. While my account of representation isn't a rigorous definition with necessary and sufficient conditions, it has this advantage: it applies to many different media. Certainly gardens are among them.

Let me conclude this exploration. I have examined and rejected five theories of pictorial representation. My positive account of representation is a composite one, integrating insights from each of the theories canvassed.[95] On my view, a representation is an array of lines, shapes, and colors which refers to an object, scene, or event, either real or imagined. It does so because identifying features of the subject can be seen in—retrieved from—the representation. The relevant features are any that would aid in the visual identification of similar objects, scenes, or events in real life. Appropriately schooled viewers of the representation experience twofoldness; they are aware of both the formal array and the subject being portrayed. Viewers who have prior experience with other representations in the same system, and who are also familiar with the objects and scenes depicted—or with their component parts—will be able to "read" the representation, interpret it correctly.

4. GARDENS AGAIN

Theories of pictorial representation often take painting as a paradigm case. As a result, representations are thought of all too often as two-dimensional displays. But the question that emerged from our study of the sister-arts tradition was whether gardens might function *as* landscape paintings. This would require that gardens represent other pieces of land.[96] A garden functioning symbolically in this manner would be a three-dimensional object representing another three-dimensional object. What was said above about assimilative vision and possessed and presented properties would apply equally well to this case. That is, particular properties of the represented scene, including spatial ones, could be represented by identical properties in the representation; they could also be represented by any from a range of different properties in terms of which the original ones could be seen.

The first sort of representation could be achieved if a garden imitated the salient features of the scene it depicted. The garden could accomplish this by being a sort of model—a reduced-scale replica of all that it was to denote. There are in fact gardens that have functioned like this, many of them in the East. For example, Maggie Keswick in her book on Chinese gardens describes the hunting park of the emperor Ch'in Shih-huang. After conquering his enemies, the emperor destroyed their palaces and rebuilt them surrounding his palace "as trophies of his victories."[97] "Beyond the city limits," Keswick continues, "he walled off a vast hunting preserve, the Shang-lin Park, in which he collected tribute of rare beasts and birds and trees from the vassal states. With this, the idea of the park as a microcosm of empire began to be added to its earlier role as hunting preserve. . . . More and more the Shang-lin Park seems to have become a magical diagram, a symbol of the empire in miniature. . . . Within it eight rivers converged symbolically from the four corners of the earth."

Keswick also notes that mountains had special significance for the Chinese. The Western Mountains, together with islands in the Eastern Sea, were thought to be among the homes of the Chinese Immortals.[98] Gnarled and twisted rocks of various sizes were used to symbolize mountains; rocks coming from the bottom of Tai-hu Lake near Soochow were especially prized. Keswick coins the term "petromania" to label the Chinese passion for collecting and displaying oddly shaped stones both in gardens and in smaller indoor arrangements on scholars' desks. Christopher Thacker, in his *History of Gardens*, notes that "in China, the natural mountains and the rocks erected in gardens have always been consciously associated, and their veneration has never been interrupted."[99] Thacker mentions another garden which represents mountains in the manner I have been discussing. It is the Shih Tzu Lin or "Lion Grove" in Soochow, which "was laid out around 1350 as part of the garden surrounding a temple, to commemorate a mountain retreat called 'Lion Rock' on the T'ien Mu mountain." The "mountainous character" of the garden," Thacker continues, "is indeed overwhelming. A central lake . . . is dominated by the artificial mountain on which the Hall of the Spreading Cloud stands. This eminence is reached by twisting paths leading through, under, and over the massed and fantastic rocks."[100] Keswick discusses one other interesting aspect of this mode of garden representation. Taoists believed that miniature representations gained magical potency and enhanced their creators' likelihood of gaining immortality. Again quoting Keswick: "By recreating a mountain or a demon on a reduced scale, he could focus on its magical properties and gain access to them. The further the reproduction was in size from the original, the more magically potent it was likely to be. . . . Representations of potent sites in miniature were thus not aesthetic in origin, but were pieces of practical magic."[101]

I have been describing oriental gardens that represent through modeling and miniaturization. But just as a painter often varies or distorts the objects she depicts in order to achieve certain expressive effects, a garden designer creating a garden that represented some other piece of land might want to do something more artful and ambitious than merely making a scaled-down replica. She might want to make a statement about the represented scene rather than merely denoting it by creating a likeness. (Recall Danto's definition of works of art as things that make statements and require interpretation.)

Consider some examples. A garden in the country might represent some other rural landscape by reproducing its significant topography and flora. (Recall that Horace Walpole declared a wooded section at the head of Painshill's central lake to be Alpine. Whether this section of Painshill represents the Alps, alludes to them, or simply brings them to mind would have to be determined in the ways discussed above.) An eighteenth-century English garden might represent the English countryside and make a statement about enclosure and the loss of commons.[102] A present-day garden might represent some earlier garden landmark. For example, I might create a representation of Stourhead in my small St. Louis back yard. A garden might represent some exotic place or even a nonexistent one. Thus chinoiserie in an eighteenth-century English garden might represent Chin Shih-huang's legendary hunting park; a lush garden with fountains and orchards might represent biblical Eden or Milton's paradise; a contemporary garden might represent the world Alice entered when she went through the looking glass. And of course a representational garden needn't use as its media all or any of the materials present in the place represented. A Chinese mountain range or a particular section of the Swiss Alps might be represented entirely by topiary. (The garden at Packwood House in Warwickshire reputedly depicts the Sermon on the Mount in this manner.) Mountains might be represented not by mounds of earth or conical yews but by arrays of spiky blooms: lupine, delphiniums, gladioli, and so on. A representational garden might be more expressionist, denoting a particular piece of land not by reproducing its topography but by arousing the emotions it provokes. (This would be the garden equivalent to the work of Max Beckmann or Willem de Kooning.) And of course a representational garden, one that functioned as a painting, need not represent land only. A garden might pictorially represent water. The "dry river" in a traditional Japanese garden, consisting of smooth polished stones arranged to express the energy, flow and turbulence of a stream, is one such example. A more ambitious garden might portray the sea in any of its forms and moods.

The examples just listed have all been rather fanciful. I know of no actual gardens that function in these ways. But the crucial point once again is that such gardens are possible, they can be imagined. Functioning like a painting, representing some other piece of land, is clearly one among gardens' powers.

THE PICTURESQUE

I. INTRODUCTION

In the last chapter I argued that eighteenth-century English gardens, though declared sisters to painting as well as poetry, neither copied landscape paintings nor functioned like them. I should like now to explore two further relations that may have held between gardens and paintings in the eighteenth century: (1) gardens remind us of particular paintings or of the style of a particular painter, and (2) gardens are created using the principles and techniques of painting.

The first relationship, that gardens remind us of paintings, or that we see gardens in terms of paintings, leads to an exploration of the *picturesque*, an aesthetic category first popularized in England in the last third of the eighteenth century. The term picturesque was applied to landscapes in many guises—to landscape poems and landscape paintings, as well as to gardens and natural scenes. I should like to begin my discussion of the picturesque by singling out two gardens that seem to require us to take painting into account when we interpret them.

Charles Hamilton's Painshill Park, described in detail at the beginning of chapter 4, is the first garden that I want to mention in the context of the picturesque. Recall that Painshill resembled Stourhead in layout. Circling a central lake, viewers encountered a stylistically varied assortment of structures and an artfully designed set of vistas. Despite its similarities to Stourhead, I offered evidence that Painshill should be classed as a "painterly" rather than a poetic garden. First, particular sections of the garden were said to copy particular paintings by Salvator Rosa and Gaspard Dughet; second, no obvious iconographic program links Painshill's architectural and sculptural components in the way that so many of Stourhead's features refer to the *Aeneid;* and finally, contemporary viewers commented predominantly on visual aspects of the garden, emphasizing the composition and sequence of scenes rather than some underlying meaning conveyed.

Painshill engages the art of painting and the concept of the picturesque in both of the ways set out at the beginning of this chapter: (1) portions of the garden seem to *remind* viewers of the work of particular artists, setting in motion trains of association that link scenes in the garden to paintings visitors have seen in the past; and (2), Hamilton seems to have employed the principles of painting to construct the scenes, landskips, and vistas mentioned earlier.[1]

Before assessing these claims, let us consider one more English eighteenth-century garden. In 1758 Thomas Duncombe improved his Yorkshire estate by carving a half-mile long grassy terrace atop a steep hillside. The hill overlooked the sprawling ruins of Rievaulx Abbey, a thirteenth-century Cistercian monastery, and Duncombe's terrace was intended to provide a panoramic overview of that site. Visitors walking along the slope encountered a changing set of stunning vistas as different portions of the monastic complex came into view. The skeletal remains of the chapter church dominated the ruins. Ghostly ranks of clerestory windows topped the Gothic arches of its lower bays. Each end of Duncombe's terrace was marked by a temple, one round and in the Tuscan style, the other square with an Ionic portico. The latter temple was equipped as a "banqueting room," with frescoed walls and ceiling, elaborately carved woodwork, ornate furniture, and a subterranean kitchen.

Rievaulx Terrace was clearly a marvelous pleasure ground for its owner and his guests. In designing the terrace, Duncombe was guided by a number of precedents. His grandfather, the first Thomas Duncombe, had commissioned a similar terrace after completing his new house, Duncombe Park, in 1713,[2] while the idea of including actual ruins may well have come from John Aislabie's neighboring Yorkshire estate, Studley Royal, which incorporated the Gothic ruins of Fountains Abbey.[3] Despite these influences, Rievaulx Terrace is unique. While other English gardens had incorporated actual ruins or built artificial ones, Duncombe dispensed with the garden altogether and provided nothing but a view. In creating his terrace he appropriated that view and framed it in a way that controlled and orchestrated each viewer's experience. If we consider Rievaulx Terrace as the limiting case of an English landscape garden, we can see that it marks the culmination of an aesthetic revolution. It epitomizes eighteenth-century taste for the picturesque.

Rievaulx Terrace, a view of the ruined abbey. Photograph by David Conway.

2. THE PICTURESQUE

The picturesque figured in discussions of eighteenth-century English gardening. In fact, some garden historians acknowledge a gardening style *called* the picturesque, associated primarily with the work of Humphry Repton. But the concept played a much broader role in eighteenth-century cultural life. Christopher Hussey characterized the picturesque as an aesthetic discovery—the discovery of visual qualities. He claimed that in the picturesque era "the relation of all the arts to one another, through the pictorial appreciation of nature, was so close that poetry, painting, gardening, architecture, and the art of travel may be said to have been fused into the single 'art of landscape'."[4] The art historian David

Watkin remarks, "Between 1730 and 1830, English poets, painters, travellers, gardeners, architects, connoisseurs, and dilettanti, were united in their emphasis on the primacy of pictorial values. The Picturesque became the universal mode of vision."[5]

Despite this agreement, it is very difficult to come up with an adequate definition of the picturesque. The term was first used in the sense I wish to trace by the Rev. William Gilpin in his treatise *An Essay on Prints* (1768). Gilpin defined the picturesque as "a term expressive of that peculiar kind of beauty which is agreeable in a picture."[6] Unfortunately, this definition does not help us to identify picturesque items or understand their charms. And one source reports that "by 1801 a supplement to Johnson's *Dictionary* allowed a range of meanings which include what is pleasing to the eye, what strikes the viewer as singular or appeals to him with the force of a painting, what is expressible in painting or would either afford a good subject for a painted landscape or help in conceiving one."[7]

Despite this vagueness, a considerable picturesque industry sprang up. Gilpin traveled to remote regions of England, Scotland, and Wales throughout the 1770s. He kept journals of his tours, illustrated with pen-and-ink sketches. Gilpin subsequently published five volumes recounting his travels to, and appreciation of, the Wye Valley (1782), the Lake District (1786), the Scottish Highlands (1789), forest scenery (1791), and Cambridge, Norfolk, Suffolk, Essex, and North Wales (1809).[8] The titles of all five books included the phrase "Observations relative chiefly to picturesque beauty." They became immensely popular, serving as guides for generations of "picturesque tourists" who retraced Gilpin's steps while seeking out the scenes he had described. In *The Search for the Picturesque* Malcolm Andrews describes the picturesque in terms of the "particular pleasure of comparison and association" (39). He speaks of the "habitual exercise" of these capacities (3) and notes that "one of the chief excitements for the Picturesque tourist was the recognition and tracing of resemblances between art and nature" (39). That is, for tourists in search of the picturesque, natural landscapes came to be seen in terms of painted ones. We have seen, in connection with the grand tour (chap. 2), how a taste for landscape art arose in eighteenth-century England. Gentlemen on the tour encountered landscapes unlike any they had seen at home: first the Alps, rugged and forbidding, then the Roman campagna, replete with ruins alluding to an arcadian past. These experiences made the travelers newly receptive to the landscape paintings of the French and Italian masters.[9] Englishmen sought out, championed, and collected works by Claude Lorrain, Nicholas Poussin, Gaspard Dughet, and Salvator Rosa.

Not only were eighteenth-century tourists expected to seek out and appreciate picturesque sites, where appreciation involved noting similarities between the literal landscapes and painted ones; they were also expected to produce their own pictures. That is,

A landscape by Gaspar Dughet. Photograph courtesy of University of York Library.

picturesque tourists were to go about equipped with Claude glass and sketch pad, capturing on paper the scenes in nature that reminded them of famous landscape paintings. Very explicit directions were offered in the guidebooks for creating suitable—i.e., picturesque—pictures. The books identified "Station Points" where the tourists should pause and produce their sketches. Here is one example quoted by Andrews, instructions from James Clarke's *Survey of the Lakes* (1787) on how to paint Ullswater:

> The side-screens will be Ewe-Cragg, the rising ground in Gowbarrow park, and some other less striking objects on the right hand: on the left, a small coppice, Sandwich-Dod, Sandwich-Cascade, and Birk-Fell: the front screen will take in Glencoyn-House, Lyulph's Tower, and the picturesque ground on which they stand; whilst Glencoyn Pike, Common-Fell, Catesby Pike, and Helveylin, succeeding each other in just degrees of distinctness, close the distances (30).

Consider one more example, instructions from R. H. Newell's *Letters on the Scenery of Wales* (1821) for capturing Llaugharne Castle: "Bring the Castle exactly *within the angle* made by the sloping hill and woody steep *before* it. Then ascend or descend, till the *water* and *three* of the promontories appear above the castle. In this station the sea bounds the distance" (30).

Such a rigid approach to the appreciation and representation of landscape scenery could not but become formulaic and stultifying. Andrews explains that English landscape painters embraced principles derived from the works of Claude and Dughet. These principles included an "obligatory, mellow master-tint," a structural division of the painted scene into three distances—"a background, a strongly lit middle or second distance, and a darkened foreground"—and "the device of the *repoussoir* object, the foreground framing trees, or the tree and ruin, or mountain sides, to prevent one's eye from straying outside the canvas and to push it into the middle distance" (29).[10] Strict reliance on conventions of this sort had a deleterious effect on both landscape painting and landscape appreciation. Andrews comments, "The limitations of the Claudean orthodoxies had important consequences for the Picturesque tourist, whether or not he was himself a painter. It limited the kinds of landscape eligible for praise and study" (34).

A tension should be evident in even the limited account of the picturesque sketched so far. If "picturesque" is glossed according to Gilpin's usage to mean "whatever might look good in a picture," then any and every landscape scene is potentially picturesque. That is, the term is so all-inclusive as to be almost meaningless. If, on the other hand, the ideal landscape to be imitated and appreciated is that which exhibits the structure of a painting by Claude, then many other sorts of appealing landscapes are overlooked, for instance, those that would be represented by Dutch and Flemish masters, by Rosa and Girtin, and so on. In sum, our initial approach to the picturesque via Gilpin's guidebooks and the tourist tradition they generated has led to a standoff between two equally unhelpful interpretations. The first—"like a picture" [any picture]—is too broad, while the second—"like a Claude"—is too narrow. I would like to begin again and examine a more theoretical take on the picturesque, one generated by the debate later in the century between Sir Uvedale Price and Richard Payne Knight. While neither theorist in the end provides us with a more satisfactory link between literal landscapes and pictured ones, the details of their disagreement are interesting in and of themselves and illuminate garden history in a number of ways.

3. PRICE AND KNIGHT

Let me briefly set the scene. Born three years apart, Sir Uvedale Price (1747–1829) and Richard Payne Knight (1750–1824) became neighbors and friends. Price was educated at Eton and at Oxford. Knight, sickly as a child, was educated at home and never went to university. As young men both inherited Herefordshire seats and both embarked on grand tours. Price came into the estate of Foxley at the age of fourteen, the same age at which Knight inherited Downton.[11] From 1774 to 1778 Knight built Downton Castle, a crenellated, irregular country house whose asymmetrical plan Nikolaus Pevsner declares "extremely unusual" for the time. Moreover, Downton's medieval exterior with round and polygonal towers and battlements belied its Grecian interior with classical orders throughout and a round dining room in imitation of the Pantheon.[12]

Price described the three major preoccupations of his life as "pictures, scenery, and music."[13] Pevsner calls him a "one-book author" compared to Knight who wrote on topics ranging from the worship of Priapus to the Greek alphabet to judgments of taste—though Pevsner says of three publications on the picturesque that appeared in 1794, "One of these was a masterpiece: Uvedale Price's *Essay on the Picturesque*."[14] Knight became a member of the prestigious Society of Dilettanti in 1781 and was proud of his independent status as a scholar.[15] Both men wrote more than one work on landscape and the picturesque. Knight's initial effort, *The Landscape* (1794), a "didactic poem," was followed by a much more ambitious aesthetic treatise, *An Analytic Inquiry into the Principles of Taste* (1805), while Price revised his *Essay on the Picturesque* (1794) for expanded editions in 1796–98 and 1810,[16] and he published *A Dialogue on the Distinct Characters of the Picturesque and Beautiful* (1801) to counter a note Knight had added to the second edition of *The Landscape*.[17]

A painting by Thomas Hearne of Richard Payne Knight's estate, Downton. Reproduced by permission of the Victoria and Albert Museum.

Although their discussions of the picturesque became increasingly acrimonious, Price and Knight initially agreed in their judgments of landscape and of art. In fact, Knight invited Price to publish his *Essay* jointly with *The Landscape*. Price declined and the two works appeared separately in 1794. In the ensuing years doctrinal differences drove the two theorists apart. While they may have agreed in admiring rugged scenes, busy paintings, and "unimproved" gardens, the reasons behind their judgments differed significantly. Let me compare their theories as presented in Price's *Essay on the Picturesque* (1794) and Knight's *Analytic Inquiry into the Principles of Taste* (1805).

4. SIR UVEDALE PRICE

Price's *Essay* begins with a discussion of the art of laying out grounds. On page one he asks "Is the present system of improving founded on just principles of taste?"[18] His answer is no. Thus Price's theory grew out of practical concerns with gardening and with landscape. His main target throughout the *Essay* was the landscape gardener Lancelot ("Capability") Brown, whose design principles Price found wanting.

Brown was perhaps the most famous gardener of the eighteenth century. He is said to have improved between 120 and 140 great country estates.[19] Brown learned the rudiments of landscape gardening and design during seven years of employment at Kirkharle Tower, Northumberland. He soon began receiving commissions to confer about other properties. Among the well-known gardens he improved were Stowe, Chatsworth, Claremont, Kew, and Blenheim (where he received £21,500 for ten years' work.[20]) In 1764 Brown was appointed master gardener at Hampton Court. Brown earned his nickname from his habit of saying of each estate he was invited to improve that it "had capabilities." He developed these capabilities by destroying the formal gardens and geometric plantings of his predecessors and replacing them with more natural elements. Brown's gardens featured rolling lawns, limpid lakes, clumps and belts of trees, and meandering roads and paths. They were notable for their *lack* of such traditional garden elements as terraces, temples, statues, fountains, and, above all, flowers. Brown generally brought the lawn right up to the edge of the house and dammed any available streams to make a large, central lake. At Blenheim Palace, considered by many his most successful commission, he altered the topography, eliminated the gardens, and flooded Vanbrugh's thirty-room bridge.

Price denounced Brown's formulaic gardens as monotonous and bald and compared him to a quack dispensing a single nostrum for all complaints (199 n.). Throughout the *Essay* Price disparaged Brown's inventiveness. Sometimes he attributed his assessments to anonymous others, for example, a "friend" who declared "he was quite certain there was not a housemaid in Blenheim to whom [Brown's great water] would not immediately have occurred" (259 n.). Elsewhere, Price speaks sarcastically of "the famous Mr. Brown, who has so fixed and determined the forms and lines of clumps, belts, and serpentine canals, and has been so steadily imitated by his followers, that had the improvers been incorporated, their common seal, with a clump, a belt, and a piece of made water, would have fully expressed the whole of their science, and have served for a model as well" (187). Another time Price compares Brown to a slug or snail trailing slime: "Former improvers at least kept near the house, but this fellow crawls like a snail all over the grounds, and leaves his cursed slime behind him wherever he goes" (268 n.).

Harewood, designed by Capability Brown. Reproduced by permission of Lord Harewood.

Perhaps Price's cleverest attack against Brown occurs early in the *Essay* when Price imagines a painting by Claude Lorrain improved in the style of Brown—the terrain smoothed, the undergrowth cleared, the buildings whitened (12 ff.). Price says that a "Brownian painter" would most immediately note the lack of "that leading feature of all modern improvements," the clump, and would paint some in in the most conspicuous places. Next, noticing the connection and continuity—trees, bushes, and thickets linked together, growing alongside one another—the painter would declare "All this rubbish must be cleared away." He would then alter the painting to make the ground smooth and level and each group of plants separate and distinct. The trees shading the picture's ruins, temples, and palaces would be "expunged" (13) so that no architectural detail remained hidden. Finally, the Brownian painter would clear and level the banks alongside the water, paint out any plants, tussocks, stones, and stumps, and "clean and polish" the foreground, thus completing the ruination of a masterpiece of landscape art. Price closes with a thoroughly rhetorical query: "Is it then possible to imagine that the beauties of imitation should be so distinct from those of reality, nay, so completely at variance, that what disgraces and makes a picture ridiculous, should become ornamental when applied to nature?" (16) The answer, obviously, is no. This whole thought experiment was designed to convince his readers that Brownian principles of design generate appalling landscape paintings, as well as appalling landscape gardens.

Price believed that proper gardening ought to borrow its principles from the art of painting. He argued that the leading principles of that art—those concerning "general composition, grouping the separate parts, harmony of tints, unity of character, [and] breadth and effect of light and shade" (8–9)—were equally applicable to the art of gardening. And he suggested that improvers treat painting as "a set of experiments of the different ways in which trees, buildings, water, etc., may be disposed, grouped, and accompanied in the most beautiful and striking manner" (5).

If Price's *Essay* merely exhorted gardeners to compose gardens the way painters compose paintings, it would not be very valuable. For although gardens delight all our senses, their primary appeal is visual, and gardeners are necessarily aware of such "painterly" concerns as color, texture, balance, form, perspective, and light and shade. There is more to Price's theory, however. He isolated a set of qualities which allowed him to mark what was missing in the gardens of Capability Brown and to establish criteria for successful improvements. These qualities comprise the picturesque.

Price's account of the picturesque was inspired by and modeled after Edmund Burke's work, *A Philosophical Inquiry into the Origins of Our Ideas of the Sublime and Beautiful* (1757). In the *Inquiry,* Burke argued that the sublime and the beautiful were distinct aesthetic categories, associated with distinct qualities and giving rise to distinct passions. Burke initially sorted all passions under the two headings "self-preservation" and "society." The passions concerned with self-preservation were those connected with pain and danger. Since terror and astonishment would typically be aroused in dangerous or threatening situations, these were the passions generated by the sublime.

Burke defined the sublime as follows: "Whatever is fitted in any sort to excite the ideas of pain, and danger, that is to say, whatever is in any sort terrible, or is conversant about terrible objects, or operates in a manner analogous to terror, is a source of the *sublime;* that is, it is productive of the strongest emotion which the mind is capable of feeling."[21] Obscurity, power, privation, vastness, infinity, difficulty, magnificence, loudness, and more were among the qualities associated with the sublime.[22]

Burke subdivided the social passions into two further categories, (1) those concerned with sexual attraction and generation, and (2) those concerned with what he called "society in general." Category (2) involves social pleasures—for example, "good company, lively conversations, and the endearments of friendship" (43)—generated by such passions as sympathy, imitation, and ambition (44). Aesthetic beauty pertains to this second group of social passions.[23] In discussing the art of tragedy, Burke takes up some questions about imitation first posed by Aristotle in the *Poetics*. Burke notes, "It is a common observation, that objects which in the reality would shock, are in tragical, and such like representations, the source of a very high species of pleasure" (44). But rather than attribute this pleasure entirely to our delight in imitation, Burke also suggests that we actually enjoy others' misfortunes: "I am convinced we have a degree of delight, and that no small one, in the real misfortunes and pains of others" (45). He explains this not as a sign of our degeneracy or evil, but as a divine mechanism intended to heighten our sympathy with others: "and as our Creator has designed we should be united by the bond of sympathy, he has strengthened that bond by a proportionable delight; and there most where our sympathy is most wanted, in the distress of others" (46).

Given the importance Burke attributes to the social passions that link us to others, it is not surprising that he defines beauty in terms of the pleasures they promote: "By beauty I mean, that quality or those qualities in bodies by which they cause love, or some passion similar to it" (91). Burke is careful to distinguish love—the passion that effects our connection with "society in general"—from lust—the passion concerned with sex and generation, although he often uses the same word for both.[24] The beautiful, then, is linked to love just as the sublime is linked to terror. And, just as the sublime is associated with such qualities as obscurity, power, privation, and vastness, so too the beautiful is associated with such qualities as smallness, smoothness, gradual variation, delicacy, and clear but mild coloration. Burke summarizes his discussion of beauty at the end of part 3 in these words: "On the whole, the qualities of beauty, as they are merely sensible qualities, are the following. First, to be comparatively small. Secondly, to be smooth. Thirdly, to have a variety in the direction of the parts; but fourthly, to have those parts not angular, but melted as it were into each other. Fifthly, to be of a delicate frame, without any remarkable appearance of strength. Sixthly, to have its colours clear and bright; but not very strong and glaring. Seventhly, or if it should have any glaring colour, to have it diversified with others" (117).

Applying Burke's definitions, a storm at sea, a gloomy forest, a lion, tiger, or rhinoceros, are all sublime (60), while a swan, a rose, and a garden by Brown are all beautiful

(94–95). Price admired Burke's system, but thought it incomplete.[25] Many pleasing objects fit into neither of Burke's categories.[26] For example, a landscape painting by Gaspar Dughet lacked both the serenity of a Claude and the terror of a Rosa, yet Dughet's work was greatly admired in the eighteenth century. To explain such anomalies, Price proposed the picturesque—an intermediate category situated between the beautiful and the sublime and structured like them.

Price named intricacy and variety as hallmarks of the picturesque. He believed that they were great sources of human pleasure (17), and that they aroused in us the passion of curiosity. In fact, Price defined intricacy in terms of this passion, calling it "that disposition of objects which, by a partial and uncertain concealment, excites and nourishes curiosity" (18). Borrowing from Hogarth, Price declared that the beauty of intricacy was "that it leads the eye a kind of wanton chace" (198). He concluded that "intricacy in the disposition, and variety in the forms, the tints, and the lights and shadows of objects, are the great characteristics of picturesque scenery" (18).

In a later chapter, Price offered a more systematic definition of the picturesque in terms of three somewhat different characteristics: roughness, sudden variation, and irregularity. He called these "the most efficient causes of the picturesque" (45). Whether we attend to the first pair of qualities cited by Price—intricacy and variety—or to the trio mentioned later—roughness, sudden variation, and irregularity—it is clear that Price's theory makes the picturesque an objective property. *Any* object can count as picturesque if it exhibits roughness, sudden variation, and irregularity, or intricacy and variety. Furthermore, Price maintained that the picturesque extended to all our sensations, not merely sight, and that it prevailed throughout nature (40–41). By way of illustration, he discussed the picturesqueness of such diverse objects as water, trees, buildings, ruins, dogs, sheep, horses, birds of prey, women, music, and painting (chap. 3).

To support his theory, Price constructed various examples in which beautiful objects were contrasted with picturesque ones. He compared a Grecian temple to a Gothic palace, a calm, clear lake to a rapid, raging stream, a smooth young beech to a rugged old oak, a horse to an ass, a sheep to a goat, Belisarius or Marius to beggars and gypsies, and so on. In each case the first item was beautiful, the second picturesque. Such comparisons point to one clear doctrinal difference between Price's account of the picturesque and that of William Gilpin. While Gilpin addressed all his tourist guides to travelers in pursuit of picturesque beauty, Price defined the picturesque in contradistinction to the beautiful. Thus on his view, the composite concept "picturesque beauty" could not arise. This is underscored by the title of his work, *A Dialogue on the Distinct Characters of the Picturesque and the Beautiful* (1801).[27]

Price devoted part 2 of his *Essay* to applications of his theory to the art of improving. He criticized at length the style of Capability Brown. Special venom was reserved for two of Brown's signature items, the clump and the belt. For example, Price declared that "the great distinguishing feature of modern improvement is the *clump;* whose name, if the first letter was taken away, would most accurately describe its form and effect" (190). And again, "the belt lies more in ambuscade, and the wretch who falls into it, and is obliged to walk the whole round in company with the improver, will allow that a snake with its tail in its mouth is, comparatively, but a faint emblem of eternity" (192–93). More important, Price criticized Brown's gardens in terms of the picturesque principles just deduced. He objected to Brown's clumps because they contained trees of the same age and growth, planted in regular circular patterns. Unlike natural groups, which mixed timber trees with thorns and hollies and were full of openings and hollows, Brown's clumps were "as like one another as so many puddings turned out of one common mould" (191). Price insisted that smoothness and verdure could not make amends for want of variety (243), but instead became insipid and monotonous. In his chapter on water, he argued that water's most striking property was its ability to produce mirrorlike reflections. Yet the smooth banks of Brown's artificial lakes lacked just those objects—trees, bushes, roots, tufts, tussocks, stones, lichens, mosses, and more—which would make their reflections varied and interesting.

Price concluded with the wish that gentlemen with a taste for drawing and painting, and a knowledge of their principles, would do their own improving instead of hiring a professional to "torture their estates" (276). Such gentlemen should take art and nature as their models.[28] Price hoped that this would yield "a great variety of styles of improvement and all of them with peculiar excellencies" (276). Though Price's remarks seem to advocate any and every style of gardening, his discussion throughout the *Essay* stresses the beauty of picturesque scenes—those characterized by intricacy, variety, and sudden variation. And, Price claimed that the most successful improvers were those who "*leave . . .* or create the greatest variety of *pictures*" (286).

Price's conclusion shows his theory to be far from seamless. On the one hand, his attack on Brown is an attack on a particular style of gardening. Price doesn't advocate replacing it with some *other* dominant style, for he believes it is impossible to find one formula that suits all places (199). Price's advice that amateur improvers seek models in works of art thus defends an extremely weak sense of the picturesque, a sense in which *all* gardening is picturesque. The fact that gardens, like paintings, require attention to color, texture, balance, and so on, was not a discovery that was new to the eighteenth century. Garden designers and spectators alike had long been aware of these parallels.[29]

On the other hand, the distinctive part of Price's theory introduces a second and

The park at Petworth, showing Brown's trademark clumps. Photograph courtesy of the National Trust.

stricter sense of the picturesque, one defined in terms of roughness, sudden variation, and irregularity. Note that this second sense has nothing to do with painting. All sorts of objects can have the three essential traits, and many paintings lack them. I would guess that Price settled on these three qualities by asking what was missing in the gardens improved by Brown, and not by giving any thought to painting per se. Thus even though some gardens may be picturesque in Price's second sense, this establishes no particular affinity between gardening and painting.

5. RICHARD PAYNE KNIGHT

I have argued that Price's *Essay* suggests two accounts of the picturesque and that neither one is satisfactory. The fact that painters and gardeners share compositional concerns and techniques does not explain the sudden vogue for the picturesque. And Price's fascination with irregular and intricate objects and scenes does not link the picturesque to the art of painting. I want to turn now to the opposing theory of Richard Payne Knight to see whether it provides a more helpful understanding of eighteenth-century taste. Knight shared Price's disdain for the work of Capability Brown, yet his *Analytical Inquiry into the Principles of Taste* offers a definition of the picturesque quite unlike that of Price's *Essay*. It was written from very different motives and reflects very different influences.

Even a brief examination will show that the *Inquiry* and the *Essay* differ in scope. Knight's work is much more ambitious than Price's. Knight was not addressing the relatively narrow issue of garden improvements; he was attempting to construct a full-fledged theory of taste, in the tradition of Gerard, Allison, Shaftesbury, and (ultimately) Kant. Accordingly, he organized the *Inquiry* by mental faculties, beginning with chapters on each of the five senses, followed by others on the association of ideas, imagination, judgment, and the passions. In addition, Knight's work is much more erudite than Price's. While Price's debt to Burke is clear, Knight's treatise is scattered with references to such figures as Plato, Aristotle, Locke, Berkeley, Hume, Reid, Newton, and more. Overall, Knight set out to answer the question "Is there a standard of taste?" And his attempt incorporated many of the intellectual currents of his time, among them associationism, subjectivism, and theories of the operations of the mind.

Knight discussed the picturesque in his long central chapter on the imagination. He differed most strikingly from Price in denying the picturesque a distinct objective character.[30] Declaring that Price's "great, fundamental error" was "seeking for distinctions in external objects which only exist in the modes and habits of viewing and considering them" (196), Knight located the picturesque not in the external world but in the observer's mind. That is to say, for Knight the picturesque was a mode of association.

Knight ascribed all intellectual pleasures to the association of ideas. He enunciated the basic principle of association as follows: "To a mind richly stored, almost every object of nature or art that presents itself to the senses, either excites fresh trains and combinations of ideas, or vivifies and strengthens those which existed before" (143). He offered various examples to illustrate this thesis. A peasant and a scientist, he claimed, would respond to the natural world quite differently. "Every insect, plant, or fossil, which the peasant treads upon unheeded, is, to the naturalist and philosopher, a subject of curious inquiry and speculation" (143). An uninformed observer would see the heavens as a blue vault with twinkling fires, while a learned viewer would be aware of "unnumbered worlds, distributed through the boundless vacuity of unmeasurable space; and peopled, perhaps, with different orders of intelligent beings" (144). And finally, mention of London or Paris would raise very different ideas in the minds of those who had only heard of these cities, those who had visited them briefly, and those who had resided a long time in either capital (145).

While taste, for Knight, was based on feeling and sentiment rather than belief and opinion (3), a similar relativity applied with regard to judgments of taste.[31] That is, people differently versed in the arts could be expected to appreciate painting, music, and poetry in different degrees. This was because "much of the pleasure, which we receive from painting, sculpture, music, poetry, etc. arises from our associating other ideas with those immediately excited by them. Hence the productions of these arts are never thoroughly enjoyed but by persons, whose minds are enriched by a variety of kindred and corresponding imagery" (145).[32]

Knight defined picturesque objects and circumstances as those so connected to other objects in nature and circumstances in society as to "be enabled to excite similar or associated trains of ideas, in minds so enriched, and consequently to afford them similar pleasures" (146). He also claimed that such objects and circumstances would *only* afford pleasure to perceivers conversant with the art of painting (146). The following long passage spells out the mechanism by which association constitutes the picturesque:

> This very relation to painting expressed by the word *picturesque,* is that which affords the whole pleasure derived from association; which can, therefore, only be felt by persons who have correspondent ideas to associate; that is, by persons in a certain degree conversant in that art. Such persons being in the habit of viewing, and receiving pleasure from fine pictures, will naturally feel pleasure in viewing those objects in nature, which have called forth those powers of imitation and embellishment. . . . The objects recall to the mind the imitations, which skill, taste, and genius have provided; and these again recall to the mind the objects themselves (154–55).

There is a certain reciprocity at work here. A connoisseur, viewing a picturesque scene, is reminded of various paintings it resembles, but later, viewing a painting, his thoughts turn back to the scene. Each enlivens the other and each acquires new meaning imported by intellect and imagination and not provided by sense alone.

Clearly, the picturesque as Knight conceived it is a subjective matter. It is shaped in each instance by the interests, experience, and reflectivity of the perceiver. To emphasize this point, Knight noted that we call opposite kinds of things picturesque. He listed among examples human figures—the boors of Ostade, the peasants of Gainsborough, the warriors of Rosa, the apostles of Raphael, and the bacchanalians of Poussin. Trees—the giant oaks of Ruysdael, the full grown pine or ilex of Claude, and the stumpy decayed pollard of Rubens and Rembrandt. And horses—the shaggy worn-out cart horse of Morland or Asselyn and the pampered war horse of Wovermans.[33] Knight concluded that we can't hope to enumerate or analyse all things that are picturesque. "To attempt to analyze, class, or enumerate the objects in nature, which are, in this proper sense of the word, *picturesque* would be vain and impractical; as they comprehend, in some degree, every thing of every kind, which has been, or may be represented to advantage in painting" (154). Thus his approach and Price's are diametrically opposed.

One might object that Knight's theory makes the picturesque ubiquitous. *Anything* can be picturesque, so long as it reminds *someone* of a picture. My Airedale might remind someone of a painting by Stubbs, but so too might my bright red Swingaway can opener. Knight offered no provisions for ruling out such "aberrant" associations.[34] He insisted that association constitutes a mechanical operation of the mind, one we can't influence or control (136), and later he claimed "though we may analyze the principles of mental, as well as of corporeal pleasures, we can never discover the full extent of their operation" (232–33).

Some mitigating factors might undercut this objection. An individual's associations are limited not only by his memory and experience, but also by his culture. Within a particular society, popular trends and tastes give us a shared basis for association. For example, eighteenth-century Englishmen of Price's and Knight's class who had shared the experience of the grand tour, read many of the same books, and purchased many of the same prints would tend to think of similar paintings in similar circumstances. For such men, the works of Claude, Rosa, and Dughet became a sort of shorthand representing the three categories of the beautiful, the sublime, and the picturesque.[35] These considerations do not, however, defeat the objection to Knight's view raised above. For although such commonalities might well in *fact* constrain the picturesque, it remains promiscuous in *principle*.[36]

We know that Price and Knight agreed in practical matters of garden improvements. How did their judgments compare with regard to the picturesque? Price described many rough and irregular natural scenes in the course of the *Essay* as he tried to persuade improvers of the attractiveness of rugged lanes, broken banks, gnarled roots, and overhanging trees. Would Knight have deemed such scenes picturesque? His theory of association counters Price's view, since perceivers acquainted *only* with beautiful and sublime paintings would not judge the scenes picturesque. That is, Downton, Foxley, and other rugged and varied landscapes would not remind these viewers of any landscape paintings of their acquaintance. Yet Knight also in places defines picturesque objects in terms reminiscent of Price's definition. For example, while discussing Flemish and Dutch painters, Knight says that "those objects and combinations of objects, which exhibit blended and broken tints, or irregular masses of light and shadow harmoniously melted into each other . . . are the objects and combinations of objects, which we properly call *picturesque*" (150).

Conflicting strands emerge here in Knight's theory, much as they did in Price's. One strand suggests that Knight could mount a physiologically based argument to show that picturesque scenes would be universally admired. Let me briefly sketch that argument. Throughout the *Inquiry,* Knight distinguished purely sensory pleasures from those involving intellect and imagination. At the level of sensation, he argued, we are initially drawn to simple qualities but come to find them insipid and to prefer mixtures and diversities (46). "Colors, as well as sounds and flavors, are more pleasing when harmoniously mixed and graduated, than when distinct and uniform" (62). Again, "harmonious combinations of tones and flavors are more grateful than single ones," the eye prefers "tints happily broken and blended, etc." (151). Since such varied combinations are just those which mark Price's picturesque, Knight's remarks seem to provide physiological grounds for supporting Price's view. Transferred to the macrolevel, they encourage us to reject the smooth, monotonous gardens of Capability Brown.

In the end, this argument fails to effect a rapprochement between Price and Knight because Knight believed that taste was determined not by sensory factors but by intellectual ones. Knight maintained that the beauties of light, shade, and color were the only ones which affect the eye. He also held that painting imitates only the visible qualities of bodies. As a result, painting allows us to appreciate visually pleasing but otherwise offensive objects—decayed trees, rotten thatch, tattered worn-out dirty garments, and fish markets (70). Yet it doesn't follow that we prefer such objects overall. As Knight aptly noted, if this were the case we would admire not only such variegated objects as zebras, multicolored tulips, and jasper or porphyry columns, we would also prefer pimpled faces to smooth ones (88). We do not prefer pimpled faces, and the reason is that "all the pleasures of the intellect arise from the association of ideas" (143).

Knight made clever use of satire to establish his point that taste is independent of any physiologically based preference for variety. Noting that "irregularity of appearance is generally thought essential to picturesque beauty" (199), Knight remarked that "no painter has ever thought of making a man or animal more picturesque by exhibiting them with one leg shorter than the other, or one eye smaller than the other" (199). An even more telling passage addressed an example from Price's work *A Dialogue on the Distinct Characters of the Picturesque and the Beautiful* (1801). One of the three participants in that dialogue commented on the picturesque appeal of a rambling and irregular parsonage, and another went on to reply, "I think there is a sort of resemblance between the good old parson's daughter and his house. She is upright indeed, and so are the walls, but her features have a little of the same irregularity, and her eyes are somewhat inclined to look across each other like the roofs of the old parsonage. Yet a clear white skin, clean white teeth, though not very even, and a look of neatness and cheerfulness, in spite of these irregularities, made me look at her with pleasure."[37] Knight venomously observed that to be consistent, Price should have extended the asymmetry beyond the girl's face. "The same happy mixture of the irregular and the picturesque must have prevailed throughout her limbs; and consequently, she must have hobbled as well as squinted; and had hips and shoulders as irregular as her teeth, cheeks, and eyebrows" (201–2).

Knight's theory, then, carefully distinguished sensory pleasure from the picturesque.[38] The physiology of our senses guarantees that certain sorts of blended and variegated sights, sounds, smells, and tastes will please. In fact, in his closing chapter on novelty, Knight proclaimed that "change and variety are . . . necessary to the enjoyment of all pleasure; whether sensual or intellectual" (426).[39] Yet, the picturesque transcends this sensory base in two respects: first, variety and irregularity don't guarantee a picturesque object or scene; and second, objects and scenes that *are* picturesque are not recognized as such by all perceivers, but only by those with the requisite knowledge of painting. Thus Knight resisted the objective pull of Price's theory.

While Knight's comments about the parson's daughter constitute an effective reductio of Price's position, in the end the two quarreling theorists were not that far apart. Both ended up endorsing freedom and variety in taste *and* in gardening. Price's exhortation that gentlemen improve their own estates and discover a variety of uniquely excellent styles was echoed by Knight's closing diatribe against rules of taste. Knight argued that critics, like casuists in morals, have "attempted to direct by rules, and limit by definitions, matters which depend entirely on feeling and sentiment: and which are therefore so various and extensive; and diversified by such nice and infinitely graduated shades of difference, that they elude all the subtleties of logic, or intricacies of calculation" (233). Knight insisted again and again that general rules cannot reach every possible case.[40] This I take it is Knight's answer to the opening question of his *Inquiry*. There is no standard of taste, nor should there be, because all such standards are inevitably misleading.

6. TRANSFER OF TECHNIQUE

While neither Price nor Knight favored squinting women with pimpled faces, both undoubtedly preferred Rievaulx Abbey in ruins just as they preferred lanes rutted and woods overgrown. Their attempts to justify these preferences and support them in theory comprise an interesting and important episode in the history of taste. I have tried to show that their efforts to identify the category *picturesque* pulled in different directions. While they may have agreed in their assessments of landscape gardeners and landscape paintings, they did *not* agree regarding what was picturesque and why. Moreover, Price's and Knight's theories of the picturesque, once their details are set out, have no essential connection to the art of painting. Price defined the picturesque in terms of objective qualities—roughness, irregularity, intricacy, sudden variation, and the like—which aren't possessed by each and every painting, and which characterize many objects that are not paintings. Knight defined the picturesque in terms of subjective qualities—individuals' associations—but these may be mistaken or idiosyncratic and thus fail to pick out any paintings at all.

There remains one interesting eighteenth-century debate which grew out of the preoccupation with the picturesque; this debate has consequences for garden history and for the proposal that gardening and painting are sister arts. I have in mind a dispute between Sir Uvedale Price and the garden designer Humphry Repton concerning the claim that gardening and painting share principles and technique. This claim represents the weakest possible interpretation of the view that painting and gardening are sister arts. The debate between Price and Repton became quite convoluted. In this final section I will try to outline and critique its main twists and turns.

We have already met Sir Uvedale Price. Humphry Repton, born in Bury St. Edmunds in 1752, came to the profession of landscape gardening late in life. After trying various ways to earn his living—textile manufacturer, merchant, civil servant, essayist, art critic— he suddenly decided, some five years after the death of Capability Brown, to set himself up as a landscape gardener. Repton was skilled at drawing and sketching, and his circle of acquaintance from his earlier years included experts in botany and horticulture.[41] Dorothy Stroud writes that within two years Repton "had firmly established himself as the leading landscape designer of his day."[42]

A hallmark of Repton's practice were his Red Books, leather-bound volumes in which he outlined his suggestions for potential clients. The Red Books described the improvements Repton had in mind and illustrated them through an ingenious system of flaps and slides that allowed comparison of each scene before and after its proposed alteration.

Above and opposite: a pair of illustrations by Thomas Hearne (engraved by Benjamin Thomas Pouncy) for Richard Payne Knight's poem *The Landscape* (London, 1794). The scene above is titled *A Brownian Landscape*. Reproduced by permission of the Yale Center for British Art, Paul Mellon Collection.

Some garden historians go so far as to identify a picturesque style of gardening, with Repton as its main proponent. In many respects, Repton carried on the design traditions of his predecessor Brown, whose gardens helped spark the picturesque movement by generating such antipathy in Price and Knight. Fleming and Gore report that after his father's death (in 1783), "The son of Capability Brown . . . gave Repton access to his father's papers, tacitly admitting him as his successor; and, to an extent, Repton did consider himself in this role."[43] There were, however, stylistic differences between Brown's and Repton's creations. Comparing the two designers, Dorothy Stroud notes that Repton's "plantations

This scene is titled *A Picturesque View of the Same Landscape*. Reproduced by permission of the Yale Center for British Art, Paul Mellon Collection.

tended to be thicker, while the small buildings in the grounds frequently assumed a rustic rather than a classical character."[44] Repton also objected to placing a belt of trees all around an estate; he planted groups of trees atop hills in a manner quite different from Brown's clumps;[45] also, he advocated a formal treatment, including flowers, terraces, and fountains, in the area directly around the house.[46] Though initially enthusiastic about the design principles defended by Price and Knight, Repton soon had second thoughts and distanced himself from their views. In the end, both his gardens and his gardening principles seem too eclectic and too conciliatory to merit the label "picturesque."[47] Nevertheless, his debate with Price regarding the applicability of principles of painting to the art of gardening illuminates one last, attenuated sense of that term—one highlighting similarity not of form, nor of association, but of technique.

Repton and Price began discussing gardens, painting, and the picturesque because Repton felt that both he himself, as well as Brown, with whose work he was identified, had been unfairly attacked in Price's *Essay*. Price sent him an early copy of that work, and Repton was so distressed that he wrote "A Letter to Sir Uvedale Price, Esq.," of which he says that

> this letter, which has been written at various opportunities during my journey into Derbyshire, has insensibly grown to a bulk which I little expected when I began it: I shall therefore cause a few copies to be printed, to serve as a general defense of an art which, I trust, will not be totally suppressed, although you so earnestly recommend every gentleman to become his own landscape gardener.[48]

Repton also included the letter as a footnote to the Appendix of his volume *Sketches and Hints on Landscape Gardening* (1794). Price in turn responded with a book-length "Letter to H. Repton, Esq., on the Application of the Practice As Well As the Principles of Landscape-Painting to Landscape-Gardening" (subtitled "Intended as a Supplement to the Essay on the Picturesque").[49] The subject of the exchange between the two authors was the extent to which the principles of painting could be applied to the art of gardening.

In his *Essay*, Price defined the "great leading principles" of painting as general composition, grouping the separate parts, harmony of tints, and unity of character (64). He went on to add "breadth and effect of light and shade" to the list, noting that it is essential to painting but "at first sight hardly seems within the province of the improver" (64). A good deal farther on in the *Essay*, Price adds one last item to his list—connection—declaring that the "defect, the greatest of all [of the present system of improving] and the most opposite to the principles of painting, is want of connection—a passion for making everything distinct and separate" (179).[50]

These are the principles on which Price believes landscape gardening should be based. I shall discuss the principles themselves—and the underlying assumption that each art *has* a set of leading principles—in more detail below. In exhorting gentlemen to be their own improvers, Price is urging them to study the masterpieces of landscape painting, extract these principles, and apply them in designing their estates. Thus he states in the *Essay* that:

> If a taste for drawing and painting and a knowledge of their principles made a part of every gentleman's education; if, instead of hiring a professed improver, to

torture his grounds after an established model, each improved his own place according to general conceptions drawn from nature and pictures, or from hints which favorite masters in painting, or favorite parts of nature suggested to him, there might in time be a great variety in the styles of improvement, and all of them with peculiar excellences (230).

Price returns to this same theme in the *Letter:* "It is true that I have very earnestly and generally recommended it to gentlemen who have places, that they should qualify themselves for becoming their own landscape gardeners, by one of the most pleasing and liberal of all studies; that of the principles of painting, the works of painters and of nature" (119–20). Elsewhere Price notes that men of liberal education who pass time at their country seats are continually among landscapes (120–21), and he predicts that "with the least attention to pictures and to composition, the principles of landscape gardening would insensibly press themselves upon their minds" (*Letter*, 121).

Price does qualify his advice to this extent: he doesn't recommend that improvers study art exclusively; they must also study nature. Thus he remarks that "nothing can be farther from my intention . . . than to recommend the study of pictures in preference to that of nature, much less to the exclusion of it. Whoever studies art alone, will have a narrow pedantic manner of considering all objects" (*Essay*, 3).

Repton initially agreed with Price's views. Some time before publication of Price's *Essay* and Repton's *Sketches and Hints,* the two had taken a tour together down the Wye River valley.[51] Both allude to the journey in their letters. Price recalls advising Repton, as they admired the striking scenery, to study "what the higher artists have done, both in their pictures and their drawings" (43). He also notes that Repton seemed *not* sufficiently acquainted with the work of the great masters, since he did not make the sorts of references to paintings that might have been expected:

> I will frankly own, that from all the conversations which have passed between us, I had (perhaps rashly) conceived that you were not very conversant in them: I cannot recollect, amidst all the romantic scenes we viewed together, your having made any of those allusions to the works of various masters which might naturally have occurred to a person who had studied, or even observed them with common attention (43).

Repton himself remarks that "During the pleasant hours we passed together amidst the romantic scenery of the Wye, I do remember my acknowledging that an enthusiasm for the picturesque had originally led me to fancy greater affinity between *Painting* and *Gar-*

dening than I found to exist after more mature consideration and greater experience" (70 n.). He places a similar disclaimer in a later edition of *Sketches and Hints:* "The want of duly considering the affinity between painting and gardening is the source of those errors and false principles which I find too frequently prevailing in the admirers or connoisseurs in painting: and I do not hesitate to acknowledge that I once supposed the two arts to be more intimately connected than my practice and experience have since confirmed" (57).[52] The contemporary garden historian Edward Hyams admiringly quotes his predecessor, Marie-Louise Gothein, who in her work *Geschichte der Gartenkunst* (1928) declared Repton "the first man to free himself from the exaggerated idea of a similarity between painting and landscape gardening" (131).

In *Sketches and Hints* Repton identifies four principles of landscape gardening. These include such recommendations as "display the natural beauties of every situation" and "disguise the boundary to give an appearance of extent."[53] Interestingly, there is no overlap between these and the principles of painting cited by Price. This may be because Repton's principles are taxonomic rather than practical. They do not tell us how to design gardens— where to dig, what to plant, what architectural features to incorporate. Rather, Repton offers his principles in order to distinguish the modern style of landscape gardening from what he calls the ancient style. (These differ above all in their degree of what we would deem naturalness.) Overall, Repton offers three arguments in the course of his writings for rejecting the theoretical relationship Price proposes between painting and gardening. The first argument concerns differences between painted scenes and natural ones; the second concerns a conflict between aesthetic or picturesque values, on the one hand, and comfort and convenience, on the other; the third concerns claims of expertise. These arguments are convoluted, and they tend to blend into one another. Let me outline the first two.[54]

Here is Repton's first argument. In chapter 8 of *Sketches and Hints,* he lists five differences between scenes in nature and pictures on canvas, all of them owing to technical facts about optics, vision, and linear perspective. They are:

(1) The painter paints each view from a fixed spot, while the gardener "surveys his scenery while in motion" (53).[55]

(2) A garden or a scene in nature encompasses a "quantity of view, or field of vision . . . much greater than any picture will admit" (53).

(3) The prospect or view down a steep hill is one of the most pleasing of all scenes, but one that cannot be painted.

(4) The painter's light can come from any point of the compass but "can only be made strong by contrast of shade" (54).

(5) Foregrounds are treated differently in gardening and in painting: "the neat gravel walk or close-mown lawn would ill supply the place, in painting, of a rotten tree, a bunch of docks, or a broken road, passing under a steep bank, covered with briers, nettles, and ragged thorns" (54).[56]

In addition to these five conditions, which guarantee that our experience of gardens will be quite unlike our experience of painted landscape scenes, Repton notes some further differences in the knowledge required of painters, on the one hand, and garden designers, on the other. He claims that gardeners' practical knowledge in "planting, digging, and moving earth" will rein in the painter's luxuriant imagination. He also points out that the garden designer must have "competent knowledge of surveying, mechanics, hydraulics, agriculture, botany, and the general principles of architecture" (iv). Having established that the experience of a garden is unlike the experience of a painting, and that an artist who can paint a marvelous landscape scene may not have the knowledge needed to design a landscape garden, Repton sarcastically proposes that "If . . . the painter's landscape be indispensable to the perfection of gardening, it would surely be far better to paint it on canvas at the end of an avenue, as they do in Holland, than to sacrifice the health, cheerfulness, and comfort of a country residence to the wild but pleasing scenery of a painter's imagination" (70 n.).

Repton's remarks about sacrificing health, cheer, and comfort to wild scenery may seem both hysterical and beside the point, but his debate with Price eventually becomes focused on comfort and convenience, two "emotional" consequences of landscape. Here is how their debate becomes reoriented. Technically, Repton's claims are correct. (We have seen earlier that no painting can provide the exact same experience as viewing, in the normal way, the scene it represents.) But the fact that painted and natural landscapes yield different experiences does not establish that the principles of painting have no application to landscape gardening. That claim would be a non sequitur. So, Repton hasn't yet established his point.

For a time, the exchange between Repton and Price shifts to Repton's point 3, above, the one concerning scenes that can't be painted. Near the end of his "Letter to Price," Repton expands on this example, saying "I trust the good sense and good taste of this country will never be led to despise the comfort of a gravel walk, the delicious fragrance of a shrubbery, the soul expanding delight of a wide extended prospect, or a view down a steep hill because they are all subjects incapable of being painted" (18–19). In his reply, Price devotes considerable space to discussing painted prospects. He concedes there is a technical sense in which a view from a high prospect cannot be painted. While "the *general* effect of looking down from a height on lower objects" (143) has been "perpetually expressed" in painting, no painting can capture "the *immediate and uninterrupted progress* of the descent" (143). But this, he argues, no more undermines the claims of painting to represent landscape than does the painter's inability to express the warbling of birds, the fragrance of flowers, or the motion of deer. Price closes the discussion with an apology: "Had I not so often heard this circumstance mentioned, and with great triumph, by the adversaries of painting, I should be ashamed of having said so much about an impossibility, that seems to have no more to do with the application of the principles of painting to objects of sight, or with the affinity between painting and gardening, than the impossibility of painting real sounds, real smells, or real motion" (144).

Initially, this looks like another flawed argument. I suppose the position Price sets out to topple is this: if there are certain scenes that can't be painted, then the principles of painting don't apply to all varieties of natural landscape and so can't serve as principles of landscape gardening. But Price soon changes his tune. The new claim is not that such scenes can't be painted, but that they don't make *good* paintings (140)! Unlike views from prospects, gravel walks, shrubberies, and close-mown lawns *can* be painted. But because they lack interesting texture and detail, they are not suitable for the foreground of a landscape painting. (In fact, Price includes prospects in this category as well. Noting that the view from a prospect generally comes from the highest and most open part of a hill, he claims that such a view necessarily lacks the sort of foreground and second distance required in a good landscape painting [130].)[57]

One further change is rung on this theme as the debate continues. Good paintings, for both Repton and Price, exhibit three distances; the foreground is textured, not bare. But if we imagine a garden which realizes or reconstructs such a painting, our preferences suddenly change. Burdocks and rotting trees, briers, thorns, and nettles are the best occupants, aesthetically, of the foreground of a landscape painting. By contrast, trimmed shrubs, cropped lawns, and gravel walks are best suited to surround (constitute the "foreground" of) a house or its outbuildings. Similarly, what makes for a good foreground in a painting does not make for a good foreground in a garden.[58]

Repton makes this point repeatedly. In chapter 7 of the 1794 edition of *Sketches and Hints* he derides Knight, saying "the enthusiasm for picturesque effect seems to have so completely bewildered the author of [*The Landscape*] that he not only mistakes the essential difference between the landscape painter and the landscape gardener; but appears even to forget that a dwelling-house is an object of comfort and convenience" (59). Comparing Downton and Foxley, the estates of Knight and Price, Repton notes that Price is more willing to sacrifice picturesque beauty to neatness near the house, but points out that "by this very concession [Price] acknowledges, that real *comfort*, and his ideas of *picturesqueness*, are incompatible."[59]

For his own part, Repton states "I am not less an admirer of those scenes which painting represents; but I have discovered that *utility* must often take the lead of *beauty*, and *convenience* be preferred to picturesque effect, in the neighborhood of men's habitation" (60). In the "Letter to Price," Repton reiterates that "*in whatever relates to man, propriety and convenience are not less objects of good taste, than picturesque effect*" (70 n.). Declaring that both he and Brown were admirers of wild scenery, Repton claims that the lesson Brown took from his studies in Needwood forest, and that he himself took from his experiences in the forest of Hinault, was this: "*that the landscape ought to be adapted to the beings which are to inhabit it*—to men, and not to beasts" (77). While the landscape painter may treat people as mere "staffage" to balance or fill his composition,[60] "The landscape gardener does more:—he undertakes to study their comforts and convenience" (77).

In a sense Repton and Price are arguing at cross-purposes. There are few particular claims on which they would disagree. Neither author would sacrifice safety or comfort to picturesque effect. Neither would mass rotting wood, beetling rocks, and clusters of thorns at the foundations of a house or the forefront of a garden. And both would admire landscape paintings in various styles—by Claude, Poussin, and Wilson as well as Rosa, Gainsborough, and Dughet.

Do the principles of painting in fact apply to landscape gardening? Repton concludes his letter with an extended and awkward trope. He claims that painting and gardening are not "sister arts, proceeding from the same stock, but rather congenial natures, brought together like man and wife; while, therefore, you exult in the office of mediator betwixt these two 'imaginary personages,' you should recollect the danger of interfering in their occasional differences, and especially how you advise them both to wear the same articles of dress" (74 n.). Whether we construe painting and gardening as sisters, or as husband and wife with a tendency to cross-dress, the claim that they share a set of principles turns out to be rather empty. Price tries to defend this claim by showing that Repton is caught in a pragmatic contradiction. That is, Price suggests that Repton's practice belies his principles. Since he sketches the proposed changes for each garden commission in a Red Book, he is *using* painting (and thereby its principles) to design each garden. But this too seems in error. We must distinguish here painting as a system of representation, and painting as a set of aesthetic principles. Repton's practice employs painting in the first sense, to portray gardens. Nothing follows about the use of the principles of painting to compose or design gardens.

In fact, there is a deeper question here—*are* there principles of painting in the second sense? Presumably, such principles would guide artists in the creation of excellent paintings. Would they guarantee such results? Rules regarding composition and technique can be followed in creating, say, a landscape painting. Here as in the other arts, no set of rules can guarantee success. In fact it was a common eighteenth-century belief, supported by both Pope and Hume, that genius shouldn't be constrained by rules.[61] Setting aside the question of quality, what role might remain for rules or principles of landscape painting?

Repton defines landscape as "a view capable of being represented in painting," and goes on to add that it has two, three, or more well-marked distances.[62] But this is too general to differentiate among landscapes. Compositional principles, if they can be formulated at all, would operate at one of two levels, that of of particular genres, or that of what Wollheim called general and individual style. Thus John Barrell, in his book *The Idea of Landscape and the Sense of Place,* isolates what he considers the structural principles which characterize landscapes by Claude. Claude's landscapes, he argues, share a fairly high viewpoint, tremendous depth, an area of light set just below the horizon which immediately attracts the eye, framing trees or buildings in the foreground, a series of planes alternating light and dark, the penultimate one in sunlight, and a road or bridge running diagonally and linking the planes.[63] Would following such compositional principles yield a Claudean painting? Surely one would also have to make stipulations about subject matter, color and tone, brushwork, and so on.

Similar comments apply if we pick other landscape styles or genres. Consider, for example, what Anne Bermingham in her book *Landscape and Ideology* calls the rustic landscape tradition, associated with the work of Gainsborough and Constable. Bermingham defines this genre by saying that "Rustic landscapes differ from topographical studies in that their main intention is not to portray a famous spot, view, or monument but instead to evoke the countryside and rural life. The rustic landscape is not easily or satisfactorily assimilated into classical-romantic polarities."[64] The principles delimiting this genre would primarily address subject matter and its treatment rather than formal or technical matters.[65] Note that in each case (1) identifying a style or genre of painting, and (2) instructing painters in the creation of works of that type are correlative tasks guided by the same set of principles.

I have been suggesting that there are not principles of painting per se, but rather principles that delimit one or another genre or style of painting. Few of these would seem to be principles that would translate readily to garden design. As discussed in chapter 4, it is possible to create gardens that imitate, model, or allude to particular paintings or to particular genres or styles of painting. But each such garden would be singular, and the method of establishing this referential connection to a particular painting or group of paintings would most likely not be repeated. That is, it would not be a necessary or regular aspect of garden design.

If this is correct, then it follows that any principles shared by the arts of gardening and painting would be extremely general. They would be at the level of "Pay attention to color, balance, and texture; use perspective to create an illusion of depth; achieve unity of composition." Note that we are now at the level of principle cited by Price in his *Essay.* I suggest that such principles are without guiding force. That is, knowing that general composition, harmony of tints, breadth of light and shade, and connection are factors that we attend to in viewing paintings and that painters attend to in painting them, tells us nothing about what sort of composition and which varieties of tonal harmony, light and shade, and connection are desirable. Inevitably *all* paintings have some composition or other, some tonal relationships—harmonious or not, some degree of connection. But to grant this is to say nothing about whether the paintings in question are landscapes or portraits, linear or painterly, representational or abstract, excellent or appalling. Since features like those listed by Price have no normative force, I propose reconstruing them as *elements* of painting, reserving the term "principles" for rules or features that guide our actions in important ways.

I believe that an equivalent result holds for the art of gardening. That is, there are no principles of gardening, per se. There are principles or rules of thumb that guide the design of specific types of gardens—water gardens, terrace gardens, knot gardens, Zen gardens, shade gardens, desert gardens. And, at a more general level, there are elements of gardening that correspond to the elements of painting noted above. These claims can be supported by browsing through any contemporary books on garden design. For example, Alice Recknagel Ireys, in a volume entitled *Garden Design,* lists the following six principles of garden art: scale, proportion, unity, balance, rhythm, and focal point.[66] (I would once again denominate these elements rather than principles, since every garden possesses them to some degree—except perhaps for unity—and since merely having some scale or other, some proportion or other, and so on, doesn't guarantee quality.) A more ambitious text, also entitled *Garden Design,* by five authors aided by the Publication Board of the American Society of Landscape Architects, lists the following as elements of the garden: paving, turf and ground covers, steps, walls, and fences, gates and windows, structures, seats and benches, water, ornaments, light, and the plant palette.[67] These are not shared with painting in the way that Price's elements are; they are more garden ingredients than garden techniques. An earlier chapter of the same text breaks the garden down into experiential units—landmarks, landings, entries, corridors, vertical changes, water—and opportunities—places for exploration, gathering, dining, play, contemplation, and work.

In sum, these and other primers instructing readers in garden design do not make any explicit comparisons with painting. They do not mention particular principles or techniques of that art, nor do they invariably mention elements shared by painting and gardening. One final way to test Price's claim about the transfer of technique is to look at the actual practice of particular garden designers. Russell Page, for example, in his book *The Education of a Gardener,* first published in 1962, says "I know now that one cannot be taught to design gardens academically or theoretically. You have to learn the ways and nature of plants and stone, of water and soil at least as much through the hands as through the head."[68] (Compare this claim with the discussion of academies of gardening in chapter 2.) Yet at the same time, he says "Whether I am making a landscape or a garden or arranging a window box I first address the problem as an artist composing a picture; my pre-occupation is with the relationships between objects" (Preface). Later he notes "At the drawing-board, I work out my composition in terms of levels" (70). Yet do these procedural remarks indicate any deep relationship between the arts we are examining? Page lists the following as "timeless elements" of gardens: light and shade, earth, stone, and water, foliage and flowers (49). Thus the elements of gardens differ from the elements of paintings, and the transfer of technique that we have been exploring in this second chapter on gardening and painting turns out to be at a level so general as to have no effect on the actual process of garden design.[69] All one can conclude is that certain basic elements attended to by painters—color, texture, form, balance, composition, perspective, light and shade—also play a role in the creation of gardens.

7. CONCLUSION

Let us return now to the eighteenth-century concept of the picturesque, with which we opened this chapter. While this concept figured in and enhanced the appreciation of certain types of landscape, and also fueled the criticism of a particular style of landscape garden—that associated with Capability Brown—the picturesque did not figure centrally in garden design.[70] I believe that no particularly revealing connection between gardens and painting emerges from a study of the picturesque. Yet there has been considerable interest in this aesthetic category. Why did it flourish in the period we have been examining, and why did it decline?

In assessing the apparent popularity of the picturesque, we must realize that the concept has been greatly stretched. So far we have been examining the picturesque primarily as it applied to landscape aesthetics, and derivatively to garden design. Yet even in this regard, the label "picturesque" has been extended to such chronological extremes as to become almost meaningless; this is in addition to the strain imposed by internal tensions and inconsistencies like those in the theories of Price and Knight.

The chronological difficulties I have in mind are exemplified by a book by Morris Brownell taking Pope as a paradigm example of a picturesque gardener.[71] For instance, Brownell writes that Pope's treatment of landscape reveals "a sensibility to picturesque landscape in natural scenery explicit enough to allow us to infer his adherence to something like an aesthetic of picturesque scenery."[72] Of the interpretations of the picturesque we have canvassed so far, Brownell's approximates the last and weakest, the one I have labeled "transfer of technique." Given that Pope was gardening some seventy-five years before the publication of Price's *Essay,* and thirty-eight years before the publication of Burke's *Inquiry,* to which Price's work was indebted, it seems very unlikely that Pope was gardening in a style that fitted the late eighteenth-century use of the term "picturesque."[73] Again, Edward Hyams, in his book *The English Garden,* labels all English gardens in the first half of the eighteenth century "picture-gardens."[74] The eighteenth-century travel literature discussed in chapter 2 above further blurred the boundaries of the picturesque, since rugged mountain scenes like those along the Welsh border—scenes reminiscent of the paintings of Salvator Rosa, and worthy, therefore, of the label "sublime"—were called picturesque, as were those in the lake country.

Hunt gives a simple account of the rise of the picturesque. He attributes it to loss of learning. Hunt claims that as patronage for the arts expanded in the eighteenth century, viewers were increasingly less equipped to puzzle out the meanings of complex emblematic works. Expressive and, ultimately, picturesque works were much more accessible to audiences no longer schooled in the classics.[75]

Hunt's interpretation recalls passages quoted earlier in this chapter from Christopher Hussey and David Watkin. These authors identified the picturesque with the discovery and celebration of visual values. Yet celebration of the visual can cause other concerns and values to be downplayed or expunged. For some commentators, the picturesque as characterized by Price and Knight is morally problematic, since it singles out humble, rustic scenes (although the picturesque requires variety, a variety of jewels, baubles, and silks would not do) without any concern for their origins or limitations. Malcolm Andrews, in *The Search for the Picturesque,* suggests that "the Picturesque enterprise in its later stages, with its almost exclusive emphasis on visual appreciation, entailed a suppression of the spectator's moral response to those very subjects which it could least hope to divest of moral significance—the ruin, the hovel, and rural poverty" (59).[76]

Andrews takes his analysis one step farther, proposing a link between the characteristically humble picturesque subjects and the viewpoint from which they were painted:

"The social descent—palace to ruin to hovel—has an interesting analogy with the painter's changing viewpoint in the eighteenth century" (61). The picturesque viewpoint was a low one,[77] in direct contrast with the high prospects and panoramic vistas of earlier topographical paintings. For Andrews, this change is psychologically revealing. He concludes that the picturesque fixation testified to a crisis of sorts throughout England: "The repudiation of the high viewpoint in late-eighteenth century Picturesque theory suggests a failure of confidence" (63). That is, in repudiating the synoptic point of view characteristic of earlier prospect poems and topographical paintings, practitioners of the picturesque were also repudiating the certainties of the Augustan Age, expressing their doubts about man's ability to conquer and harness nature.

Other theorists offer similarly deep readings of the eighteenth-century psyche. For example, Anne Bermingham, drawing on the work of John Barrell, argues that the cult of the picturesque arose just when enclosure of the English countryside was accelerating. The natural world was romanticized precisely when it was in fact disappearing. Bermingham suggests that "In its celebration of the irregular, preenclosed landscape, the picturesque harkened back nostalgically to an old order of rural paternalism" (70). Later, she claims that the picturesque "mystified the agency of social change so that fate, and not the economic decisions of the landowning classes, seemed responsible. In this respect, the picturesque represented an attempt to wipe out the fact of enclosure and to minimize its consequences" (75). To some extent she concurs with Andrews, stating "A profound pessimism lay at the root of picturesque theory" (70).

With these last accounts of the picturesque we have come quite far from Price's and Knight's criticisms of the bald, monotonous gardens of Capability Brown; far, too, from the Rev. Mr. Gilpin's enthusiasm for the actual sights and scenes of his native land. These later theories, linking the picturesque with enclosure and sweeping economic change, with insecurity and malaise, assume a close connection between landscape and well-being. In fact, the way we relate to landscape can both determine and reveal our mental and emotional states, as well, of course, as our social class, politics, and ideology. These connections raise questions that will be explored in subsequent chapters. How do we experience landscape, and in particular, gardens, given that they do not function precisely like their sister arts, painting and poetry? And, what is the fate of gardens today, given that many of the social and economic changes cataloged by Hunt, Andrews, and Bermingham have continued apace?

1. Monet's garden at Giverny. Photograph by Mick Hales.

2A. *(opposite top)* Stowe, the Temple of Ancient Virtue. Photograph by David Conway.

2B. *(opposite bottom)* Stowe, the Temple of British Worthies. Photograph by David Conway.

3. *(above)* This view of a contemporary garden in St. Louis designed by Chuck Freeman exemplifies two appeals gardens make to our imagination: invitation and enclosure. Photograph by Jerry Naunheim, Jr., courtesy of the *St. Louis Post-Dispatch*.

4. *(opposite)* The Odette Monteiro Garden, designed by Roberto Burle Marx. Photograph by Stuart Wrede.

5. *(above)* Naumkeag, designed by Fletcher Steele. Photograph by Everett Scott.

6. *(opposite)* The Stella Garden by Martha Schwartz. Photograph courtesy of Martha Schwartz.

7. A postmodernist garden? Clifford Davis's array of rubber ducks and plastic daisies combines eclecticism and kitsch. Photograph by Eric Crichton.

8. An aircraft carrier bird-table in Ian Hamilton Finlay's garden, Stonypath. Reproduced by permission of Ian Hamilton Finlay. Photograph courtesy of Reaktion Books.

THE BEHOLDER'S SHARE

I. INTRODUCTION

The title of this chapter pays homage to *Art and Illusion,* E. H. Gombrich's ground-breaking study of the psychology of pictorial representation, first published in 1960. In part 3 of that work, entitled "The Beholder's Share," Gombrich examines the beholder's contribution to illusionistic representation. Arguing that all images are inherently ambiguous, Gombrich establishes that viewing pictures is not a passive experience. Since no picture presents the world exactly as it appears—as it would appear to what Ruskin termed "an innocent eye"—viewers must arrive at interpretations of the images and pictures they confront. They do so, Gombrich claims, by drawing on knowledge and expectation, facts about the conditions under which the picture is viewed, and their experience of other pictures and other works of art. In this chapter, I would like to conduct a similar study of the art of gardens. That is, I would like to investigate our experience of gardens, noting not only the ways in which we actively respond to these works, but also the ways in which gardens (garden designers) manipulate and control our reactions.

Of course, our experience of a garden and the nature of that garden are correlative notions. Different gardens will evoke different sorts of experiences in their visitors, and how each garden affects us depends in large part upon that garden's characteristics. In chapter 1 I indicated the great variety of gardens that have flourished in different times and places, the great variety of functions gardens can and have performed. This richness makes it unlikely that there is anything so simple as *the* experience of the garden. Nevertheless, I believe there are important commonalities to be noted about gardens and their relation to attention, enclosure, invitation, and, finally, reality (that is, the physical world).

2. SENSE

As I claimed in chapter 1, gardens appeal to all of the five senses: sight, hearing, smell, taste, and touch. The smells of a garden can include not only the fragrances of flowers and herbs but also the acrid odor of mulch and the fetid smells of dampness and rotting vegetation. A small area at the St. Louis Botanical Garden is given over to a scent garden. Designed for blind visitors, the garden features small braille plaques which identify a variety of strongly-scented flowers and herbs in raised brick beds.

Few gardens appeal to the sense of taste if this means providing something we actually savor as we observe or stroll through the garden. But the appeal to this sense can be promissory rather than actual. Gardens present us with all manner of delicacies whose tastes we can anticipate or imagine. We can also see other creatures—birds, bees, butterflies, slugs—feasting on garden bounty. This provides a sort of vicarious reminder of the pleasures—and relativity—of the sense of taste.

With regard to the sense of hearing, we are regaled with sounds ranging from people's passage through the garden—footfalls, echoes, and conversations—to the noises of birds and insects, the sounds of wind, rain, and other weather, the splash of water, natural or artificial. Weather and terrain stimulate our sense of touch as well. The warmth of the midsummer sun, the cooling relief of a breeze, and the sting of driving rain are all components of garden experience. The various textures of the paths under foot—packed sand, shredded bark, intricately laid brick—also contribute. I often feel inclined to touch, stroke, or pat the plants I pass by in a garden—an urge that must be repressed in the twelve-acre desert garden on the estate of Henry Huntington in San Marino, California. This garden groups together plants of similar species and therefore similar geometry. The clusters of echoing forms—balls and tussocks, tubes and spikes—have a strong tactile appeal that is enhanced, if anything, by their fierce covering of thorns. A garden so strongly geometric, which forbids (or at least strongly penalizes) the exercise of touch, intensifies our appreciation of form and structure and supports Berkeley's claim in the *New Theory of Vision* that distance and size are perceived immediately not by sight but by touch.

Despite the ways in which our senses of smell, taste, hearing, and touch are activated in a garden, the primary appeal of gardens is to our sense of sight. A garden is, after all, a

Braille markers, scented plants, and Solari bells adorn a section of the Missouri Botanical Garden designed for blind visitors. Photograph by author.

The twelve-acre cactus garden at the Huntington Library and Botanical Garden. Reproduced by permission of the Huntington Library, San Marino, California.

particularly delightful thing to view. Gardens can provide expansive views—vistas and panoramas—and also more microcosmic delights—attractive groupings of plants, exquisite blossoms, compelling shapes and colors. The sorts of concerns discussed one chapter back under the heading "a transfer of technique" are particularly relevant here. A painter working on a canvas takes into account such factors as color, texture, variety, balance, composition, shading, and perspective. These very same concerns motivate the garden designer. Such painterly concerns and techniques—i.e., those that transfer from the art of painting—will appeal primarily to the sense of sight.

It is easy to think of ways in which gardens delight the sense of sight. And, most of these examples will point to commonalities between gardens and paintings—color, composition, and so on. It might seem harder to think of actual techniques that are shared between these two arts, so consider for a moment the case of perspective. The system of linear perspective developed by Alberti, Brunelleschi, and in others in the fifteenth century allowed artists to represent three-dimensional scenes on a two-dimensional surface. How is this relevant to garden design, which operates, after all, in the three-dimensional medium of landscape? Perspective is certainly mentioned often in seventeenth- and eighteenth-century accounts of gardening. Horace Walpole, in his well-known encomium of the garden designer William Kent, declared that "The great principles on which he worked were perspective, and light and shade."[1] Alexander Pope wrote in a letter to his painting instructor, Charles Jervas, that Twickenham was a place to "practice on a larger terrestrial canvas the principles of perspective and variety that he had learned from him a few years earlier."[2] Pope explained the technique more fully in a letter to Spence: "You may distance things by darkening them and by narrowing the plantations more and more toward the end, in the same manner as they do in painting, and as 'tis executed in the little cypress walk to that obelisk."[3]

One intriguing study of perspective in garden design concerns an earlier gardener, André Le Nôtre. Hazlehurst's *Gardens of Illusion* emphasizes the ways in which Le Nôtre crafts garden illusions—features which appear to have properties they in fact do not have. Many of these illusions are perspectival: they take effect when the garden is viewed from a privileged vantage point, often one within the chateau. We have seen (chap. 2) how Le Nôtre adjusted the size of the basins punctuating Versailles's Grand Canal to make them appear equal from afar. An example involving illusions of shape as well as of size comes from Le Nôtre's earlier work at Fontainebleau. There, Hazlehurst reports, the Grand Parterre, though not in fact square (it measured 310 by 395 meters) was designed so that "viewed from the west, either from the raised terrace or through the opening from the Allée de la Clausée, the parterre and pool would have appeared square as a result of foreshortening."[4]

The examples just cited may well seem to be cases where garden viewers are tricked—deceived by the garden designer. It is important to emphasize the degree to which the eighteenth-century gardens discussed here manipulated and controlled their visitors' experiences.[5] Consider two often overlooked features of the English garden: paths and benches. Paths of course prescribe a route through the garden. Given that many eighteenth-century gardens were laid out as a circuit, the paths were to be walked in one direction only. Thus they controlled the order in which visitors encountered various garden features. Moreover, the particular view from any given section of the path could be aimed, framed, and focused by the use of plantings to direct attention and channel the line of sight. William Kent trained in Italy as a painter before he turned to garden design, and Horace Walpole's account of him in *The History of the Modern Taste in Gardening* stresses Kent's use of painterly techniques.[6] Walpole writes of Kent that

> where the view was less fortunate, or so much exposed as to be beheld at once, he blotted out some parts by thick shades, to divide it into variety, or to make the richest scene more enchanting by reserving it to a farther advance of the spectator's step. Thus selecting favorite objects, and veiling deformities by screens of plantation, . . . he realised the compositions of the greatest masters in painting.[7]

A contemporary author, Peter Martin, notes Kent's use of an opposite effect, one designed to unify pictorial scenes. Martin claims that at Chiswick Kent "increased visual movement from area to area by lessening plantations separating them."[8] Recall that in chapter 4 I quoted a number of authors who compared walking through a garden with viewing a series of pictures. It is techniques like Kent's that serve to demarcate each individual "sketch" or "snapshot" in the series.

Another aspect of control is the management of surprise. Kenneth Woodbridge says of Stourhead that "the walk round the garden is planned as a sequence to be correctly followed, with calculated vistas and surprises."[9] And consider Walpole's more detailed description of Alexander Pope's garden. Here is Walpole on the experiences that unfold as one exits Pope's grotto and walks through the garden: "The passing through the gloom from the grotto to the opening day, the retiring and again assembling shades, the dusky groves, the larger lawn, and the solemnity of the termination at the cypresses that lead up to his mother's tomb, are managed with exquisite judgement."[10] "Managed" is the crucial word here. Walpole shows how even within the scope of five acres, Pope incorporates variety and contrast and arranges these to build to a climax at the end of the garden axis.

A second example of managed surprise occurs at Charles Hamilton's estate at Painshill. There visitors following a path down a steep terraced hill enter a Gothic temple and only then see the broad vista that opens up below. The Painshill circuit exemplifies a further aspect of the control exercised by eighteenth-century gardens, namely, that visitors remain mystified about the gardens' overall structure or scheme. Paulson writes of poetic gardens like Stowe and Stourhead that the visitor lacks a "mental map" or sense of the whole.[11] At no point does the entire garden come into view. "You don't know what is over the hill or around the bend until you see it, and then, were you to go beyond the emblem placed before you and try to project a ground plan, you would probably produce a faulty one."[12] While a glance down the two-mile central axis of Versailles reveals a good deal of

Watercolor by F. Nicholson showing a path at Stourhead. Reproduced by permission of the British Museum.

that garden's structure, no comparable view exposes the layout of Stourhead or Stowe. The monuments of these gardens succeed one another in a "narrative" order as the visitor follows the circular path. Moreover, the monuments are reencountered from different points of view, seen newly juxtaposed, framed by changing foreground scenes. Such experiences naturally engender curiosity and surprise as the viewer tries to puzzle out the garden's scheme—its physical layout and the meaning of its monuments.

Benches were often arrayed along garden paths. They served to further underscore the garden program, for a bench invites reflection. In effect it says about the scene revealed, "Here is something worth contemplating." Thus the individual "pictures" that make up part of a visitor's visual experience of a garden are delineated through topography and planting—devices which physically limit what is in one's field of vision—while benches serve to punctuate and emphasize these visual experiences. They impose a rhythm on the viewer's journey through the garden and mark some vistas as more important than others.

Everything said so far is predicated on the notion of proceeding through the garden in the prescribed manner. There was one correct way of viewing many of the gardens described above. As already noted, visiting gardens became a popular entertainment in the eighteenth century. Sometimes visitors would be conducted around the estate by one of the gardeners. For example John Parnell, in his account of a visit to Painshill in 1763, writes that he rang at the main gate and was met by a gardener who led him on an extensive tour after asking his name and writing it down in a book.[13] Guidebooks were written to facilitate visits to other gardens.

Did viewers resist the gardens' control, strolling in the "wrong" direction or forsaking the paths altogether to ramble through the grounds? Perhaps such rebellion would be unlikely for first-time viewers, who would be anxious to see the garden at its best and tease out its iconographical program, if any. But what might happen with repeated viewings of a given emblematic garden? It is commonly claimed that great works of art reward repeated encounters, that they are so rich, so deep, that they can always yield new insights and new pleasures. Is this true of gardens, especially those of the period we've been examining? In particular, what of the gardens' owners? How would they conduct themselves when alone in the garden, not showing it off to guests? Would they walk in their garden day after day? Would they proceed along the paths in the prescribed manner? Would they attend each time to the garden's iconography, ponder the subtlety of its message?

Horace Walpole addresses such questions in his *History of the Modern Taste in Gardening*. He writes:

> The Doric portico, the Palladian Bridge, the Gothic Ruin, the Chinese Pagoda, that surprise the stranger, soon lose their charms to their surfeited master. The lake that floats the valley is still more lifeless, and its lord seldom enjoys his expence but when he shows it to a visitor. But the ornament whose merit soonest fades, is the hermitage, or scene adapted to contemplation. It is almost comic to set aside a quarter of one's garden to be melancholy in. Prospect, animated prospect, is the theatre that will always be the most frequented.[14]

Walpole suggests that a garden's follies and architectural features are those of which an owner will tire soonest. I agree that in a poetic or emblematic garden those features tied to the iconography—what Paulson referred to as "objects of a high degree of denotation"—will not reward sustained interest, at least not in their limited meaning-bearing role.[15] How often in walking the circuit at Stourhead can one profitably think of Aeneas and his journey to the underworld? I don't think it follows that one would tire of the garden monuments themselves, but one would cease according them merely instrumental value. Repeated encounters with a given temple, ruin, or bridge need not lead to surfeit if one treats the monument visually, as part of an always-engaging, ever-changing picture. We have probably all experienced the charms of getting to know a particular piece of land. As a dedicated runner who regularly jogs the same four-mile route in an urban park, I can truthfully say that I never tire of the experience. I am always aware of the small changes wrought by the time of day, the season, the weather, as well as of the animation provided by insects, birds, dogs, skaters, cyclists. By analogy, it seems perfectly possible to treat the Stourhead circuit more like the circuit of Painshill—a route that is to be traveled in one direction only, yielding interest and variety, climaxes and surprises, but whose architectural features are not intended to tell a story or reveal a moral.

Walpole proposes that animated prospect is the most continually rewarding garden feature. John Dixon Hunt offers a similar argument in his historical overview of eighteenth-century gardens. He suggests that the emblematic garden was supplanted by the expressive garden in the second half of the century as viewers became less willing—and less able—to "read" poetic gardens. Rather than the hard work of puzzling out the fixed meanings of such gardens, viewers desired landscapes that would mirror their feelings and moods. Thus Hunt says of Stowe's Grecian Valley, designed more than ten years after the Elysian Fields, that it

> makes no claim upon our intellect. The subtle varieties of the valley afford a landscape that seems to answer our moods, that allows a unique and individual response by each visitor to its unobtrusive character. It expresses us and our changing moods, or such is the illusion it encourages."[16]

The answer to our question, then, about tiring of a garden seems to be this: we are most likely to tire of a garden's cognitive component, the meaning conveyed by its iconographic program. Most gardens present ever-changing sensory stimuli. Even the most austere of all gardens, a Japanese *kare-sansui* consisting of rocks and raked sand, will yield changing visual and tactile sensations as the sun moves behind clouds, a breeze springs up, and so on. But the aspect of a garden which Hunt, and Whately before him, focus on—the garden's ability to answer our changing feelings and moods—derives not from sensory appreciation or intellectual analysis but from imaginative play. Let us consider this faculty in more detail.

3. IMAGINATION

Many eighteenth-century treatises divide our mental powers into three faculties: sense, imagination, and understanding.[17] While sensation was explained as a kind of receptivity, a capacity to receive stimuli (ideas) directly from the external world, imagination was considered more active. It was explained as a faculty that allows us to summon up ideas of things when no longer in their presence and also to alter and combine ideas to create images of things we have never actually experienced. Although ideas of sense were claimed to be stronger and more vivid than those perceived by the imagination, the latter faculty performs essential cognitive and creative tasks. Hume argued that the imagination helps form our conception of a world of enduring objects independent of our experience,[18] while Kant accorded to the imagination the function of unifying the manifold of sensation. This activity is a prelude to any knowledge whatsoever.[19]

The quintessential work on gardening and imagination is the series of eleven essays, "On the Pleasures of the Imagination," written by Joseph Addison for *The Spectator*, which he edited with Richard Steele from March 1711 to December 1712.[20] Addison contributed a number of series to the periodical, on topics including Italian opera, English tragedy, *Paradise Lost,* and "True and False Wit." The series "On the Pleasures of the Imagination" is of special interest to us because it employs important examples concerning our appreciation of landscape, and because it offers a three-part theoretical framework purporting to classify our pleasurable responses to scenery of all sorts.

Addison opens his series of essays by declaring sight to be "the most perfect and most delightful of all our Senses" (535). Since it is sight that provides imagination with its ideas, Addison defines the pleasures of the imagination as "such as arise from visible Objects, either when we have them actually in our view, or when we call up their Ideas into our Minds by Paintings, Statues, Descriptions, or any like Occasion" (536–37). Pleasures arising from objects actually before our eyes he deems primary pleasures of the imagination; pleasures arising from objects which are remembered or fictitious he deems secondary (537). Addison maintains that such pleasures are more readily available than those of the understanding:

> It is but opening the eye, and the Scene enters. The Colours paint themselves on the Fancy, with very little Attention of Thought or Application of Mind in the Beholder. We are struck, we know not how, with the Symmetry of any thing we see, and immediately assent to the Beauty of an Object, without enquiring into the particular Causes and Occasions of it (538).

Addison often cites landscapes as sources of the primary pleasures of the imagination. He mentions both gardens and natural landscapes, but claims that each type is best appreciated when it most resembles the other. Consider some examples. "A beautiful prospect delights the soul as much as a Demonstration" (538); "Such are the Prospects of an open Champain Country, a vast uncultivated Desart, of huge Heaps of Mountains, high Rocks and Precipices, or a wide Expanse of Waters . . . [that] we are flung into a pleasing Astonishment at such unbounded Views" (540); "Groves, Fields, and Meadows, are at any Season of the Year pleasant to look upon" (542); "There is nothing that more enlivens a Prospect than Rivers, Jetteaus, or Falls of Water, where the Scene is perpetually shifting" (542); "We take delight in a Prospect which is well laid out, and diversified with Fields and Meadows, Woods and Rivers" (550); "Our English gardens are not so entertaining to the Fancy as those in France and Italy, where we see a large Extent of Ground covered over with an agreeable mixture of Garden and Forest" (551); "A Marsh overgrown with Willows, or a Mountain shaded with Oaks, are not only more beautiful, but more beneficial, than when they lie bare and unadorned" (552).

Addison also cites landscapes as sources of secondary pleasures of the imagination, especially landscapes described by great poets. Thus he says that Virgil's *Georgics* "has given us a collection of the most delightful Landskips that can be made out of Fields and Woods, Herds of Cattle, and Swarms of Bees" (565). Addison points out the advantages that a poet has over a landscape gardener: "He may draw into his Description all the Beauties of the Spring and Autumn, and make the whole Year contribute something to render it the more agreeable. His Rose-trees, Wood-bines, and Jessamines, may flower together, and his Beds be covered at the same time with Lillies, Violets, and Amaranths" (569). Finally, while cataloging Addison's references to the secondary pleasures of the imagination yielded by gardens and natural landscapes, I must include one much-quoted passage from an earlier issue of the *Spectator* (no. 37), where he describes the country seat of a reclusive widow named Leonora. Its delights do not arise simply from authorial manipulation of the seasons:

> The Rocks about her are shaped into Artificial Grottoes, covered with Woodbines and Jessamines. The Woods are cut into shady Walks, twisted into Bowers, and filled with Cages of Turtles. The Springs are made to run among Pebbles, and by that means taught to murmur very agreeably. They are likewise collected into a beautiful lake, that is inhabited by a Couple of Swans, and empties it self by a little Rivulet which runs through a green Meadow.[21]

What are the sources of pleasure in these landscapes, natural and artificial, real and fictional, that Addison has described? In the first *Spectator* essay, he points out several salutary aspects of landscape vistas, connections with appropriation, freedom, and health. Regarding the first of these, Addison remarks that a man of Polite Imagination "often feels a greater Satisfaction in the Prospect of Fields and Meadows, than another does in the Possession. It gives him, indeed, a kind of Property in every thing he sees" (538).[22] The imagined appropriation that Addison calls to our attention here derives in part from our ability to survey vast stretches of land. In fact the ambiguity in the word *survey*, which means both to scan a landscape visually and to measure and map it with instruments, preparatory to sale or development, underscores Addison's point. As we survey—scan—a scene, we take in its details. They come into our visual range and, metaphorically, into our possession. Recall that James Turner and Carol Fabricant added a sexual dimension to this theme: in circumstances where the glance penetrates (say, a grove, copse, or thicket) and thereby possesses a scene, the situation structurally resembles some versions of heterosexual intercourse.

In the examples just discussed, where we view and metaphorically possess a panoramic scene, this effect stems in part from actions we imagine ourselves performing. Seeing a path entering the woods, we imagine ourselves following it; seeing a high wall, we imagine ourselves peering over it; seeing a distant temple or folly, we imagine ourselves exploring it; seeing a stream or lake, we imagine ourselves crossing it; seeing a steep hill, we imagine ourselves climbing it and enjoying the new view from the top. These effects aren't confined to actual landscapes. Similar imaginings enliven our interactions with landscape paintings. Arnold Berleant stresses the role of such imagined actions in his book *Art and Engagement*.[23]

A crucial difference between real landscapes and represented ones is that, with the former, we can interact both in imagination *and* in reality. That is, we can imagine certain actions—walking, climbing, wading, entering, peering, glimpsing—but we can often go ahead and carry out those actions as well. Nevertheless, imagination remains a centrally important means for exploring and enjoying natural landscapes. In some cases imagination is a natural prelude to action, for instance, when we deliberate and then choose to walk along a particular path. In other cases, we are for practical reasons restricted to imagination alone. Thus, while viewing an extensive prospect of the sort praised by Addison, I can imagine ascending a craggy peak or following a road to the horizon when either task is clearly beyond my physical abilities. In sum, a central feature of our enjoyment of gardens, and of other natural landscapes as well, is imagining ourselves performing some sort of action in that landscape, or in response to it, coupled with the possibility of actually going on and doing one or all of these things. Let me call this feature of gardens *invitation*.

All gardens invite us to explore them perceptually and through movement. We take up these invitations by exercising our imagination, our senses, and our bodies. While perhaps the quintessential example of an "invitational" landscape feature is a path receding into the distance, even small confined gardens without paths or prospects invite us to explore them in myriad ways. A walled Islamic garden with a paved surface and central fountain still invites us to imagine performing various exploratory tasks: pacing the garden's perimeter, dipping a hand in the fountain, seeing over (or through!) the wall.

I arrived at my claims about invitation by beginning with Addison's discussion of prospect and (imagined) appropriation. Addison notes two other benefits that flow from our experience of landscape and of gardens: freedom and health. Regarding the first of these, he declares:

> A spacious Horison is an Image of Liberty, where the Eye has Room to range abroad, to expatiate at large on the Immensity of its Views, and to lose it self amidst the Variety of Objects that offer themselves to its Observation. Such wide and undetermined Prospects are as pleasing to the Fancy, as the Speculations of Eternity or Infinitude are to the Understanding (541).

The claim about freedom derives from the points I have been making about imagination. Just as an extensive prospect allows us to see and therefore to imaginatively possess a large piece of land, so too the extensive exercise of our imaginative faculties in response to a landscape scene allows us to experience a species of freedom. We are free to perform any variety of imagined sensing or moving within the landscape we are examining. In fact there are no limits to what we can imagine, short of the law of noncontradiction. Descartes in his fourth *Meditation* claimed that our imagination, unlike our understanding, is godlike and unbounded. There is nothing we cannot attempt in our imagination. In viewing a garden, even one we don't own and cannot physically explore, we are still free to engage in all manner of imaginative interactions. Visiting a garden by Capability Brown, I can imagine crossing the central lake even though I can't swim that far and no rowboat is in sight. I can even imagine performing actions that violate the laws of nature. For example, I can imagine flapping my arms and lazily flying across Brown's lake. It is because there are no limits on our ability to exercise the imagination, short of the impossibility of imagining logical contradictions like a round square, that imagination provides the utmost in freedom.

A further consequence of viewing a landscape or garden, Addison remarks, is its benefit to our health. This may not seem so clearly connected to our imagination as to, say, our body and its component systems. In a garden we breath fresh air, exercise our limbs, soak in vitamin D from the sun, and so on. But Addison insists that we benefit emotionally as well.

> The Pleasures of the Fancy are more conducive to Health, than those of the Understanding, which are worked out by Dint of Thinking, and attended with too violent a Labour of the Brain. Delightful Scenes, whether in Nature, Painting, or Poetry, have a kindly Influence on the Body, as well as the Mind, and not only serve to clear and brighten the Imagination, but are able to disperse Grief and Melancholly, and to set the Animal Spirits in pleasing and agreeable Motions (539).

Recent work by the psychologists Stephen and Rachel Kaplan supports Addison's claims. Their research shows that both gardens and wilderness settings provide "restorative experience." Such settings, the Kaplans argue, permit escape or withdrawal, fascinate us and hold our attention, and encourage exploration and understanding. Moreover, the actions and responses they demand of us are compatible with our purposes and inclinations.[24] For these reasons, the Kaplans maintain, gardens restore our ability to direct our attention, an ability which is taxed and weakened by the demands of modern life.[25] Other researchers have shown that merely viewing a landscape scene through a window provides measurable psychological benefits. Typical studies here compare the days of recuperation required by surgery patients who did, versus those who did not, have a view of greenery through their hospital window. Such studies suggest that even imagined or vicarious interactions with the landscape can provide both physical and psychological benefits.[26]

I have been following up on Addison's suggestion that gardens can buoy us emotionally and improve our health. A contemporary geographer, Jay Appleton, makes an even stronger claim. He argues that our landscape preferences are biologically based, linked to considerations of safety and survival. In his book *The Experience of Landscape*, Appleton claims that we evaluate all landscapes in terms of prospect, refuge, and hazard.[27] His view is known as prospect-refuge theory.

Two assumptions underlie Appleton's view, first, that "men and women . . . perceive their surroundings in much the same way as other animals perceive their habitat," and second, that when our habitat is construed as a "theater for survival," the kinds of information needed most immediately are "those that relate to self-preservation from sudden, unexpected danger."[28] Appleton suggests that we maximize our chances for survival by availing ourselves of two sorts of environmental opportunities—sight and concealment. That is, we want unimpeded views of others while we remain hidden from them. Thus the two variables of his theory: prospect provides a vantage point, while refuge provides concealment.

There are certainly times when safety and survival shape our assessments of landscape. Consider soldiers fighting on inhospitable terrain, golfers threatened by a sudden summer thunderstorm, or lost hikers seeking shelter for the night. But can it be that such considerations affect our interactions with the surrounding landscape in situations where we aren't threatened or in danger? Suppose we are strolling through one of the English gardens mentioned above. Do we make conscious calculations about sight and concealment as we investigate Painshill, West Wycombe, or Stourhead? Granted, we might climb a hill or promontory eagerly anticipating the view that will unfold; we might seek the privacy of a wooded glade or deserted temple. But such choices are pragmatic rather than self-preserving. They do not bear on our survival.[29] We might also prefer sections of the garden that afford neither of the variables Appleton champions. For example, I find the path that skirts the long finger of Stourhead's central lake, beyond the Temple of Flora, particularly delightful. Its sandy curves are soft underfoot, and it leads through varied plantations of striking, mature trees. Yet this portion of the Stourhead circuit lacks panoramic vistas and offers little seclusion. Finally, in strolling through any of these gardens, we are likely to be occupied with various concerns besides viewpoint and privacy, prospect and refuge. We might muse about each garden's history, its owner, its iconography, its follies, its plants, and so on, not to mention countless matters not connected with the garden at all (a lover's face, plans for dinner, traffic on the motorway, tasks left undone). In sum, either the twin concepts on which Appleton builds his theory do not concern us greatly as we examine and explore a garden, or they come into play instinctually, subconsciously.

It may well be that Appleton would happily concede this claim. But I don't think his theory is strengthened if we posit instincts for prospect and refuge. Recall the controversy that greeted E. O. Wilson's book *Sociobiology* (1975), which attempted to derive conclusions about human nature from observations of animal behavior.[30] While survival remains a preeminent concern for animals and insects in any type of landscape, it is rarely relevant to humans exeriencing a pleasure garden. Rather than explain our experience and appreciation of landscape in evolutionary terms—an instinct for survival, manifested by concern with prospect and refuge—it seems wiser to seek correlates of Appleton's variables that will apply to our situation as cultural beings.

I have already introduced the term "invitation" to signal the way in which gardens and other landscapes engage us in imaginative and actual explorations. Applied to the view from a high prospect, invitation encompasses curiosity, knowledge, appropriation, and control as well as the apprehension of danger. I believe this aspect of our experience of gardens is complemented by another aspect which I shall call "enclosure." Enclosure too has a significance beyond Appleton's notions of concealment and survival; it indicates a basic sensory and kinesthetic notion of surroundedness, of being surrounded. It can also signify comfort, security, passivity, rest, privacy, intimacy, sensory focus, and concentrated attention. These properties and attributes can be valued for themselves as well as for their instrumental worth.

Michael Van Valkenburgh, a Cambridge landscape architect and head of Harvard's Graduate School of Design, was quoted in a recent *Home Design* supplement to the *New York Times Magazine* regarding the concept of immersion. His account of immersion is quite similar to my notion of enclosure. According to the article, Van Valkenburgh declared himself

> interested in what he calls "immersion," in being surrounded by landscape and having the experience of being changed by it. "And how you can qualify the immersion, whether through fragrance or foliage," he adds, "so that it becomes a visceral thing."[31]

The example of being immersed in a fragrance—say, of honeysuckle, hyacinth, or lily of the valley—reminds us that immersion and enclosure can affect all of the sense modalities. Any sensation so strong, striking, or persistent as to block out or distract us from other sensations is one in which we are, at least temporarily, immersed. Chocolate mousse so rich and exquisite that I savor it and ignore everything else is a form of immersion (though not, I grant you, one likely to be supplied by a garden!). It is more likely that gardens will immerse us by appealing to our senses of touch, sight, sound, and smell.

A contemporary example of a garden which emphasizes enclosure is Sissinghurst in Kent, designed by Vita Sackville-West and Harold Nicholson beginning in 1930. Many commentators speak of this garden as divided into a series of rooms. Rectilinear hedges of box and yew surround and subdivide the garden's six acres. Within this small compass, a number of different areas are defined: the Rose Garden, the White Garden, the Cottage Garden, the Herb Garden, the Purple Border, the Lime Walk, the Moat Walk, the Tower Lawn, and the Orchard. Within each garden area, a teeming array of varied plants catches our attention and demands close scrutiny; a strong rhythm of interest and expectation is set up by a pattern of paths, vistas, arches, peepholes, and so on, linking each area. "Vista" here means not the long allées of Versailles, but a compressed view along a path terminating with an urn or sculpture, or a tantalizing glimpse into an adjacent garden section. Views into the surrounding countryside are cut off by hedges and walls, but knowledge of the prospect from Sissinghurst's central tower and the 360-degree panorama it reveals (a stunning bird's-eye view of the gardens themselves which makes their compact structure clear, with fields, hedgerows, and rolling hills trailing off to the horizon in all

Sissinghurst, an avenue of pleached limes. Photograph by Edwin Smith.

directions) heightens visitors' curiosity. Harold Nicholson described the garden as "a combination of expectation and surprise," and "a succession of intimacies."[32] Both phrases indicate the central role played by enclosure in this delightful space.

Overall, enclosure, like invitation, appeals to our imagination as well as to our senses.[33] Enclosure brings about a focusing of attention. It redirects us to microcosmic features of our surroundings and encourages us to reflect on our sensory and bodily engagement with them. This working out includes imaginative extrapolations of features of our pre-

At Sissinghurst, glimpses from one section of the garden into another tease and entice viewers. Photograph by Edwin Smith.

sent experience. It triggers trains of thought in which we sample more deeply qualities and aspects of the present scene. Thus, just as invitation prompts us to imagine possible ways of engaging and (physically) exploring the vistas that spread out before us, enclosure prompts us to imagine heightening and intensifying the experiences framed by the boundaries that enclose and surround us.[34] Garden grottos exemplify this dynamic. Dank, dark, and enveloping, they heighten our perception by the very fact of blunting our vision. The grotto at Stourhead triggers both the responses I am trying to characterize, combining as it does sculptures (of a nymph and river god) and a fountain in a darkened space with a "window" offering a vista out across the lake to the Temple of Apollo situated high on the hill.

The two garden features I have been discussing, invitation and enclosure, are complementary (see color plate 3). Gardens of quite opposite sorts may feature one or the other; the two might also coexist in different parts of a given garden, or even in a single or adjacent garden locales. Consider two distinctive features of eighteenth-century gardens, grottoes and ha-has. As I claimed above, grottoes tend to intensify tactile, auditory, and olfactory sensations by dimming our sense of sight. Thus they are devices that enhance enclosure or immersion. By contrast, ha-has permit uninterrupted vistas by visually connecting foreground, middle distance, and background. They thus enhance the invitational aspects of a garden.

One might object that I have simply taken Appleton's theory and replaced his theoretical terms, "prospect" and "refuge," with two near synonyms, "invitation" and "enclosure." But I arrived at the terms "invitation" and "enclosure" by pondering the *experience* of being in gardens of various types, not by assessing Appleton's theory. It is an advantage of my terms that they can and do enter into our conscious assessments of our surroundings. I think they flag qualities that are, for modern-day human beings, more widely applicable than Appleton's terms, and also of more interest and importance.

There is one further difficulty with Appleton's theory. Once we grant that the assessments he posits may not be entirely conscious on our part, then how are we to distinguish these from other calculations and influences percolating at the subconscious level? I have in mind here more personal memories and associations that help determine our landscape preferences. I may like a certain landscape—say, a woodland pond—because it reminds me of landscapes of my youth and happy times spent there. I may dislike certain landscapes for equally personal or idiosyncratic reasons, not all of which are accessible to memory. In avowing a preference among landscape scenes, I don't think I can determine just which factors have influenced me the most. That is, I can't be sure whether I am being influenced by phylogenetic factors like the instincts Appleton acknowledges, by quirks of personal history unfolding over "one life,"[35] or by my perceptual and imaginative engagement with the scene at hand and the pleasures that engagement provides. (Clearly with this last alternative I am trying to flag my own theoretical constructs, invitation and enclosure.) The theory I endorse, then, is one that recognizes all these levels and leaves open the possibility that they might operate simultaneously. My account of landscape preference allows multiple causation, and this seems preferable to a theory like Appleton's, which appeals only to inaccessible primal instincts.

So far I haven't yet discussed the most extraordinary, or perhaps I should say most prescient, aspect of Addison's *Spectator* essays. I have in mind his three-part classification of natural scenes into those that please through greatness, those that please through novelty, and those that please through beauty. Writing in 1711, Addison here anticipates by some forty-five years Edmund Burke's divison of aesthetic response into the beautiful and the sublime, while the heyday of the category of the picturesque, which parallels Addison's notion of novelty, was to wait another eighty-three years.[36]

Although Addison introduces the categories greatness, novelty, and beauty in his second essay on the pleasures of the imagination, he doesn't make clear their relation to that faculty. Burke and Price would later define their aesthetic categories, the sublime, the beautiful, and the picturesque, in terms of distinctive qualities that arouse them and distinctive passions that accompany them. Addison does tie each category to an emotion. For example, speaking of greatness he says that "Our Imagination loves to be filled with an object, or to graspe at any thing that is too big for its Capacity. We are flung into a pleasing Astonishment at such unbounded Views, and feel a delightful Stillness and Amazement in the Soul at the Apprehension of them." (540) In his third essay, Addison goes on to speculate that this association was instilled in us by God: by making us "naturally delight" in the apprehension of things "Great or Unlimited," he guarantees that part of our happiness will arise from contemplation of his being.

Why are the pleasures just described pleasures of the imagination rather than of sense or of understanding? To appreciate something that is great and unbounded—Addison's examples include "the Prospects of an open Champain Country, a vast uncultivated Desart, of huge Heaps of Mountains, high rocks and Precipices, or a wide Expanse of Waters" (540)—we must have working organs of sense. (This is why, drawing on Descartes, I would insist on what I call the bodily basis of imagination.) In addition, to classify such perceptions, to realize that they fall within the category "great and unbounded," we must use our intellect. What role then is played by the imagination? Addison, so far as I can determine, does not speculate about the mechanisms involved in this procedure. It may well be that certain comparisons are rehearsed. Perhaps we classify a particular panorama as great and unbounded by summoning up images of other sites with which we are familiar and realizing that they are smaller in scale. Although "great" as Addison uses it is a relative term (nothing is great simpliciter, but only when measured against some standard or other), I doubt that deliberate comparisons must be made each and every time we acknowledge the greatness of a scene. Nevertheless, to deem a scene great, or beautiful, or novel, we must not only perceive it and apply some label; we must also be struck by it, register certain aspects, imaginatively enter and savor that scene. In the end, however, the explanations present-day psychologists and linguists would offer for our use of the terms "great," "beautiful," and "novel" is of less import than the fact that these terms or close synonyms figure in accounts of landscape scenery offered by thinkers spanning the eighteenth century.

4. UNDERSTANDING

We use our intellect or understanding in various ways as we experience a garden. Some of them have been discussed extensively already. In working out the iconographic program of a garden like Stowe or Stourhead, we are clearly solving an intellectual puzzle. The faculty that eighteenth-century philosophers called the understanding is crucially involved. Granted, the distinction between imagination and intellect is not a clear one. We might stipulate that (1) the imagination is involved whenever we create, entertain or manipulate mental images, but that (2) when we do this in the service of further ends—problem solving, for instance, or recollection—the intellect is involved. Recall the discussion in chapter 3 of alternative interpretations of Stourhead. In identifying, individuating, and choosing among such interpretations, we are formulating claims, weighing evidence—in short, using the understanding. It is also the case that we use our understanding or intellect whenever we work out the associations generated by a given monument, inscription, or scene. This aspect of gardens was treated in the chapter on the picturesque, since a number of theorists have defined the picturesque as a largely associative operation. And finally, Hume, in his "Essay on the Standard of Taste" listed good sense as one of the five characteristics of a good critic. Good sense is needed for certain sorts of intellectual assessments of works of art. The examples Hume mentions are working out the part-whole relations within the work, and identifying the artist's goals and determining whether they have been met. Clearly these mental tasks come into play in our interactions with gardens.

Besides using our intellect to work out the meaning of a given garden or garden feature, or to critically assess a particular garden, we also use this faculty when we think of gardens in general, that is, whenever we think philosophically about the nature and powers of gardens. I hope such thoughts have been triggered by the entirety of this book. In the closing section of this chapter, I would like to explore some possibilities concerning the ontological status of gardens. I am not here exploring or summarizing the work of eighteenth-century thinkers as I did in the previous section. Rather, I would like to work out the status of gardens as it would be acknowledged by present-day logicians and aestheticians.

Borrowing from some work by Mara Miller, I propose to develop the notion that gardens are virtual worlds. I shall combine this with material about twofoldness adapted from Richard Wollheim to end up with my final claim: that gardens are at once parts of the real world—actual pieces of land—and also virtual worlds—coherent sets of possible sensory stimuli.

It was Susanne Langer, in her book *Feeling and Form* (1953), who first introduced the notion of virtual objects and virtual worlds into aesthetic analysis.[37] Langer characterizes art by contrasting it with ordinary physical reality. She states that every work of art tends to appear "dissociated from its mundane environment. The most immediate impression it creates is one of 'otherness' from reality" (45). This account of art is reminiscent of Edward Bullough's earlier theory of psychical distance, which insisted that we put art "out of gear" with our practical interests and concerns; Langer's remarks also recall the Kantian tradition which posits disinterestedness as a mark of the aesthetic. Langer goes on to describe this situation in terms of virtual reality:

> An image is, indeed, a purely virtual "object." Its importance lies in the fact that we do not use it to guide us to something tangible and practical, but treat it as a complete entity with only visual attributes and relations. It has no others.

Virtual objects exist in the natural world. Langer claims that the most striking examples are visual: she mentions rainbows and mirages (48); later she adds mirror images to the set of examples. Once again Langer distinguishes virtual reality from the everyday physical world:

> The space in which we live and act is not what is treated in art at all. The harmoniously organized space in a picture is not experiential space, known by sight and touch, by free motion and restraint, far and near sounds, voices lost or re-echoed. It is an entirely visual affair; for touch and hearing and muscular action it does not exist. . . . Like the space "behind" the surface of a mirror, it is what the physicists call "virtual space"—an intangible image (72).

In this last passage, Langer indicates the origin of the notions of virtual objects and virtual space: the science of physics. Let us briefly consider some of the ways the term "virtual" is used in this discipline, in order to see how this usage might transfer to the aesthetic realm. Physicists acknowledge virtual objects, virtual images, virtual particles, virtual processes, virtual cathodes, and virtual work. The simplest of these concepts to grasp is that of virtual image. Consider the experience of standing in front of a full-length mirror. Under normal conditions, we see a reflection of ourselves. A person appears to be located as far behind the mirror as we are in front of it. Moreover, the person resembles us except that everything is reversed left to right.

Our mirror double does not really exist. That is, what we see is not a real person behind the mirror but the utterly persuasive appearance of one, an illusion created when light is reflected by the mirror and sent back to our eyes. This theme of irreality recurs with all the other uses of "virtual" in the physics vocabulary. For example, a virtual process in quantum mechanics is one "which contributes in a stage of a theoretical model but is not, by itself, physically realizable,"[38] while a virtual cathode "acts as if it were a source of electrons," although in fact it is not.[39] Virtual processes and virtual particles are so called because they violate the law of conservation of mass and energy,[40] and thus they too cannot really exist.[41]

These examples should suffice to convey the flavor of the term "virtual" as it has been used in physics. Virtual processes, entities, etc., are not actual, but their existence is postulated to explain certain effects. They differ from theoretical terms as these are explicated by at least some philosophers of science.[42] Langer introduced the term "virtual" into her aesthetic vocabulary to flag a (visual) experience not caused in the standard way. Like an illusion, a virtual object or scene is appearance divorced from reality. But this description sounds too paradoxical. Langer speaks of certain works of art as presenting to us a "sheer visual form instead of a locally and practically related object" (47). She adds that the artist's image "exists only for perception, abstracted from the physical and causal order" (47). These remarks suggest that we aren't deceived by the virtual objects presented by, or contained in, works of art, because our experience of art is detached from all practical connections and concerns. But I don't think this is correct. We don't just passively register works of art, taking in their sensory surface. (Recall the discussion of disinterestedness in chapter 1.) Rather, we interact with them along the various dimensions Langer mentions—physical, causal, practical. Moreover, our experience of the work can be probed, explored, expanded, using all our mental faculties—sensation, imagination, and intellect or reason.

It might be better to put things this way: with virtual objects, we have many of the sensory experiences we would have if there were a real object present; it is *as if* there were an object there. But we are not deceived as we are in the case of illusion. A crucial difference, then, between aesthetic and quotidian experience, is the fact that with the former we know that we are in the presence of a work of art, say, a representation. For example, studying a photograph of the Lime Walk at Sissinghurst, I know that it is a photograph, that it is *of* the Lime Walk, that it bears a certain *causal relationship* to the Lime Walk, and so on. A painting of a fictitious garden raises more complex ontological problems. Once again I know that it is a painting, that it represents a garden, but since there is no such garden in the world, it isn't strictly correct to say that it is a painting *of* a garden. Nelson Goodman would flag these ontological distinctions by claiming that the painting is a garden-painting as opposed to a painting of a garden. The grammatical stipulation is meant to indicate cases of fictional reference—reference to what does not exist. Returning to our painting, some commentators would say that the painting is not of anything in this world but that it nonetheless depicts (and thereby creates) a fictional world—the world of the work. With a painting, the world of the work is the world represented. How can this notion be extended to gardens, especially nonrepresentational gardens?[43] Contributions from three philosophers might prove helpful here: Richard Wollheim's notion of twofoldness, Arthur Danto's account of the material counterpart of a work of art, and Nicholas Wolterstorff's definition of the world of a work.

Wollheim uses the term "twofoldness" to describe our experience of pictorial representation. He claims that in viewing a representational painting we are *simultaneously* aware of both the painted surface and the image seen in that surface. He takes this to be the crucial phenomenological trait of painting.[44]

It might seem that twofoldness cannot apply to gardens, at least not to those gardens which lack representational aspirations or programs. In such cases there is one and only one thing to view—the garden itself, its contours, plants, follies, fountains, etc. Let me divide my answer to this question into two cases. Consider first those gardens that are representational. (Recall that in chapter 4 I argued that gardens *can* represent, that is, they can function like realistic paintings and portray other locales, either real or make-believe. While gardens in the Western tradition do so rarely, in China it was quite common for gardens to represent in this manner.) Let us assume, for the sake of discussion, that Henry Hoare's garden at Stourhead does indeed retell the story of the *Aeneid* and that its central lake represents Lake Avernus, as Paulson and Woodbridge claim. With this garden, so interpreted, the notion of twofoldness can apply. We have two entities—(1) the physical garden, located in Wiltshire, dating back to the eighteenth century, featuring a central lake, many temples, several bridges, hundreds of trees, etc., and (2) the depicted realm—ancient Italy, Lake Avernus, the entrance to the underworld, etc.—*represented by* the physical constituents of the garden. I see no reason to question our ability to experience both these aspects simultaneously. We see the central lake, know that it is a feature of the Wiltshire landscape created in Henry Hoare's time, and we also know that in the world of the garden iconography, it is Lake Avernus.

How would this account apply to a nonrepresentational garden, one without any sort of iconographical program? Consider Charles Hamilton's garden Painshill, discussed in chapter 4. Created in the same era as Stourhead, Painshill resembles that garden in many respects (hilly circuit laid around a central lake, varied temples, calculated vistas). Yet Painshill doesn't narrate any particular story or moral; it functions more like a painting than a poem. Nevertheless, I think a similar ontological distinction applies in this case. We still can distinguish (1) the physical garden, a particular chunk of, in this case, Surrey, from (2) the world of the garden, a virtual world as Langer used that term, grounded in the physical garden, in the sense that the experiences which constitute the virtual garden are sensory experiences of (and triggered by) its physical base.

I have introduced Richard Wollheim's terminology because I believe we are simultaneously aware of the physical garden and the virtual garden. However, the claim I am trying to establish could also be couched in terms drawn from Arthur Danto. In his book *The Transfiguration of the Commonplace,*[45] Danto distinguishes between a work of art and its material counterpart. This distinction emerges from what I have called his doppelganger examples: pairs of indistinguishable objects, only one of which is a work of art, or alternatively, sets of indistinguishable objects each of which is a different work of art. We discussed some of these examples in chapter 1—red squares, blue neckties, etc.—and went on to imagine some garden versions as well. Danto believes such examples show that an artwork cannot be identified with its material base or counterpart (101), most importantly because the work will have aesthetic properties which its counterpart lacks. Works of art, on Danto's view, make statements. They require interpretation and this "consists in determining the relationship between a work of art and its material counterpart" (113). Interpretation thus sets works of art apart from mere real things. It locates the aesthetic properties unique to those works, and it explains what the works are about and what they say about their subjects.

Consider Danto's terminology applied to gardens. What I have called the physical garden—the hills and valleys, flowers and trees, lakes and streams, follies and fountains—would be what Danto labels the material counterpart. Presumably, all of these features could be present without constituting a work of art. The garden-as-art is a certain arrangement of terrain, water, flora, sculpture, and architecture which possesses aesthetic and expressive qualities and which makes a statement and requires interpretation. Two questions arise in extending Danto's view to gardens. First, could the material counterpart, the mere piece of land, exist without the correlative work of art? And second, what account are we to give of *non*representational gardens, those without an iconographical program? Consider again some Dantoesque pairs: an English landscape garden by Capability Brown and a similarly configured stretch of farmland, a painterly garden like Painshill and an identical demesne with some functional outbuildings and some Roman ruins. In the latter case—where the ensemble is not a work of art, yet might be indistinguishable from something that is—it is hard to imagine how some of the architectural features could have been put in place without at least some aspirations toward art—especially the Gothic pavilion and Turkish tent! What would it be for these garden structures to be considered merely utilitarian? Could they be viewed as decorative yet not as works of art? Similarly with Henry Hoare's Stourhead, we can readily define its material counterpart by abstracting and isolating the physical entities—trees, paths, bridges, temples. But again I cannot conceive a story which would explain how that material counterpart alone could have been constructed and not have been a work of art. Wouldn't this require that the various garden features be arrayed without any consideration given to their classical origins, their Claudean echoes, or to any visual interest whatsoever?

My inability to imagine "mute" material counterparts to Painshill and Stourhead might simply show that I am culturebound, of limited imagination. Let us consider a garden entirely lacking in artificial decorative features. The hardest case for the claim I am trying to defend would be a naturalistic English landscape garden. What here would constitute the "virtual garden," to borrow from Langer? Or, to rephrase the question in Danto's terms, what statement can be derived by interpreting the material counterpart of this garden? What does the garden *say?*

I don't see why this question, posed of a landscape garden, should be any more problematic than a similar question posed of a (naturalistic) landscape painting. If nothing else, any such painting says, "Here's how the world looks to me"; it reveals the artist's point of view on a slice of reality. A landscape painter might be making a myriad of further statements in painting a particular scene—statements about artistic technique, artistic tradition, economic justice, or Christian morality. But the important point is that none of these further, more reflective, levels of meaning is necessary. A landscape painting which aspires simply to convey the look of a certain piece of land, as filtered through a given artist's vision, technique, and style, is thereby a work of art. Yet an even more emphatic statement can be made by a garden. Whereas a realistic painting might, at the very minimum, say to its viewers, "This is how I see the world," a naturalistic garden can say to its audience, "I made this world." How that made world compares to the natural world, the degree to which the garden designer did or did not alter the site, contributes importantly to the further content of the work's statement, to the interpretation it demands of viewers.

Our goal, then, is to understand the garden as virtual world, as the world of a work of art. What, for example, are the boundaries of that world? Which of our experiences, as we wander through the physical garden, are experiences of—inform us about—the virtual garden? To help answer these questions, I shall borrow from the work of Nicholas Wolterstorff. In his book *Works and Worlds of Art*,[46] Wolterstorff proposes a highly technical account of the world of a work of art. His analysis is based on consideration of two narrative art forms, literature and drama. He says, "What the structuralists call the *story* of a narrative is one species of what I call the *world* of a work. The genus as a whole includes as well the worlds of such nonnarrative works as individual representational paintings, dramatic performances, and passages of prose and verse consisting wholly of state descriptions and including no indication of happenings" (108).

As Wolterstorff construes things, worlds are projected by artistic acts. The act of fictionally projecting a world is neither true nor false, though subsequent descriptions of the worlds thus created can be evaluated in this manner (109).

In part Wolterstorff's presentation is made difficult by its reliance on complex formalisms; also by its ready appeal to two metaphysically murky entities, propositions and states of affairs. Wolterstorff in fact identifies these, declaring "I hold that propositions and states of affairs are just the very same entities—that the proposition that Carter is from Georgia is identical with the state of affairs of *Carter being from Georgia*" (127). One final complication of Wolterstorff's theory is his distinction between a proposition or state of affairs (1) existing and (2) occurring. The former requires only that it be possible that someone believes the proposition in question (127) (an example here would be "Wolterstorff drinking green tea"), while the latter applies to states of affairs that now obtain ("Gore being Vice President") or have obtained ("Napoleon invading Russia"). Wolterstorff also cites examples of states of affairs which do not at any time occur ("Napoleon invading Ethiopia") or could not at any time occur ("me being married to someone who lacks a spouse") (127). I would like to try to make use of some of Wolterstorff's positive proposals without getting mired in the metaphysical difficulties they entail.

Let us then consider Wolterstorff's method for determining the world of a given work of art and see whether it can be extended to the art of gardens. Since Wolterstorff concentrates initially on literary works, the first propositions he includes in a work's world are those asserted in the text. Wolterstorff calls these the propositions or states of affair *indicated* by the author. This set includes both propositions stated directly and propositions merely suggested or implied. Wolterstorff gives the label *elucidation* to the activity of discovering what the author has so indicated.

The process of filling in is more complicated, however. Some propositions, though not explicitly endorsed, are nevertheless entailed or required by those that are. Wolterstorff defines *extrapolation* as "the activity of determining what is included in the projected world beyond what the author indicated" (116), and he suggests that interpretation consists in elucidation plus extrapolation.

Various paradoxes arise even when Wolterstorff's scheme is applied to the art of literature. For example, since necessary truths are entailed by any proposition whatsoever, the world of every work will include all logical and mathematical truths. And, should any author knowingly or unknowingly include a contradiction in the body of his work, then the world of that work will include every other proposition since an impossible proposition entails all propositions (117). Wolterstorff copes with these difficulties by introducing the notion of *strands*—sets of maximally comprehensive compossible conjunctions (118). Rather than follow him any further over this difficult terrain, let us consider some of the difficulties that arise when we try to apply his explanatory base, the pair (proposition, state of affairs), to the art of gardens.

One problem arises immediately. It concerns the relation between words and pictures. As various clichés can attest ("A picture is worth a thousand words" and so on), these two symbol systems have quite different powers. Nelson Goodman and Susanne Langer before him devoted considerable effort to demarcating the respective capacities of depiction and description.[47] Words are obviously more suited to convey complex arguments and detailed narratives, but it is pictures rather than words that more adequately communicate the look of things. Imagine the challenge of trying to convey in words the exact look and feel of whatever room you are in as you read this page. Compare now the task of conveying it through some visual medium—sketch, painting, photograph, whatever. I think this exercise alone shows the futility of seeking an exact verbal equivalent for any visual experience. But—isn't this just what is required if we are to adopt Wolterstorff's program and construe the world of any work of visual art as a set of propositions? Admittedly, Wolterstorff equates propositions and states of affairs. But since we can only identify and individuate states of affairs using the propositions with which they are paired, the problem persists. To delineate the world of a given garden, we must affix verbal descriptions to visual experiences.

One might grumble at this point that the notion of the world of a garden has not panned out, it has turned out to have merely metaphorical value. That is, the objection might continue, a garden is like a world in that it is a demarcated area of space; that's all there is to it. Let us take one last crack at this notion by reflecting on our experience of gardens of several different types—poetic and painterly, expansive and self-contained, formal and natural. A garden like Stourhead proved the easiest to assimilate to this model. Because of its iconographic program, Stourhead can be interpreted as both narrative and representational. The garden tells us about Aeneas and ancient Italy, and in doing so, we might claim, it represents that other realm. I suggested that Wollheim's notion of twofoldness was adequate to explain this case.

What about Painshill? There is no mythical realm to which that garden explicitly refers. This case, I suggested, could be assimilated to that of a realistic landscape painting. As we saw in chapter 4, some landscape paintings are topographical, they depict actual places, while others are ideal, they portray made-up locales. I don't know that the world of a landscape painting by, say, Claude Lorrain can be adequately paraphrased by a set of statements or propositions purporting to name everything depicted. Rather, one might want to begin characterizing the world of the painting through ostension—by simply pointing *to* the painting and claiming that the world of the work contains everything clearly depicted. Many of those items can be specified—trees, lakes, temples, etc.—but some are indeterminate, others ineffable. I believe the best way to characterize the world of such a work is to *begin* with ostension and then *continue* the task with the logical operations Wolterstorff describes, namely, elucidation and extrapolation. If the painting shows trees and a lake, then it follows that there are plants in its world, that photosynthesis takes place in that world, and that that world has not been blighted by nuclear winter.[48]

Imagine a similar strategy applied to Painshill. To indicate the world of the garden (the garden as virtual world) we begin with ostension. We indicate (remember that this was a technical term for Wolterstorff) the physical garden itself—the steep vine-clad banks, the meandering stream, the Alpine forest, the restored temples, and so on. We include in the embrace of this ostension all that is required (entailed) by the items we have delimited. What are the boundaries of the virtual garden—what determines its metaphysical as opposed to its physical domain? Much here depends on style and intent. Horace Walpole praised William Kent and his contemporaries for opening up the closed formal gardens of the seventeenth century and realizing that "all nature was a garden." Kent's work at Rousham was designed to take advantage of a broad view looking out over the river Cherwell and the distant Cotswold hills; Claremont in Devonshire sits in a dramatic wide valley between rising banks of hills. With each of these gardens, the view out is as important as any of the views within. (Recall the discussions of appropriation above and also in chapter 3.) The world of the garden contains these expansive views; part of these gardens' statements has to do with the ways in which the country can be surveyed and commanded (Rousham) or can crowd around to dwarf and humble (Chatsworth).

A quite different sort of effect prevails in gardens without broad vistas, for example, Twickenham or Sissinghurst. Here the world of the garden is not enlarged by the inclusion of calculated vistas looking off beyond its borders; instead it is complicated, drawn in upon itself, and enriched by relationships between and among its parts. These too were knowingly created by the gardens' designers and are meant to be part of a visitor's experience. We have discussed various ways in which gardens control viewers' perceptions, experiences, and thoughts. In such cases, the world of the garden is enlarged to include not only its obvious physical features but also relations among them. Consider the following examples, drawn from accounts of Pope's garden at Twickenham: the narrowing of the cypress alley culminating in the memorial obelisk to Pope's mother; the contrast between the central groomed swath of the bowling green and the strips of wilderness on each side; the coziness of the bench surmounting the largest of the mounts; the energy of the ever-changing rivulet that courses through the grotto; the natural camera-obscura effect by which images of boats on the Thames are projected onto the walls of the grotto's inner chamber. These features of Pope's garden, which would have been apparent to any sensitive visitor,[49] are in effect perceptual and expressive *elucidations,* in Wolterstorff's sense of that term, of the world of the garden. They concern not just the garden's physical contents—what Danto would call its material counterpart—but the experiences they engender in visitors with normal perceptual and intellectual capacities. That is, certain relationships between and among the elements would have been noticed; certain emotional tones would have been felt; certain trains of thought would have been explored.[50]

I have here adapted Wolterstorff's insights so as to consider the world of a garden not a complex state of affairs nor a very large set of propositions but rather a set of possible experiences. Those experiences which the garden designer clearly expected of all "normally equipped" visitors (i.e., visitors with well-functioning organs of sense, unblunted emotions, and an ability to reason), I class among those we elucidate from the garden. What might count as experiences extrapolated from the garden? These would be experiences beyond those indicated by the artist. Wolterstorff himself admits that there is no clear dividing line between elucidation and extrapolation.[51] Perhaps, then, experiences requiring heightened sensitivity or more care or effort than is normally lavished on a landscape or a garden would count among those extrapolated from the garden. Examples here might include all those cases of complex iconography dismissed by Whately as more emblemat-

Rousham, the view out into the surrounding countryside. Photograph by Edwin Smith.

ic than expressive, the sort that Hunt deemed too taxing for late eighteenth-century viewers. (Recall the riverside array of monuments designed for Pope's garden and explained in dense detail by Maynard Mack.)

We could also exploit anachronism to devise experiences extrapolated from a garden. Certainly, insights gleaned from Freudian, Marxist, or feminist theories would not have been intended by designers of eighteenth-century English gardens. Yet such gardens might well convey messages about voyeurism, the alienation of labor, or the oppression of women to modern-day viewers. Such messages would, I suggest, be ascribed to the world of the garden on the basis of extrapolation. Clearly, extrapolation applies to nonprogrammatic gardens as well as to gardens that convey a well-orchestrated iconography. Here is one last example of an extrapolated feature of a nonprogrammatic garden. A group now restoring Painshill to its eighteenth-century state has decided to include only species of plants that would have been available to its owner Charles Hamilton as he designed the garden. All varieties added to the landscape since his time will be removed. Thus there are certain botanical facts about the physical garden in Hamilton's time that were not explicitly indicated by him but that collectively confer the aesthetic quality "authenticity" on the twentieth-century reconstruction of that garden and on its virtual counterpart.

My claim, then, is that gardens are simultaneously physical and virtual worlds and are experienced as such by us. Borrowing from Nicholas Wolterstorff's notion of the world of a work of art, I have offered an account of the world of a garden, at least of one that aspires to be a work of art. Of course each actual viewer brings cultural baggage (values, clichés, and concepts) and personal quirks (memories, preferences, and associations) which would shape his or her experience of any given garden. While we might choose to relativize the world of a garden to the first of these variables, the time and culture in which it is viewed,[52] I would resist more radically relativizing the notion. The world of the garden is an objective, nonphysical realm. Though we may each have different thoughts and feelings as we stroll through a given garden, we enter a shared virtual garden, one composed of the maximally compossible set of experiences elucidated and extrapolated from that physical realm.[53]

One might object that my account makes the experience of gardens no different from the experience of traditional architecture. Each is a space or domain that we enter; each is physical and complex; each sustains a rich set of perceptual, expressive, and semantic relations. Moreover, certain writers characterize the experience of architecture in ways that resemble my claims about gardens. For example, Nelson Goodman, in "How Buildings Mean" claims that

A painting can be presented all at once—though our perception of it involves synthesizing the results of scanning—but a building has to be put together from a heterogeneous assortment of visual and kinesthetic experiences: from views at different distances and angles, from walks through the interior, from climbing stairs and straining necks, from photographs, miniature models, sketches, plans, and from actual use.[54]

Roger Scruton, in a more ambitious work, *The Aesthetics of Architecture,* argues that architecture is properly apprehended through imaginative (as opposed to literal) perception. The crucial characteristics of imaginative perception, for Scruton, are freedom and choice; it "reflects a special mode of attention and a special intellectual aim." [55] And, Scruton claims, "In all architectural experience the active participation of the observer is required for its completion. Each determinacy that is offered provides the basis for a further choice, and the idea of a building that can be experienced in its entirety in only one way is an absurdity" (94). He continues: "Ordinary perceptual experience . . . is compelled by its object. We are passive in respect of such experience as we are passive in respect of our beliefs. But we are not passive in respect of the experience of architecture, which arises only as the result of a certain species of attention" (95). Scruton also notes that we apprehend architecture through all of our senses, not just through the sense of sight, and that we see architecture in terms of nonvisual concepts such as warmth, mass, solidity, and distance (what other philosophers have called expressive or aesthetic predicates.) These too are claims I have made about our experience of gardens.

Despite these points of similarity, it is not correct to say that my account conflates our experience of gardens and our experience of architecture. It is true that buildings, both classical and contemporary, appeal to the same faculties—sense, imagination, and understanding—that I have been discussing. That is, in appreciating a Gothic cathedral or a Palladian villa, a postmodern skyscraper or a Levittown tract house, we notice the structure's visual, tactile, and auditory properties, its relation to its site, the works it alludes to, the statements it makes, the emotions it evokes. All this is true of our approach to gardens as well.

Yet important differences separate our experiences of architecture and of gardens. First, these arts employ quite different materials. As I stressed in chapter 1, there is no essential definition of a garden; a garden needn't have any plant material at all. But most gardens do, and accordingly they make statements about our place in and relation to nature. Buildings do enclose us, but they do not, in addition, as do most gardens, make us think about wilderness, other species, interdependence, the passage of time, the limits of control.[56] Second, the dichotomy inside/outside which seems applicable to most traditional architectural structures (for example, houses) doesn't apply comfortably to gardens. Gardens have boundaries, but they are not often designed to present a facade, to offer a particular appearance to someone outside looking in. Inside and outside also get blurred when we consider the views and lines of sight that are meant to be part of the experience of a given garden and the appropriations these can effect. Finally, to adapt some terminology from Nelson Goodman, gardens, unlike most works of architecture, are both replete and dense throughout.

This is not the place to explain the details of Goodman's theory.[57] Let me just summarize one of his examples to show the use to which I want to put his terms. Discussing representations, Goodman asks us to compare a Hokusai drawing of Mount Fujiyama with an electrocardiogram. Both, we are to suppose, trace the exact same pattern on the page. Yet Goodman maintains that the first is a picture and the second a diagram. The crucial difference is that with the Hokusai many things matter: the nature of the line, its thickness, its color and intensity, the quality of the paper, the absolute size overall. With the electrocardiogram all we care about is which coordinates the jagged line crosses. Goodman's point is that in a picture almost any variation can have aesthetic import.[58] Gardens, I want to claim, function like drawings rather than diagrams. Every square inch of a garden can be planned. (In this sense gardens metaphorically share the density of the real number line, which inspired Goodman's formalism.) Any sensory aspect of a garden can matter, can come to command our attention and be of aesthetic import. This holds true irrespective of the garden's style, whether it is natural or artificial, compact or expansive. While I think of architects as creating space and volume by assembling walls, floors, and roofs, garden designers do not just define spaces but they fill them as well.

GARDENS AND THE DEATH OF ART

I. INTRODUCTION

I have argued in this book that gardening was, at least for a time, a high art, a full sister to painting and poetry. Examining the gardens of eighteenth-century England, I have attempted to document the sophistication of this art form—the complex meanings gardens of the time conveyed, the daunting demands they placed on viewers and interpreters. But what of gardens today? In the sombre postscript to *Nature Perfected,* his lavish survey of garden history, William Howard Adams suggests that gardening as a high art is now moribund:

> The garden as a work of art, an aesthetic composition beyond the pursuit of horticulture, therapy, or extravagance in support of power, has all but disappeared from the modern world. . . . Few gardens of the twentieth century have been widely admired as works of art worthy of serious investigation and analysis. The psychological and metaphysical speculation that gardens once provoked is out of the question.[1]

In this closing chapter, I would like to investigate the death knell Adams sounds for the art of gardening. Our initial questions in chapter 1 about gardens' status as art prompted a prolonged investigation of the nature of gardens *and* the nature of art. The fates of gardens and of art will be similarly linked in this chapter. That is, to determine whether or not Adams's bleak assessment of gardening's present-day status is justified, I shall first set out and critique some general claims about the death of art.

2. THE DEATH OF ART

Many writers have, like Adams, pronounced the death of some particular art—representational painting, classical music, poetry—generally as corollary to a broader thesis about the death of art overall. Perhaps the most persuasive proponent of this view is Arthur Danto. In a recent series of papers Danto has refined a Hegelian view according to which "art is really over with, having become transmuted into philosophy."[2] Danto's pronouncement suggests that art will end in apotheosis rather than decline. Instead of competing with other distractions or entertainments, it will transform itself into philosophy. I want to investigate Danto's claim in what follows, but let me note a few important qualifications to my project. First, my comments will be culture-bound. I shall be talking primarily about the artworld of a particular time and place—the United States at the end of the twentieth century. I am not in a position to comment more globally. But I believe that the conclusions I draw about the death of art in my own culture may illuminate other segments of the artworld as well. And second, in using Hegel's philosophical system I make no claim to be voicing the views of that philosopher; I shall grapple with his system only enough to understand Danto's adaptation of certain Hegelian insights.

The claim that art is dead can be variously interpreted. Does the statement lament the loss of a single work of art? Of a given art in its entirety? Or of all the arts of a given epoch? The first possibility is the most unlikely. Recall George Dickie's institutional theory of art, which defines a work of art as "(1) an artifact, (2) a set of the aspects of which has had conferred upon it the status of candidate for appreciation by some person or persons acting on behalf of a certain social institution (the artworld)."[3] Dickie's theory tells us how ordinary everyday objects (quilts, utensils, scrap metal, urinals) can change their status and become works of art. But we lack a parallel account to explain the *demotion* of artworks into quotidian things.

The label "work of art" is a defeasible one, and certain conditions, if they obtain, prevent an object from retaining that status. A work of art discovered to be a fake or forgery might turn out to be not art at all. For example, an etching might lose its claim to be a work of art if it were a spurious Rembrandt manufactured in 1996 with the aid of a Xerox machine. But note the complexities of this situation. Nothing prevents an artist today from xeroxing Rembrandts and calling that her art.[4] In today's artworld, it seems, anything goes. There are no grounds for ruling out as art such bizarre offerings as bottled excrement and self-scarification. My concern, however, is whether the status "work of art," once attained, can be lost. Can a bona fide art object cease to be art while remaining physically intact?[5]

Nelson Goodman gives the example of a museum commandeered during wartime, its paintings taken from the wall and set up to represent the location of enemy troops.[6] But this strikes me not as an example of paintings ceasing to be works of art, but rather of works of art temporarily put to another symbolic use. The canvases don't lose their original representational and expressive powers during the military briefing, though additional ones are superimposed on them. They don't cease to be paintings.

What story could be told about that more drastic change? "It *was* a painting, an array of pigment on canvas depicting the artist's native village and expressing his love for it as well as his fascination with flatness and with the brush-stroke–like fronds of the palm trees, but now . . ." To withdraw the status "work of art" seems to require denying the painting's expressive and representational powers as well as somehow retrospectively canceling the artist's intentions, intentions which helped determine that work. I don't question our ability to reinterpret and reevaluate artworks as time passes, but I don't see how an art object's constitutive properties can be revoked or denied.[7]

Are we to conclude that the status "work of art" is a problematic or peculiar one? I don't think it is so unlike the other examples of conferred status which Dickie discusses in his article—for example the status of being husband and wife, conferred by a marriage ceremony, or the status of being a college graduate, conferred by a graduation ceremony. A B.A. would most likely be revoked if a graduate were found to have cheated or falsified his records, and a marriage would be annulled if one of the spouses were found to be a bigamist. These cases resemble that of a work of art found to be a forgery and demoted to the status of mere real thing.

We do not have a ceremony to demote works of art the way divorces undo marriages, there being no equivalent cultural need. No pain, suffering, unhappiness, or inconvenience accrues from having the status "work of art" stay in place throughout the physical life of the object so promoted. By contrast, much pain and suffering probably would accrue if that phrase from the marriage vows, "till death us do part," were strictly enforced.[8] There is, then, this asymmetry in our artworld: ordinary objects can be promoted into works of art, but works of art cannot sink back and become everyday real things. It follows that the death of art cannot occur through the individual deaths of each and every work of art in a given artworld or culture.

A second interpretation of the death of art locates art's demise at the level of the individual arts. Certainly today there are entire arts which count as dead. Consider, for example, tapestry, or stained glass.[9] The prime examples of these arts date back to the early Middle Ages. Pictorial tapestries adorned the great halls of medieval castles and fortresses, and expanses of stained glass bathed Gothic cathedrals in what appeared to be a manifestation of divine light. To give a few sample dates, the rose windows at Chartres were completed in the early thirteenth century; the unicorn tapestries in New York's Metropolitan Museum were woven between 1495 and 1505; and France's famous Gobelins factory produced tapestries based on Raphael's Vatican frescoes during the reign of Louis XIV. We haven't ceased to admire these wondrous works, yet neither art is central in our culture today. No major artist uses these media to make a serious statement. Why have they failed to flourish?

No doubt these arts declined for complex reasons. Relevant factors might include technological changes and pressures (a crucial ingredient becomes scarce, a secret process is lost or forgotten); new social and cultural arrangements (church patronage declines, an urban bourgeoisie evolves); and changes in the artworld itself (the passing of the Gothic style deprives certain arts of their niche). However, the most significant factor may well be the development of successor arts which performed the same tasks with greater power and ease. Oil painting, for example, holds considerable advantages over the arts of tapestry and stained glass. It offers the artist a richer palette, a more expressive surface, and a subtler range of contour, line, modeling, and shade. A painting can be completed more rapidly than a window or weaving of comparable scale; it also requires fewer assistants and fewer tools. Stained glass and tapestry both permit effects which can't be captured in paint. (Consider the translucence of glass, the texture of yarn.) Still, oil gradually became the preeminent pictorial medium, and I believe that the "death" of both stained glass and tapestry can be traced to its growing popularity.

Not all arts declined in this manner. Compare the fate of the art in question here, landscape gardening. In 1770, Horace Walpole declared gardening, painting, and poetry to be "Three Sisters, or the Three New Graces who dress and adorn Nature."[10] Yet gardening today is not a full-fledged sister to painting and poetry. Granted, suburban enthusiasts plant flowers, tend lawns, and beautify their lots; their urban counterparts devote equal effort and attention to window boxes and rooftop plots. But they don't do so with the sense that they are creating high art. The splendors of Stourhead and Stowe can't be replicated on a smaller scale. And, few today can afford to garden on the scale of the eighteenth century. As a result, gardening as it was known in Walpole's time has ceased. Undoubtedly this is due more to economic factors than to changes in taste or the appearance of a successor art. Changing patterns in recreation may also have contributed to the decline of lavish gardens, since the pleasures enjoyed by eighteenth-century aristocrats on their estates—walking, riding, hunting, conversing—are less popular in our electronic age.

All three arts—tapestry, stained glass, and landscape gardening—are dead in the sense that artists today no longer produce major works in these genres. We haven't ceased to admire past examples of these arts, but any examples produced today are likely to be backward-looking reprises of earlier forms and concerns. (Note that this is just how Danto characterized art in the posthistorical age. See below.) The problems besetting these arts do not, however, threaten the rest of the artworld. There is no contagion which might spread from art to art. If I am right that some arts die when supplanted by more vigorous successors, then this process could not eventuate in the death of art. Like an artistic version of natural selection, it could only leave the artworld stronger.

Danto's prediction that art will end by becoming transmuted into philosophy invites a third interpretation of the death of art. Like the Hegelian vision it is based on, Danto's view suggests that art dies through the simultaneous death of *all* the arts. Danto tells one version of this Hegelian story in the closing sections of his paper "The End of Art." He suggests that the proper model of art history is the *Bildungsroman,* "the novel of self-education which climaxes in the self's recognition of the self" (110), and he speculates about posthistorical life, calling it "a kind of philosophical *Club méditerranée*" (113). Hegel's vision of the future springs from his entire systematic philosophy. How is Danto to persuade us to accept *his* version of Hegel's vision? How can he prove that art will end as he says? In his essay Danto explores two accounts of the history of art.[11] I shall label these the mimetic model and the Hegelian model. The first sees art as progressing toward ever greater realism and verisimilitude; the second sees it as progressing toward ever greater theory-ladenness and self-absorption. We are meant to find the second story more plausible and therefore to accept Danto's view of the history—and future—of art. Let us examine these two tales.

3. THE MIMETIC MODEL

To characterize the mimetic model of art history Danto borrows a phrase from E. H. Gombrich and construes stylistic history as "the gradual conquest of natural appearances" (86). According to this view, primitive artists had the desire, but not the ability, to reproduce natural appearances. The discovery of perspective and the invention of new materials and techniques allowed artists to come closer and closer to the goal of optical duplication. The culmination of this progression would be a work of art which exactly reproduced the visual experience (or, in Gibsonian terms, the optical array) caused by actual objects and scenes. Danto describes this goal more technically as "the elimination, in favor of a kind of direct perception, of mediating inferences to perceptual reality facilitated by cues" (87). The progress of art history thus stems from "an imperative to replace inference to perceptual reality wherever possible with something equivalent to what perceptual reality itself would present" (88).

The model of art history just sketched is best suited to the art of painting. Danto broadens the scope of this model by incorporating a number of technological advances. He starts by proposing the moving picture as the obvious heir of the oil painting or "stationary" picture. Just as the discovery of perspective allowed artists to show spatial relationships directly which were previously conveyed through cues (such as occlusion and differential size) (87), so the invention of cinema allows the direct presentation of movement. "Movies directly reach the perceptual centers involved in seeing movement, and so function at a sub-inferential level" (89). Moviemakers have also experimented recently with ways of extending their medium beyond visual reality to include the other four senses as well. Consider "smellies," in which scents are released into the theater at appropriate times or provided to patrons on scratch cards. 3-D movies like Andy Warhol's *Frankenstein* equip viewers with special stereoscopic glasses in pursuit of tactile values. And some filmmakers have even wired their viewers to create "feelies."

Danto predicts that holographic images will be the next step in this progression, since they overcome the parallactic discrepancies of fixed-point perspective and produce images which "appear, like visions, full but impalpable, in our very midst" (93–94). Palpability will then be the last frontier. Once conquered, it will yield an art form where "for every perceptual range R, an equivalent could be technically generated" (97). The result, according to Danto: "Then art would be over with just as science would be over with when, as was thought to be a genuine possibility in the nineteenth century, everything was known" (97).

There is much to criticize in this picture of art history. Let me briefly examine four objections to the mimetic model. The first concerns its ethnocentrism. In judging the work of other times and other cultures by present-day standards, it surely begs some questions. For example, why assume that Egyptian artists were frustrated by their inability to capture natural appearances? How do we know that that was ever their goal? Perhaps we, looking back over the history of Western art, impose a teleology that was never there. Some historians claim that optical fidelity has been the artistic aim of only two previous cultures, ancient Greece and Renaissance Europe (90). Danto disagrees, arguing that the Chinese, for example, *would* have used perspective had they known about it. "Often one finds clouds and mists used to break up lines which, had they been allowed to be continuous, would have looked wrong; and a culture sensitive to optical wrongness may be described as committed to goals it has not learned to achieve" (90).

I don't find Danto's argument conclusive because we can imagine alternative accounts of Chinese art which are equally plausible. Suppose that the spatial qualities of Chinese painting facilitate the expression of certain attitudes toward nature—say, the attribution of magical powers to mountains. If this were the case, Chinese acquainted with Western perspective might well prefer their system and judge its "optical wrongness" an acceptable cost for such expressive power. My intuitions and Danto's reach a stalemate here. We may never know whether artists of another time or culture were striving to reproduce natural appearances or pursuing quite different goals. When clear-cut evidence to decide between these views is lacking, we can only defend one or another side by staunchly asserting a murky and complex set of counterfactuals.

In addition to leveling the charge of ethnocentrism, we can also criticize the account of perception underlying the progressive model of art history. Psychologists working on picture perception suggest that the goal of recreating natural appearances is unattainable. In the article "Perceiving Space from Pictures," Ralph Haber argues that no array of pigments on canvas can present exactly the same visual experience as looking at a natural scene unless the viewing conditions are artificially constrained and the scene itself is artfully chosen.[12] Among the differences Haber cites are these: most paintings fail to transmit as great a range of light and color as does a real scene; few paintings take into account the limitations of human vision such as the disparities between foveal and peripheral vision; once hung on a wall, a painting broadcasts in various ways the message that it is flat. The factors of distance, motion, and binocular vision contribute even further to the differences between real and painted scenes.

One might object that a goal can be pursued asymptotically, approached closer and closer yet never attained. If pictures and real scenes are related in such a manner, then the perception argument just sketched doesn't defeat the mimetic model of art history. However, there is something more unsettling about that model—its goal seems radically misconceived. As Danto has noted in many of his writings, there is something paradoxical about mimesis.[13] If the goal of imitation is pursued too avidly, then it shades off into illusion. That is, the perfect copy is no longer a copy but rather an original, a genuine piece of reality. And so, "mimetic art fails when it succeeds, when it gets to be like life."[14] Let me call this the paradox of imitation. Danto states the paradox as follows: "Once one has completed the mimetic program, one has produced something so like what is to be encountered in reality that, being just like reality, the question arises as to what makes it art."[15]

This paradox constitutes a third argument against the mimetic model. To succeed, imitative art must maintain a discernible gap between art and life. Yet as Danto notes, the mimetic model erases this gap and demands the logical invisibility of the medium. "It is the aim of imitation to conceal from the viewer the fact that it is an imitation, which is conspicuously at odds with Aristotle's thought that the knowledge of imitation accounts for our pleasure."[16] Awareness of the medium is one of the many "conventions of dislocation" which inform the audience not to respond to artworks as if they were real.[17] For example, our knowledge that Robert Cottingham's immense photo-realist painting *Barrera Rosa's* is in fact a painting rather than a photograph or real scene allows us to respond properly to it and appreciate its virtuosity. The mimetic model of art history seems to overlook this essential aspect of imitative art.[18]

None of the three arguments discussed above conclusively refutes the mimetic model. We can pursue goals even though they are misconceived, poorly chosen, incoherent, or unattainable. Thus it remains possible that art history is and has been the gradual conquest of natural appearances. Still, Danto rejects this view. He does so because the mimetic model cannot accommodate all the arts. In particular, because it cannot accommodate the art of literature.

We have seen that some gardens are mimetic. As such, they represent other gardens (as the Luxembourg Gardens, designed for Marie de Médicis, recall portions of the Boboli Garden she knew in her youth), other pieces of actual terrain (as the hunting park of Emperor Ch'in Shih-huang represented the conquered lands of his enemies), or sites that are merely fictive (as all paradise gardens can be said to recreate a vision of Eden). But these are exceptions. Many great gardens perform no representational tasks. Thus gardens might in and of themselves constitute a counterexample to the mimetic model under discussion. But a much more telling defeat of that model comes from the art of literature. Consider the claim that literature has gotten better at capturing natural appearances. One might urge that literature, not being a pictorial art, can't capture any appearances at all. But this is not Danto's point. Aristotle's suggestion in the *Poetics* that literature imitates human action defines one broad sense in which literature is imitative. Danto rejects not the notion of literary imitation, but that of literary progress.[19]

What might count as progress in literature? Are there any literary resources we have now that weren't available to, say, the ancient Greeks? Are there literary breakthroughs comparable to the discovery of perspective or the invention of oils? Suppose, anachronistically, that one of Aristotle's peers attempted to write a novel. He would have been unable to use as his central conceit arcane facts about the structure of DNA or the existence of black holes in space; he would presumably have been equally unable to describe his heroine's conflicts in Freudian terms or his hero's angst in terms of Marxist alienation; his plot would not mention condominiums, Cuisinarts, E-mail, or the threat of nuclear war. Yet none of these inabilities prevents our imagined novelist from writing a convincing, realistic account of life in the fourth century B.C., since the comparisons and analyses not available to him were not features *of* that life. Accordingly, he doesn't seem to be disadvantaged vis-à-vis a novelist of the 1990s.

If it is possible that the complexities of a society's life outrun the descriptive resources of its language, then in that society there *is* room for progress in literature. But Danto insists that this can't happen.[20] He maintains that with regard to language, "there is no logical room for the concept of progress" because "the descriptive resources of the natural languages [are] equivalently universal" (98–99).[21] Concluding that the progressive model of art history "finds its best examples in painting and sculpture, then in movies and talkies and, if you wish, feelies" (99), Danto rejects it as a partial and therefore unsatisfactory account.

In fact Danto's discussion provides additional grounds for judging the first model of art history incomplete. Once we take the nonvisual arts into consideration, we can no longer speak in terms of perceptual equivalents. Certainly the notion doesn't apply to literary imitations. Yet this leaves us unable to place a metric on artistic representations in general and unable therefore to compare their success.[22] In sum, once the concept of art is appropriately broadened, we can no longer compare artworks in terms of verisimilitude and can no longer view art history as the gradual conquest of natural appearances. Danto ought, then, to have rejected the first model of art history on these grounds.

While the mimetic model won't do as an account of all the arts—nor even of all painting—it remains possible that the model applies to some arts at some times. And in fact Danto writes in just this vein in his paper "Approaching the End of Art."[23] He argues that painters pursued the goal of optical duplication and that this progression reached a climax with the discovery of perspective (17). The advent of cinema ended this phase in painting's history.[24] Once cinema displaced their art, painters had to rethink the meaning of their practice. Out of this "immense problem of self-definition" (19) arose what Danto calls painting's "great philosophical phase from about 1905 to about 1965" (25). This phase can *not* be explained on the mimetic model. To understand it, we must turn to Danto's second, Hegelian, model of art history.

4. THE HEGELIAN MODEL

This second model of art history—which Danto endorses—resembles the first in being progressive and pointing toward the end of art; it differs in including all the arts. This model is based on the daunting metaphysical system of G. W. F. Hegel. One commenta-

tor on Hegel, Stephen Bungay, explains Hegel's view as follows.[25] Art is a form of Absolute
Spirit which embodies truth in a sensuous medium. As such, it stands midway between
thought and nature.[26] Art is a product of human freedom, and it fulfills its highest function when it expresses awareness of humankind's deepest interests and concerns.[27] Art
must be understood as a unity of form and content, a relationship akin to that between
body and soul (37–38). Beauty is art's Ideal, because in it form and content are identical.
No aspect of a beautiful work is superfluous. Its content completely determines its appearance, and could be expressed by no other appearance.[28]

For Hegel, the end of art is signaled by a rupture between form and content. Art, religion, and philosophy have a common content—the activity of self-reflection (33). But as
time passes and self-knowledge increases, new truths become apparent. Eventually there
will come a time when art is no longer adequate to express the highest truths of society.[29]
These more rarified truths will require a nonsensuous medium, and they will be conveyed
by religion or philosophy rather than by art.[30] Artworks of all types will continue to be
produced, but they will be reactionary products, expressing the ethos of an earlier age.
And since there will no longer be truths particularly suited to artistic expression, the relation between art's form and its content will become haphazard and contingent. Art
"moves away from its position as the 'middle' between the mind and the senses, becoming increasingly reflective and theoretical on the one hand, or losing all spiritual significance on the other" (89).

Might art really die in this manner? Danto encapsulates Hegel's system in the claim
that art becomes transmuted into philosophy. Danto seems to take this claim literally. For
instance, the opening and closing paragraphs of his paper "The Last Work of Art: Artworks and Real Things"[31] state that that paper *itself* becomes an artwork at the end (551),
and that art transforms itself into philosophy "by bringing within itself what it had tradi-
tionally been regarded as logically apart from" (562). Danto concludes that "the distinction between philosophy of art and art itself is no longer tenable" (562).

It seems clear that Danto has arrived at this view by considering the history of twentieth-century art, especially twentieth-century painting. In "The End of Art" he notes the
rapid succession of styles and movements—"Fauvism, the Cubisms, Futurism, Vorticism,
Synchronism, Abstractionism, Expressionism, Abstract Expressionism, Pop, Op, Mini-
malism, Post-Minimalism, Conceptualism, Photorealism, Abstract Reason, Neo-Expres-
sionism" (108)—and observes that works have come to depend more and more on theory for their existence as art (111). Recall Duchamp's famous urinal and the vast amount
of discussion it has generated among present-day philosophers and critics. Danto sums up

the situation with this tidy aphorism: "the objects approach zero as their theory approaches infinity" (111).

The fact that much twentieth-century art comes to us cloaked in theory doesn't by itself prove such art to be philosophy. One final piece of Danto's theory is needed to make sense of this view, namely, his claim that all art is representational.[32] "Representation" is here construed more broadly than mimesis. Art is representational not in imitating the world but in being *about* it. To explain his view, Danto invokes a metaphor—the space between language and the world.[33] He urges that art is related to reality as words are related to the world. Both stand apart from the world and bear a semantic relationship to it.[34] It follows as a corollary to this view that all artworks have interpretations, their *esse* is *interpretari*.[35]

Given this account of works of art, let us return to Danto's claim about art's end. Does art become philosophy when works of art start espousing philosophical doctrines? When the art produced now just *is* philosophy? What might this mean? Suppose that Jasper Johns's next work is a refutation of Berkeleyan idealism. This supposition is open to various interpretations. Perhaps Johns has produced a manuscript which refutes Berkeley's doctrine and exhibited that manuscript in a show. Or perhaps he has produced, say, a lithograph—a picture of a stone—which by alluding to Dr. Johnson performs the same task.[36] Then again, given the pliancy of reference, Johns could entitle any print or painting "Refutation of Berkeley." The work would then, by fiat, refer to immaterialism (though not necessarily refute it).

I believe that none of these examples captures what Danto has in mind, for art doesn't turn into just *any* philosophy—ethics, metaphysics, social and political philosophy. It turns into philosophy of art. This happens when art takes as its subject its own methods, materials, and limitations. Danto claims that modern art has evolved in just this manner: "In modern art, art became an object for itself in this sense."[37] "Much as philosophy has come to be increasingly its own subject, has turned reflexively inward onto itself, so art has done, having become increasingly its own (and only) subject."[38]

Danto cites Andy Warhol's pop-art *Brillo Box* (1964) as a seminal example. It forced viewers to work out the difference between indistinguishable objects, one an artwork, the other a mere real thing. "The Brillo box asked, in effect, why it was art when something just like it was not."[39] Danto explains further: "With Warhol, art was taken up into philosophy, since the question it raised and the form in which it raised it was as far as art could go in that direction—the answer had to come from philosophy. And in turning into philosophy, one might say that art had come to a certain natural end."[40] Minimal art, found art, and conceptual art all fit this introspective model, for a canvas painted solid white, an exhibited snow shovel, and a photographed photograph equally call into question the purpose and the bounds of art. Danto concludes that "the historical importance of art then lies in the fact that it makes philosophy of art possible and important."[41]

5. DIFFICULTIES WITH THE HEGELIAN MODEL

Danto's Hegelian model of art history was clearly created to account for recent goings-on in the artworld, in particular, to account for this century's frenzied succession of movements in the visual arts. Presumably, the same model applies to the other arts as well. Thus literature and gardening—like painting and sculpture—will end by becoming philosophy, and they will become philosophy by becoming self-reflective.[42] On this view, novels which experiment with fragmentation, ambiguity, specificity, and repetition are calling into question our traditional views about plot, character, narrative, and interpretation. They are *about* the powers and limits of literature. One might also speculate that the flurry of texts in critical theory—poststructuralist, feminist, deconstructionist, and more—all debating whether literary works have determinate meaning, are further instances of literature's transmutation into philosophy.

In many of his papers, Danto writes as if the careers of literature and painting are parallel. For instance, in "Artworks and Real Things" he gives examples from literature as well as from the visual arts. He compares not only two identical neckties (one painted by Picasso, the other by a child) and two identical paintings (one representing Newton's first law of motion, the other his third law) but also the two identical literary works described by Borges in the story "Pierre Menard, Author of the Quixote." In that same paper Danto also employs an example involving drama: the playwright Testamorbida who, a specialist in found drama, declares his latest work to be "everything that happened in the life of a family in Astoria between last Saturday and tonight, the family in question having been picked by throwing a dart at the map of the town."[43]

The fact that Danto takes his examples from various arts suggests that he views them as equally satisfying the tenets of his aesthetic theory.[44] With regard to gardens, we have seen in chapter 3 that gardens can convey complex content. There seems no reason to rule out the possibility of gardens that address issues in the philosophy of art. In particular, we can imagine imagine self-reflective gardens that address issues about the medium, powers, and limits of landscape. Such gardens would be landscape equivalents of Warhol's *Brillo Box*. (For further development of this claim, see section 6 below.)

I conclude that Danto's second model of art history can, unlike the mimetic model, accommodate all the arts. Nevertheless, a second difficulty confronts the Hegelian model.

While Danto can explain many twentieth-century trends and events, his account of the posthistorical era is problematic. Danto has not established that art is at an end.

Let me pursue this point. Art's becoming philosophy is also, for Danto, the end of art. Recall his claim, quoted above, that "with Warhol, art was taken up into philosophy . . . and in turning into philosophy, one might say that art had come to a certain natural end." Art's end is natural because it evolves from within. Danto here distinguishes stopping from coming to an end. The first is an external matter, while the second is more like a narrative closure, a story's arriving at its proper and satisfying resolution.[45] Just as life goes on after the story teller's "and they all lived happily ever after," so art continues to be produced in this, the posthistorical age. Such art no longer poses philosophical questions but it continues to serve human ends and to enhance human life.

Danto insists that we do now live in such an age, that the malaise and pluralism of the 1970s signaled the end of art. What isn't clear to me is why art can't continue to philosophize. From 1905 to 1964—"art's great philosophical phase"—art remained art but it raised philosophical questions. Danto maintains that later art styles and movements like the neoexpressionism of the 1980s raise *no* philosophical questions. Thus they signal art's end. This suggests that there is only one philosophical question art can raise, namely, the question about art's nature posed by Warhol's *Brillo Box*. But a glance at recent journals can attest that philosophers of art ponder many more questions than this. Why then isn't there more philosophy for art to do?

A further difficulty arises for Danto's theory at this point. Suppose art does find new philosophical questions to address; can it tackle them and still remain art? A tension emerges here in Danto's view. If we look back over his account, some works of art remain art while addressing philosophical questions. Warhol's *Brillo Box* (1964) is a case in point. But presumably subsequent works are are transmuted into philosophy in taking up such questions,[46] while works with no philosophical content are deemed not to be art, or to be posthistorical art.[47] In sum, it remains unclear when or whether works with philosophical content retain their status as art. Since some art remains art while becoming philosophical, and since the self-reflexive question "What is art?" is not the only philosophical question that art can raise about art, I conclude that Danto has not shown that twentieth-century art has exhausted its inquiries *or* come to an end.

6. GARDENS' FATE

Our investigation of the alleged death of art has yielded the following conclusions: particular works of art, acknowledged by a culture, cannot cease being art within that culture;

with regard to our own culture, there is no reason to accept Danto's overarching claim that art has come to an end and that we live in a posthistorical age of meaningless artistic repetition; but, it remains the case that particular arts can lose their vitality and in fact become moribund. Although a vast majority of Americans named gardening their favorite *hobby* in a Gallup survey,[48] it may well be that the *art* of gardening has come to an end. As I have argued throughout this chapter, gardening is no longer considered a fine art. Major artists do not make statements in this medium, and our sense of gardening's kinship to painting and poetry has been lost.

Yet despite gardening's decline, high art has not retreated from the landscape. A variety of art flourishes today in sculpture gardens, art parks, and more remote locations. In his introduction to an anthology aptly titled *Art in the Land,* Alan Sonfist writes of a new group of artists "whose work makes a statement about man's relation to nature." These artists often use natural substances (earth, rocks, and plants) in their work and often construct that work outside on natural sites.[49] I believe that an important relation binds these recent environmental works and the eighteenth-century landscape garden.

One author in Sonfist's anthology, Michael McDonough, claims that "The true avant-garde of architecture, the adventurous, risk-taking, experimenting, problem-seeking, redefining fringe, is not in architecture. It is in the jetties, towers, tunnels, walls, rooms, bridges, ramps, mounds, ziggurats, the buildings and landscapes, structures and constructions of environmental art."[50] In the remaining sections of this chapter, I shall challenge the genealogy McDonough has proposed. I shall argue that gardening is the true ancestor of the varied features McDonough cites, and that environmental art is gardening's avant-garde.

There are various ways of defining modernism, postmodernism, and the avant-garde. I shall focus on two such definitions and ask whether gardening could have been part of the modernist enterprise. The first mark of modernism I shall consider is that proposed by Clement Greenberg in his essay "Avant-Garde and Kitsch" (1961). Greenberg claims that abstract art develops when "turning his attention away from subject matter of common experience, the poet or artist turns it in upon the medium of his own craft. . . . These themselves become the subject matter of art and literature."[51] Arthur Danto builds a similar insight into his neo-Hegelian account of art. As we have seen, Danto suggests that art history is best modeled by the *Bildungsroman* or novel of self-discovery, and he summarizes the progress of modern art with a clever aphorism: "the objects approach zero as their theory approaches infinity."[52]

Might gardens participate in this progression? Can we imagine modernist, minimalist, and avant-garde gardens? It is certainly possible to design gardens that are spare, recti-

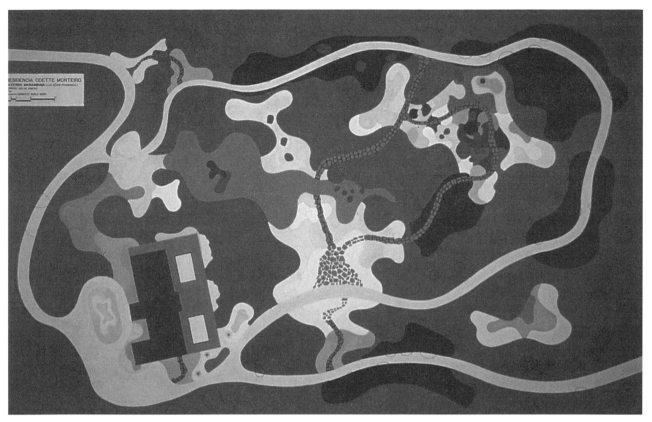

Plan of the Odette Monteiro Estate, designed by Roberto Burle Marx. Photograph by architect Haruyoshi Ono.

linear, and severe, perfectly in tune with the Bauhaus aesthetic. The Brazilian gardens by Roberto Burle Marx feature masses of color and sculptural arrays of exotic plants (color plate 4). They are said by one writer to "owe more to cubist art than to any preceding style of landscape gardening."[53] Even the plans of Burle Marx's gardens seem modernist. Their bright colors and curvilinear shapes recall works of Miro, Klee, and Kandinsky. Naumkeag in Stockbridge, Massachusetts (color plate 5), designed by Fletcher Steele beginning in the 1920s, is an American example of a modernist garden, as are more recent landscapes designed by Dan Kiley and Garrett Eckbo. There are also examples of minimalist gardens. Consider Sissinghurst's White Garden or the Red Border at Hidcote Manor in Gloucershire as landscape equivalents to Kasimir Malevitch's *White on White*. Of course, Greenbergian modern gardens would be both minimalist and introspective. The landscape equivalent to "art about art," they would question our sense of what a garden should be.

A monochromatic garden, the Red Border at Hidcote Manor. Reproduced by permission of the Harry Smith Horticultural Photographic Collection.

Such gardens might emphasize the process and materials of gardening, or deny such traditional garden values as beauty, variety, and originality. Imagine a garden that displays hoses, tools, and fertilizer as prominently as flowers, or one with nothing but marigolds covering varied settings and terrain that might otherwise lead us to expect roses, lilies, lilacs, lupine, violets, hollyhocks, daffodils, and more. More shocking gardens might dispense with plants altogether. Imagine a garden that is all trellises but no roses.

Stanley Cavell proposes a second mark of modernism in his paper "Music Discom-

This photograph of a rose garden in winter inadvertently exemplifies one of the modernist gardens I proposed—all trellis, no plants. Photograph by Elvin McDonald, courtesy of Perennial Productions, Inc.

posed" when he argues that questions of fraudulence and of trust are inextricably bound up with modern art.[54] As art becomes minimal, artistry becomes less apparent, and the responses "I could do that," "Anyone could do that," "A child could do that" ring out. Cavell is here arguing against a certain sort of serial music which he calls "totally composed." Its chief characteristic is that every aspect—notes, instrumentation, rhythm, dynamics, texture—is determined mathematically. Cavell objects to such pieces because their aleatory methods prevent composers from knowing in advance how the work will sound. And this, he claims, prevents them from composing so as to satisfy themselves.

While Cavell does not, in the end, make good his charge of fraud,[55] his discussion can be extended to the art of gardening. Like serial music or minimalist paintings, gardens invite us to meditate on change and chance. All gardening incorporates some elements of chance, for plants are affected by climate, soil, pests, and disease. A gardener could introduce additional levels of randomness by buying unlabeled seeds and bulbs, by making design choices with dice or the I Ching, or by simply ceasing to prune and weed. Gardens can also pose the issues of fraudulence and trust that Cavell finds in some modern music. Consider the gardenist's equivalent to John Cage's piece *4'33"*: well-groomed beds of soil not planted with anything at all. Alan Sonfist created a garden not unlike this. *Pool of Earth* (1975) was a fifty-foot diameter circle of fertile soil surrounded by a ring of rock in the midst of a chemical waste dump. Sonfist intended the circle to gradually reseed and rebuild the original forest. Perhaps a "found garden" would parallel even more closely Cage's views about the relative status of music and noise. Cage maintains that all sounds are worthy of attention and that music should not be specially privileged. A "found garden" which enclosed an arbitrarily selected piece of land would make a similar point about the relative status of flowers and weeds.

One garden which fits both Greenberg's and Cavell's accounts of modernism was featured in a *Home Design* magazine of the *New York Times* (1985) (color plate 6). This twenty-by-twenty-foot garden consists of brightly colored shards of Plexiglas set in a bed of gravel. A wire-and-glass table in the center of the garden replaces the traditional garden pond, and the entire ensemble is covered with a fishnet canopy dyed bright pink. Glitter-covered trash cans cluster nearby. Martha Schwartz, the creator of this garden, confessed that it was inspired by Frank Stella's relief paintings of the 1970s. The Stella Garden, as Schwartz calls it, seems a perfect example of a modernist garden. The piece alludes wittily to the progress of twentieth-century painting. It also challenges our received views about both gardening and creativity.

I don't think the existence of the Stella Garden threatens my claims about the decline of gardening. For one, the work sits, not in a public space or gallery setting, but in the artist's mother's backyard. It seems thereby insulated from the factors which generate and support an avant-garde: urban settings, political agendas, the market power of galleries and museums. The Stella Garden is also isolated in another sense. It has not, to the best of my knowledge, had any significant influence on other gardens or on other works of art.

Let me shift for a moment from modernism to postmodernism. While I am wary of trying to define this difficult and fluid term, I would include these factors in any account of the postmodern: eclecticism, irony, and antifoundationalism. In architecture, postmodernism embraces the first two factors. Consider a paradigm postmodern structure, Philip Johnson's AT&T tower in Manhattan. Rather than designing yet another glass box, Johnson created a sensuous stone-clad building adorned with a playful array of architectural details, most notably its crowning "Chippendale" pediment. Other postmodernist architects like Charles Moore and Michael Graves continued the tradition of eclecticism, juxtaposing witty quotations of various architectural styles. In such disciplines as literature and history, postmodernism advocates interpretive liberty; it decenters the traditional objectivity and certainty associated with privileged readings grounded in authorial intent. Here the factors of playfulness and antifoundationalism are combined.

Can any of these trends manifest themselves in a garden? Some contemporary gardens replace traditional structures and contents with wholly unexpected and extraordinarily kitschy items. The garden of Clifford Davis (color plate 7) photographed in Jane Owens's volume *Eccentric Gardens* consists of row after row of rubber ducks and plastic daisies all afloat on a sea of green Astroturf.[56] Other gardens documented in this volume have a playful spirit which in some ways harks back to the sixteenth-century Italian mannerist gardens with their water jokes and pneumatic tricks. No postmodernist garden would take itself as seriously as did eighteenth-century emblematic gardens or twentieth-century modernist gardens. Thus it seems unlikely that a post-modernist garden would be as large in scale as any of these earlier exemplars.

One other instance of a postmodernist garden is Ian Hamilton Finlay's Little Sparta in southern Scotland.[57] Finlay is a sculptor and concrete poet who purchased a four-acre estate in the Scottish countryside in 1966 and has been self-consciously improving it in the manner of Shenstone and Pope. Little Sparta mixes traditional garden features— ponds, temples, a grotto, a sunken garden, a Roman garden, and more—with such contemporary symbols as battleships, airplanes, and a "nuclear sail" (color plate 8). Finlay's garden is, unlike Schwarz's, open to the public and it has in fact figured in an ongoing "war" with the local tax authorities.[58] Numerous inscriptions carved in a classicizing style underscore Finlay's theme of neoclassical rearmament. The poet has taken the French Revolution with its dialectical mix of virtue and terror as the ground of both the modern era and his continuing cultural critique.

At first glance, Finlay's garden might seem a reactionary endeavor. Like its eighteenth-century predecessors, it borrows images and inscriptions from an earlier era and uses them to voice a critical view of contemporary culture. But while Stowe's and Stourhead's references to the classical world were part of the shared vocabulary of the Augustan Age, Finlay's appropriation of neoclassical style is singular and savage. Since landowners no longer improve their estates with temples, obelisks, columns, and grottos, Finlay's use of an eighteenth-century vocabulary and his juxtaposition of it with strikingly twentieth-century forms and concerns—concrete poetry, the nuclear age—mark Little Sparta as a highly self-conscious work. Finlay *uses* the neoclassical garden to make an ironic statement; he doesn't revive the garden as a viable twentieth-century art form. For this reason, Little Sparta is a paradigm case of a postmodern work of art.

7. EARTHWORKS AND ENVIRONMENTAL ART

I have been reinventing the history of gardening, grafting an imagined set of modernist gardens onto gardening's actual past. Together, these actual and imagined gardens—Sonfist's, Schwartz's, and Finlay's creations plus the aleatory, minimalist, Cagean, and found-art possibilities I have described—show that gardening could indeed have contributed to the progress of twentieth-century art. Since this supposition is, however, contrary to fact, I would like to take another approach to demonstrating gardening's powers. Turning to some twentieth-century works, the environmental art cited by McDonough, I shall see whether a lineage can be traced backwards from this art to gardening in its prime.

The category "environmental art" is extremely diverse. Let me begin with a quick typology. I am indebted here to Mark Rosenthal's article "Some Attitudes of Earth Art: From Competition to Adoration." [59] I sort recent environmental art into six categories. These categories are provisional, and they often overlap, but describing some of these works will help show their ties to gardens of the past. My categories are as follows:

1. Masculine gestures in the environment:[60]
   Heizer, Smithson, De Maria, Turrell
2. Ephemeral gestures in the environment:
   Singer, Long
3. Environmental performance art:
   Boyle, Fulton, Hutchinson, Christo & Jeanne-Claude
4. Architectural installations:
   Holt, Aycock, Miss
5. Quasi-gardens:
   Sonfist, Irwin, Webster
6. Sculpture gardens and art parks

Let me say something about each of these categories. The first contains the classic examples of what were called earthworks, works of art created by manipulating vast amounts of dirt and rock. For example, Michael Heizer's desert sculptures of the sixties include *Double Negative* (1969), in which 240,000 tons of earth were carved out of two facing cliffs,[61] and *Dissipate* (1968), in which five twelve-foot-long steel-lined trenches were dug into the floor of a Nevada desert. This category includes "additive" works as well as

Walter De Maria, *Lightning Field,* 1977. © Dia Center for the Arts. All reproduction rights reserved. Photograph by John Cliett.

excavations. In Robert Smithson's *Asphalt Rundown* (1969), a truckload of asphalt was poured down the side of a quarry in Rome, while the same artist's more famous work *Spiral Jetty* (1970) is a 1,500-foot-long spiral of rock and earth built into Utah's Great Salt Lake. Heizer's ambitious *Complex One/City* (1972–76) is a massive illusionistic structure on a remote Nevada plateau.[62] *Complex One* seems architectural, even though it can't be entered. By contrast, Walter De Maria's *Lightning Field* (1977), a one-mile-square grid containing

Above and opposite: Roden Crater, purchased and reshaped by James Turrell. Photographs courtesy of James Turrell.

640 eighteen-foot steel poles, seems more an altered landscape than an essay in architecture or sculpture. James Turrell's work in progress, *Roden Crater,* can also be construed as an all-encompassing landscape or perceptual field. With help from the Dia Foundation, Turrell purchased a mountain fifty miles northeast of Flagstaff, Arizona.[63] He is now subtly reshaping the volcanic crater and building rooms and chambers in which, as one writer eloquently puts it, "Light from lunar, planetary, and celestial events will enter the apertures, gather, refract and self-enhance in the utter darkness, and be experienced by visitors as luminous presences, not quite space nor exactly light, but rather illusions of both."[64]

I called this first group of artworks masculine because of their scale. They are also remote and inaccessible. Traveling to see them requires braving wilderness, rattlesnakes, and the desert's climatic extremes.[65] Moreover, it is not clear from what vantage point

these works *can* be seen, or are meant to be seen. For example, Elizabeth Baker states that De Maria's constructs are meant to be walked in,[66] yet venturing near *The Lightning Field* during a storm would be extremely dangerous. Many of the works are documented through aerial photographs. These reveal striking affinities between these massive works and modern minimalist painting.[67] But it is unlikely that that any ground-level spectator at the site could gain a similar view.

My second category of environmental art, ephemeral gestures in the landscape, is typified by the early work of Michael Singer. His series *Situation Balances* (1971–73) involved rearranging fallen logs to create "networks of tenuously posed trees, buttressed by stumps."[68] Later he bundled branches and reeds and placed them in marshy areas, or wove latticelike structures of strips of wood. Richard Long's work is equally modest.[69] Carol Hall describes two of his early pieces as follows: "One work was the making of a path in a field of grass by walking back and forth for several hours, another consisted of snipping off

Above and opposite: *Running Fence, Sonoma and Marin Counties, California, 1972–76,* by Christo and Jeanne-Claude. © 1976 Christo. Photographs by Wolfgang Volz.

the heads of flowers in a meadow, thus inscribing a giant X."[70] More recently, Long has been taking walks, documenting them with photographs or brief descriptions, and occasionally leaving behind geometric arrays of stones. John Beardsley remarks that the majority of Long's works seem like "physical traces of some sort of private ritual." Beardsley goes on to note that "like more monumental projects, . . . most of Long's works involve the landscape both as site and as part of the subject matter as well."[71] Interestingly, Mark Rosenthal also emphasizes the ritual aspect and the site-specificity when he summarizes the work of Long and Singer as follows: "Both view their works as ritualistic responses to the site with which they are interacting. Their largely horizontal gestures acquiesce in and complement the landscape. That these quiet gestures will be quickly erased is part of the modest ambitions of the artists when they work in nature."[72]

Some of Long's pieces—the documented walks—slide over into my third category, environmental performance art. Typical here is Mark Boyle, who, beginning in 1968, asked randomly selected people to help him create an artwork. Those who agreed were blindfolded in Boyle's studio and asked to throw a dart at a map of the world. In this manner Boyle collected one thousand randomly selected sites and has been traveling to them

since 1970. At each site he takes photographs and makes castings of various surfaces. These result in shows such as *Thaw Series* (1972), in which Fiberglas casts of square yards of melting snow were on display. Hamish Fulton is another artist I include in this category. Like Long, he makes walking his art form, but Fulton leaves behind no traces of his walks. He comes away only with photographs which document each work.

Let me add works of one more sort to my performance category. I have in mind works of art which are ephemeral, like those in category 2, but which emphasize their performance aspect by introducing artificial elements into the landscape. Paradigm cases here would include Peter Hutchinson's *Parícutin Project* (1970), in which a three-hundred-foot-long trail of bread was laid along fault lines at the mouth of a Mexican volcano and left there for six days until mold changed the bread from white to orange. The same artist's *Threaded Calabash* (1969) involved threading five calabashes onto a twelve-foot stretch of rope and securing them underwater off the coast of Tobago until the fruit became waterlogged and sank to the ocean floor. One last piece of Hutchinson's related more closely to gardens was *Thrown Rope* (1972), in which the artist planted a row of hyacinths following the configuration of a rope he had thrown.

Christo and Jeanne-Claude's works have affinities with each of my first three categories. Their most renowned environmental installations—*Valley Curtain, Rifle, CO,*

Sun Tunnels, by Nancy Holt. Photograph courtesy of Nancy Holt.

1970–72, Running Fence, Sonoma and Marin counties, CA, 1972–76, and *Surrounded Islands, Biscayne Bay, Greater Miami, FL, 1980–83*—are forceful gestures. Like Heizer's earthworks, they are massive, they can appear remote in photographs, and they can be viewed as entireties from the air (though Christo and Jeanne-Claude do not care for this point of view). However, their creations also have a performance aspect. Like Hutchinson's projects, they introduce artificial elements (orange curtain, white curtain, pink "skirt") into the landscape. And finally, the works are short-lived. Each is assembled and dismantled within a matter of days. The site is then returned to its original condition. In this respect, Christo and Jeanne-Claude's works resemble those I have labeled ephemeral gestures.[73]

Let me cover the remaining categories more quickly. I have grouped together Nancy Holt, Alice Aycock, and Mary Miss as three artists who create architectural installations in

Sun Tunnels, interior view. Photograph courtesy of Nancy Holt.

the landscape. Some of Holt's works are, like Heizer's and Smithson's, in remote desert sites, and many are keyed to celestial happenings. For example, her work *Sun Tunnels* (1973–76) in the Utah desert consists of four large concrete pipes oriented to mark the sunrise during summer and winter solstices. The pipes are also pierced with holes which map the constellations Draco, Perseus, Columba, and Capricorn.[74] Holt employs similar "locators"—pipes which focus and guide vision—in other works. It should be noted that the attunement of Holt's works to celestial events stands in a long tradition. In his account of *Roden Crater,* discussed above, Craig Adcock describes a five-thousand-year-old site near Newgrange, Ireland, where "a 62-foot-long, corbel-vaulted passage leads inward to a central chamber. At the winter solstice, the light from the rising sun shines down the tunnel and illuminates the interior space of the tomb. The entrance is constructed in such a way that the event can occur only during the winter solstitial extreme."[75] The possibility that contemporary earthworks allude to or engage previous landscapes is a theme that will be explored in more detail below. I shall argue that this trait, together with the details of site-specificity, link today's environmental works to the eighteenth-century landscape garden.

The artists whose work most clearly recalls those earlier gardens are Alan Sonfist, Meg Webster, and Robert Irwin. I have placed their work in the category quasi-gardens. Sonfist has created a number of *Time Landscapes,* tracts which reproduce an urban area's vanished native flora. Though didactic in intent, these works truly are gardens of a sort. When completed, the *Time Landscape* in New York City's La Guardia Place will exhibit three stages of a forest as it would have been in the colonial era. The ground was returned to "natural contours" before planting, and expert consultants "researched and selected native species that once grew on the site."[76] Thus Mark Rosenthal remarks that "Whereas Smithson pushes and manipulates earth to form his signature, Sonfist cultivates a garden."[77]

The first stage of Sonfist's *Time Landscape* in Manhattan was dedicated in 1978. Meg Webster's work *Pass,* installed in St. Louis's Laumeier Sculpture Park between 1990 and 1992, resembles *Time Landscape* in being a didactic piece of landscape art. (A brochure from the park calls it an "ecological sculpture.") While Sonfist's piece reconstructs the botanical past of its specific site, Webster's work refers more widely. *Pass* is meant to reproduce a variety of different habitats that can be found throughout Missouri. These include "a fruit orchard, a woodland stream, a pond, sun and shade gardens, herbs, berry bushes, a variety of prairie grasses and flowers, a clover mound and a perennial flower bowl."[78] Clearly, some of these features are reproduced in miniature in this one-and-one-half-acre site. In this respect *Pass* resembles the Chinese hunting park described at the end of chapter 4, although *Pass* refers to generic rather than specific Missouri locales.

One of the works of Robert Irwin that most resembles a garden is his Wellesley College installation *Filigreed Line* (1980), a forty-foot-long stainless steel wall, two feet at its highest, pierced by an abstract leaflike pattern, and set in a bucolic corner of the campus. The work reflects light flickering through the trees and glistening on the nearby lake. Melinda Wortz writes that the piece alters our perception of the landscape, heightening our perception of a beautiful place. Rather than calling attention to itself as art, "the work returns us to the land."[79] I also find garden resonances in some of Irwin's indoor installations which subtly alter a gallery space, say by the addition of a narrow transparent scrim just below ceiling level along one wall. Though small, and indoors, these works envelop us in a highly charged perceptual field. This effect resembles that which some viewers attribute to De Maria's *Lightning Field,* as well as that which Turrell hopes to achieve in his *Roden Crater.*

Time Landscape, by Alan Sonfist. Photograph courtesy of Alan Sonfist.

Irwin's unrealized plan for the Miami International Airport, which Arthur Danto calls Irwin's masterpiece,[80] included a number of explicit garden areas. Noting that airport art had hitherto been of the "bauble" category—"a spot of aesthetic afterthought calculated to grace a site whose essential business . . . goes on perfectly adequately without benefit of the art"—Danto claims that Irwin "basically reinvented the relationship in which art and the airport experience were to stand to one another."[81] Irwin took as his guiding principle that every airport should emblematize its city, since it is inevitably both the first *and* the last part of the city that every air traveler experiences. Moreover, Irwin took the abundance of water to be emblematic of Miami.[82] Irwin and his design crew broke the airport experience down into six repeated phases—arriving, passage, seeking, finding, waiting, and leaving—each of which, they claimed, had its own texture.[83] For his own contribution to what was to be a team effort, Irwin proposed razing a central two-story parking garage and

Filigreed Line, by Robert Irwin. © 1998 Robert Irwin/Artists Rights Society (ARS), New York. Photograph coutesy of the Pace Gallery.

replacing it with a cypress grove with native ferns and birds in a marshy lake. Pedestrian skyways would arc through it to link the various terminals. Benches and cafes would encourage travelers to pause and rest. Irwin's master plan included many other miniparks throughout the airport. Danto insists that Irwin's plan, had it been realized, would have revolutionized airport design.[84]

The final category I placed in my list was that of sculpture gardens and artparks. The Minneapolis Sculpture Garden, Laumeier Park in St. Louis, Missouri, Artpark in Lewiston, New York, Parc Lullin near Geneva, Kerguehennic in Brittany,[85] PepsiCo's world headquarters in Purchase, New York, and General Mills's headquarters in Minneapolis all resemble earlier (seventeenth- and eighteenth-century) European gardens in that all include works of art in a natural landscape. Whether these parks are functioning as gardens, or merely as museums which happen to be out of doors, depends on the relations which hold between work and site. In what follows, I shall argue that these relations are a crucial factor in understanding and interpreting these works.

8. TRACING A LINEAGE

I have described the rich variety of recent environmental art. But what might serve to connect the environmental works of today to gardens of the past? Certainly parallels abound. For example, gardening can be disruptive, like the excavations of Heizer and Smithson. Gardens can contain follies, like the constructions of Aycock and Miss. Blossoms are ephemeral, like Hutchinson's loaves and calabashes, paths and benches control a visitor's perceptions, like Holt's locators. Gardens create a total environment, like Irwin's altered rooms. But, to repeat Goodman's caution, *any* two items have some properties in common. While it is intellectually satisfying to find similarities between items as disparate as eighteenth-century gardens and twentieth-century environmental art, what, if anything, follows from this exercise?

One relation which can hold between earlier and later works is that the former influenced the latter. In his book *Influence in Art and Literature,* Goran Hermeren lists thirteen separate requirements which he claims characterize genuine artistic influence.[86] He distinguishes between direct and indirect influence, and between positive and negative influence. He notes that artists need not be aware of the influence (96), and that works of art which influence one another need not have any "obvious and easily discovered similarities" (99). Hermeren's crucial requirement is a causal one: whenever one work influences another, the artist's contact with the earlier work or with its creator is a "contributory cause" of his creation.[87]

The artistic relationship I want to characterize is looser than Hermeren's notion of influence. While I maintain that our understanding of, say, *Roden Crater, Lightning Field,* or *Time Landscape* is enhanced if we view these in light of the tradition of landscape gardening, I don't claim that Turrell, De Maria, or Sonfist was necessarily thinking back to earlier gardens, or that their works resemble such gardens in any straightforward way. For all I know, these artists never viewed or read about the eighteenth-century gardens described above. If this is so, then Hermeren's requirement of causal contact is not fulfilled, and the relation between the earlier and later works is not a simple causal one.

I propose the following principle for determining artistic legacy, for tracing a lineage from artforms of the past to those of the present. If, in understanding and interpreting later works, we see them as fulfilling some of the important functions of their predecessors, then it is proper to see the later works as descendants of those which came before. On this principle, eighteenth-century gardens and twentieth-century environmental artworks are linked if the latter works perform some of the aesthetic tasks of those gardens and do so in a in a way which recalls those original landscapes. It is not the case, however, that the later works *refer* to their predecessors. This stronger connection would hold only if the artist were aware of the earlier gardens and intended her audience to think back to them.

Artistic lineage is a complex concept, and the principle just proposed is extremely vague. I have not, in earlier chapters, developed the notion of an aesthetic task or function (though I have argued that eighteenth-century gardens did much more than merely soothe or delight). When we situate works of art historically, we note both similarities and differences between them and their predecessors. Yet not all predecessors are interpretively significant. One salient similarity which links some gardens and some environmental art is that both are built landscapes in the environment. Let me try to explain the connections I see between gardens and earthworks by taking up once again the relation of work to site. In what follows, I shall borrow some distinctions from the environmental artist Robert Irwin.

In his essay *Being and Circumstance,* Irwin proposes a four-fold scheme for classifying the relation between a work of art and its context.[88] Works can be (1) site-dominant, (2) site-adjusted, (3) site-specific, or (4) site-conditioned/determined. These categories form a continuum with each more context-bound than the preceding one.

Irwin's example of site-dominant art is a Henry Moore sculpture. Although a Moore *Mother and Child* might be displayed to greater effect in one setting than another, its meaning, purpose, and form are not affected by relocation. By contrast, site-adjusted works make some concessions to their setting—"scale, appropriateness, placement, etc." (26). These works, however, are still either made or conceived in the studio. Site-specific works are those conceived with the site in mind (27). Most of Richard Serra's sculpture falls within this category, and the artist might have defended his embattled piece *Tilted Arc* by arguing that since it would not be the *same* work of art if moved, it cannot be moved. Finally, site-determined works are those where "the sculptural response draws all of its cues (reasons for being) from its surroundings"; the site itself "determines all facets of the 'sculptural response'" (27). Here, Irwin claims, the imperatives of the site may even override the usual marks by which we recognize an artist's oeuvre.[89]

There are problems with Irwin's categories, but they let us draw some useful distinctions among works of art. We are familiar with works of art created *in response to* a particular site. Consider Cézanne's many studies of Mont Sainte-Victoire. Though these paintings testify to the artist's lifelong interest in the landscape of Provence, they aren't situated in that landscape; they hang in public and private collections throughout the world.

Other works, however, are both responses *to* a site and situated *in* that site. Examples include Saarinen's *Gateway Arch,* Serra's *Tilted Arc,* and Christo and Jeanne-Claude's wrappings and fences.[90] In some cases the relation between work and site becomes even more intimate: the site becomes in effect the *medium* of the work of art.

Consider Irwin's categories as applied to gardens and to environmental art. Surprisingly, some gardens may lack any special relation to their site. An orangery or a botanical garden is site-dominant, in Irwin's terms, if its only purpose is to produce oranges, or to display and preserve certain species of plants. The same is true of a bed of annuals planted solely to provide a striking display of color. By contrast, the eighteenth-century gardens I have been exploring do more than inhabit a site. They are responsive to that site, and they emphasize and display features which are aspects of the site itself. For example, recall that the topography of Stowe, Stourhead, and West Wycombe forms an integral part of these gardens' iconological programs.

Gardens which do not address their site, do not take it as a problem, could, it seems to me, be of botanical interest only. That is, they could only be of interest for their plantings. One might object that we could also take an interest in such added features as paths, benches, ponds, and follies, but it is hard to see how any of these could be added to a garden without taking into account prospects and viewpoints, contours and textures, the lie of the land, in short, everything that constitutes a site. Gardens which were neither site-specific nor site-determined would be in the land, but they would not make reference to it. It would not figure in our response to the gardens, and we would not take it into account in estimating the gardens' pleasures or successes.

Of course a garden's relation to its setting can be an adversarial one. Garden designers do not always surrender to the exigencies of a site. Consider Le Nôtre's ongoing campaign to form the gardens of Versailles from inhospitable swampland, or Brown's reputation for razing villages and rerouting rivers for the sake of his designs. In such cases, the gardenist carves, shapes, alters, levels, but the resulting garden is in harmony with the conquered site. At Versailles, for instance, the relentless geometric expanse of Le Nôtre's garden reveals nothing of the underlying land but expresses perfectly his monarch's reign and aspirations. Such gardens are in fact site-specific or site-determined.

Many of the environmental works described in section 6 above are also site-specific or site-determined. The pieces I classed as ephemeral gestures (those by Long, Hutchinson, and Singer) belong in Irwin's fourth category, as do Heizer's excavations, Turrell's crater, and Irwin's gallery installations. All of Holt's locator pieces are site-specific, as are Sonfist's *Time Landscapes* if we extend site to mean something like "ecological niche." All these works are in the landscape, they all manipulate that landscape, and they all make us take into account our relation to that landscape.

Nine Spaces, Nine Trees, by Robert Irwin. © 1998 Robert Irwin/Artists Rights Society (ARS), New York. Photograph courtesy of the Pace Gallery.

This then is the trait which I believe is shared by gardens, earthworks, and environmental art. It underlies their common function and grounds my claim of shared lineage. But both gardens and environmental works can possess this trait in varying degrees. Contrast one last pair of works which share some similarities: Robert Irwin's *Nine Spaces, Nine Trees* (1983) and Alan Sonfist's *Columns of Growth* (1981). Irwin's work, a grid subdivided into nine squares, occupies the roof of the Public Safety Building Plaza in downtown Seattle. The grid is constructed out of plastic-coated blue fencing, and in the center of each square sits a flowering plum tree in a cast-concrete planter. The catalog accompanying an Irwin retrospective in 1993 notes that "The plan for this project was keyed by nine columns (loading points) in the police garage below the plaza."[91] Sonfist's work, located in Louisville, Kentucky, is "a 21-foot cubic sculpture constructed of sixteen stainless steel columns in groups of four, each surrounding a native tree. Each column is of a dissimilar height and thickness that correspond to the growth pattern of the four different native trees, each representing the tree's life at ten, fifteen, twenty, and twenty-five years."[92]

How shall we classify these two works? Each is an outdoor space, planted with trees. Irwin's array responds to architectural elements of the site that viewers would not be aware

Columns of Growth, by Alan Sonfist. Photograph courtesy of Alan Sonfist.

of. Is it then site-specific at one remove, since it takes its cues not from the natural landscape but from the architecture that underlies it? Sonfist's work is also difficult to classify in Irwin's terms. *Columns of Growth* does refer to its site in a generalized way, since it features *native* trees. Moreover, once the trees are in place and growing, the work becomes self-referential since the various stainless steel columns either chart each tree's past growth or predict its future growth. We might provisionally conclude that lesser works in each of these categories—gardens, earthworks, and environmental art—are environmental art only in the weak sense that they are in a site; they are not responsive to it. Richer works are in a site, responsive to that site, at times about the site. While gardens, especially those rich in plant material, may do more to get us to *savor* a site and the variety of life it supports, environmental works also prompt heightened awareness of the sites they inhabit.

Just as eighteenth-century gardens performed many of the functions of their sister arts, painting and poetry, so many pieces of environmental art have additional layers of meaning—political messages, allusions to other works of art and to theories of agency and perception. Works like Turrell's *Roden Crater,* Heizer's *Double Negative,* Singer's fragile *Situation Balances,* and Irwin's *Filigreed Line* force us to rethink our place in the landscape, our roles as perceivers, enjoyers, consumers, destroyers. They raise profound metaphysical questions about permanence and change, about human will and agency. Thus these pieces are every bit as serious as the greatest of the early eighteenth-century gardens, and they make their points in much the same way. By inhabiting, addressing, and altering a site, they call into question our relations to landscape, nature, and art.

I began by taking issue with the claim that earthworks and environmental art are architecture's avant-garde. Since gardening is considered by many a branch of landscape architecture, perhaps not all that much turns on whether the works I have been discussing are avant-garde architecture or avant-garde gardens. What does matter is the connections, if any, that link seventeenth- and eighteenth-century gardens with twentieth-century earthworks and environmental art. I have argued that there are indeed important commonalities binding these arts.

My claim comes to this: these twentieth-century works are works of art, like gardens; they address the relation of work to site, like gardens; they can be ideological, like gardens; they can be beautiful, or sublime, like gardens. Overall, they force us to think deeply about nature itself, about our relation to nature, and about nature's relation to art. These deep-seated commonalities between the more ideological of the eighteenth-century gardens and these later works justify tracing a lineage linking one to the other. I have not claimed that the later works were influenced by the gardens that came before. It is not a causal chain I am tracing. Rather, I believe that many of today's environmental works fulfill the same functions as did those early gardens. They fill a space in today's artworld equivalent to that occupied by gardens two-and-a-half centuries ago. Yet they also bring much that is new; the environmental works I have discussed here are for the most part sustained by an entirely different structure of artistry and patronage, ownership and audience, than the grand private gardens of the eighteenth century. Nevertheless, these new works, like their predecessors, offer us signal opportunities to explore and understand our place in, and relation to, nature.

Notes

PREFACE

1. Edward Hyams, *A History of Gardens and Gardening* (New York: Praeger, 1971), 9.

2. *Webster's New International Dictionary,* 3d ed.

3. Bernard Denvir, ed., *The Eighteenth Century: Art, Design, and Society 1689–1789* (London: Longman, 1983), 295.

4. Quoted in *The Genius of the Place: The English Landscape Garden 1620–1820,* ed. John Dixon Hunt and Peter Willis (London: Paul Elek, 1975), 11. In a footnote on page 43 the editors explain that this passage was a manuscript annotation to William Mason's *Satirical Poems.*

CHAPTER I

1. Edward Hyams, *A History of Gardens and Gardening,* (New York: Praeger, 1971), 12.

2. Ibid., 42.

3. Lucy Lippard explores the connections between gardens and prehistory in her book *Overlay: Contemporary Art and the Art of Prehistory* (New York: Pantheon, 1983).

4. Pope's garden at Twickenham and Claremont are two examples of eighteenth-century gardens with bowling greens; Wollaton Hall in Nottinghamshire boasted an elaborate triple-terraced affair. See John Harris, *The Artist and the Country House* (London: Sotheby Parke Bernet, 1979), pl. x.

5. Croquet developed in seventeenth-century France. Badminton, which probably originated in India, wasn't popular in England until the nineteenth century.

6. Hyams (*History of Gardens*) reports that Pharaoh Amenhotep III made a mile-long lake in one of his parks for use in ceremonies and festivities (15).

7. Harris (*Artist and Country House*) notes that Burlington actually commissioned two sets of garden views, one to hang in Burlington House, Piccadilly, the other for Lady Bedingfield, Lord Burlington's sister (158).

8. Ibid., 160.

9. David C. Stuart, *Georgian Gardens* (London: Robert Hale, 1979), 163.

10. Laurence Whistler, Michael Gibbon, and George Clark, *Stowe: A Guide to the Gardens* (1974), 37.

11. See Warwick Wroth, *The London Pleasure Gardens of the 18th Century* (Hamden, CT: Archon Books, 1979).

12. See Perry Miller, *Errand into the Wilderness* (Cambridge: Harvard University Press, 1956).

13. Mara Miller, *The Garden as an Art* (Albany: State University of New York Press, 1993), 15.

14. Ibid., 15. I have been told that Noguchi's courtyard is for viewing only; it cannot be entered. This does not affect my desire to deem it a garden. Miller herself distinguishes between gardens meant to be walked through and those meant to be viewed from the outside and not entered physically. The latter she describes as "composed solely for imaginative entering" (37).

15. Ibid., 15.

16. Ludwig Wittgenstein, *Philosophical Investigations* (Reprint, New York: Macmillan, 1971), secs. 66–67.

17. One might claim that Capability Brown created just such gardens in smoothing and improving many eighteenth-century English estates (see chap. 5).

18. Consider that marvelous product "Meadow in a Can"!

19. Miller, *Garden as an Art*, 76.

20. Ibid.

21. Christopher Hussey, *English Gardens and Landscapes, 1700–1750* (London: Country Life, 1967), 90.

22. In some cases a designer developed entirely new sections of the landscape, in others he altered the gardens of his predecessors.

23. See, for example, papers by Derek Parfit and Bernard Williams in the volume *Personal Identity*, ed. John Perry (Berkeley and Los Angeles: University of California Press, 1975).

24. Wittgenstein, *Philosophical Investigations,* sec. 81.

25. Note that our intuitions about identity are no clearer with regard to art. Consider the *Pietà* after the attack on it by Lazlo Toth, the Cimabue crucifix after the 1966 Italian floods, or a performance of Beethoven's Fifth with a preponderance of wrong notes (Nelson Goodman's famous example). Would we be tempted in any of these cases to declare the original work no longer present? As with the examples of baldness and gardens, different answers must be legislated for different circumstances, bearing in mind our interests in each case and the ramifications each decision might have.

26. George Dickie, "What Is Art? An Institutional Analysis," in *Art and Philosophy,* ed. W. E. Kennick (New York: St. Martin's Press, 1979), 85. For more on Dickie's institutional theory, see below.

27. This criticism follows from Plato's theory of forms. See his criticism of representation in *The Republic,* bk. 10.

28. See Leo Tolstoy, *What Is Art?* (Reprint, Indianapolis: Bobbs Merrill, 1960), chap. 5.

29. Clive Bell would claim the latter two are antithetical traits.

30. For a retelling of this oft-told tale, see Francis Sparshott, *The Theory of the Arts* (Princeton, 1982), 669–70.

31. Maurice Mandelbaum first emphasized the importance of nonexhibited properties in his essay "Family Resemblances and Generalization Concerning the Arts," reprinted in *Aesthetics: A Critical Anthology*, ed. George Dickie, Richard Sclafani, and Ronald Roblin (New York: St. Martin's Press, 1989), 138–51.

32. Dickie, "What Is Art?" 89.

33. Vanda Metzger Bozicevic, "Is There a Definition of Art?"—a paper read to the American Society for Aesthetics in Santa Barbara, October 1993, p. 6.

34. Dickie, "What Is Art?" 88–90.

35. Generally, in order for an object to change in status it must persist for some length of time or be transferred from one culture to another. In the case of an object changing from nonart to art, note that it is not today's pitchforks and Tupperware that we revere, but those of other cultures and other times. Examples do

come to mind where an object's apotheosis is much more rapid. Braun appliances, Italian furniture, and Dansk china all form part of the design collection of the Museum of Modern Art in New York. See Robert Hughes, *The Shock of the New* (New York: Knopf, 1981), 199. It may well be that their creators self-consciously sought to produce objects with a dual status.

36. I don't deny that their designers intended them to be attractive, nor that viewers found them wondrous. The same is true of the quilts discussed earlier. But I think that none of these items was designed as art.

37. From "'Psychological Distance' as a Factor in Art and as an Aesthetic Principle," by Edward Bullough, reprinted in *Aesthetics: A Critical Anthology*, ed. Dickie et al., 320–33.

38. Jerome Stolnitz, *Aesthetics and Art Criticism* (Boston: Houghton Mifflin, 1960), 34–35. See also Stolnitz's history of this notion in his article "Of the Origins of 'Aesthetic Disinterestedness'," *Journal of Aesthetics and Art Criticism* 20 (1961): 131–43.

Monroe Beardsley, who also belongs in this camp, gives a more roundabout definition of aesthetic experience. He states that "To adopt the aesthetic point of view with regard to X is to take an interest in whatever aesthetic value X may possess." Beardsley goes on to define the aesthetic value of an object as "the value it possesses in virtue of its capacity to provide aesthetic gratification." He then explains aesthetic gratification as follows: "Gratification is aesthetic when it is obtained primarily from attention to the formal unity and/or the regional qualities of a complex whole, and when its magnitude is a function of the degree of formal unity and/or the intensity of regional quality." In all, these chained definitions define the aesthetic point of view so that it can only arise from what we would deem distinterested contemplation of a work's formal properties. From Monroe Beardsley, "The Aesthetic Point of View," in *The Aesthetic Point of View: Selected Essays*, ed. Michael J. Wren and Donald M. Callen (Ithaca: Cornell University Press, 1982), 19, 21, 22.

39. J. O. Urmson, "What Makes a Situation Aesthetic?" in *Art and Philosophy*, ed. Kennick, 398.

40. George Dickie, "The Myth of the Aesthetic Attitude," ibid., 444.

41. Ibid., 453.

42. The knowledge in question could be possessed either by the person who makes or selects the work of art or by someone who later promotes an object or event that wasn't art previously (or that was art but interpreted quite differently).

43. In his article "Historical Narratives and the Philosophy of Art" in the *Journal of Aesthetics and Art Criticism* 51 (1993): 313–26, Noel Carroll quotes the following passage from Jeffrey Wieand which makes a similar point: [The artist must be] "asking or answering a question, elaborating on what someone else has done or disagreeing with it, demonstrating that something is possible, and so on" (318). From Wieand's article "Putting Forward a Work of Art," *Journal of Aesthetics and Art Criticism* 41 (1983): 618.

44. Arthur Danto, *The Transfiguration of the Commonplace* (Cambridge: Harvard University Press, 1981), 44.

45. Carroll, "Historical Narratives." Subsequent quotations from this paper will be cited parenthetically in the text.

46. Elsewhere Carroll says "An identifying narrative establishes the art status of a work by connecting the production of the work in question to previously acknowledged artistic practices by means of a historical account" (318).

47. It is important that this opening description is not challenged. Thus the narrative should "begin with some art historical juncture that is recognized by all concerned to be uncontested. . . . An identifying narrative sets the stage . . . by starting with a set of circumstances already known to be artistic" (319).

48. As the foregoing has suggested, I think the elaboration must take the form of providing further description of the social institution that is the artworld and further historical accounts of individual works, artists, traditions, movements, and so on.

49. Of course there are clear-cut differences as well. Observing gardens, we often *contrast* them with

nature, categorizing them according to their degree of art and artificiality. We also think about their designer or maker, and about the work required to maintain them, to hold off nature's encroachments. Some of these responses will be explored in greater depth in chapter 6.

50. Danto, *Transfiguration*, 1–5, 33–44. In fact, Danto explored these themes in earlier papers, "The Artistic Enfranchisement of Real Objects: The Artworld," *Journal of Philosophy* (1964): 571–84, and "The Last Work of Art: Artworks and Real Things," *Theoria* 39 (1973): 1–17. The necktie example appears in the latter paper.

51. Danto, *Transfiguration*, 125, 139.

52. Miller, *Garden as an Art*, 77. Subsequent quotations from this section of Miller's book will be indicated parenthetically in the text.

53. Page 76. Miller hedges this radical claim in the course of her book. In her concluding chapter she states, "If gardens are works of art, as it now seems they are, and if they are sometimes great works of art, they are so in spite of the fact that they do not fit our definitions of art" (178). For Miller, great art "meets four criteria: excellent form, significant human content, enduringness, and adequacy of form to content" (141). She offers one example of a garden that constitutes great art, the Memorial Garden at Cliveden, but her discussion of the various components of great art suggests that she would certainly add other examples to this list, among them Stowe, Daisen-in, and Versailles.

54. This point is emphasized in Tom Leddy's paper "Gardens in an Expanded Field," *British Journal of Aesthetics* 28 (1988): 327–40.

55. "The impact of site is so crucial that it is virtually impossible to get the same effect (including specifically aesthetic effects) in two different gardens, even with identical plantings. . . . Differences in surrounding buildings or vistas contribute distinctive backgrounds that are integral to our overall impression of the garden" (75–76).

56. See Stuart, *Georgian Gardens,* chap. 17, "Kitchen Gardens."

57. Cp. Dickie's claim that "the artworld carries on its business at the level of customary practice" (89).

58. Stanley Cavell ("Aesthetic Problems of Modern Philosophy," in *Must We Mean What We Say?* [New York: Charles Scribner's Sons, 1969], 78–79) gives a marvelous reading of the metaphor "Juliet is the sun" from *Romeo and Juliet.* A bad metaphor, by contrast, would be one which does not permit such a compelling and enlightening explication—for example, "Juliet is the moon" or "Juliet is a stream."

CHAPTER 2

1. Edward Hyams, *A History of Gardens and Gardening* (New York: Praeger, 1971), 99.

2. Ibid., 157.

3. William Howard Adams, *The French Garden 1500–1800* (New York: George Braziller, 1979), 82.

4. Christopher Thacker, *The History of Gardens* (Berkeley and Los Angeles: University of California Press, 1979), 139.

5. Alfred Marie, *Jardins français classiques des 17ᵉ et 18ᵉ siècles* (Paris: Vincent, Fréal, 1949), 1.

6. Thacker, *History of Gardens,* 139–40.

7. F. Hamilton Hazlehurst, *Gardens of Illusion: The Genius of André Le Nostre* (Nashville TN: Vanderbilt University Press, 1989). For example, the construction of a new orangery south of the chateau more than doubled the size of the previous structure together with the creation of a large body of water, the Lac des Suisses, to terminate the southern transverse axis (121 ff.) balanced the features to the north—the Parterre du Nord, Cascade, and Allée d'Eau culminating at the Bassin du Dragon. But the two ends of this axis were brought into even better balance with the creation of the Bassin de Neptune at the northern end. Hazlehurst comments, "One might expect the majestic dimensions of the [Lac des Suisses] to overpower any new garden arrange-

ments in the area north of the chateau that might be undertaken to provide a satisfactory balance along the transverse axis. This possibility was avoided as a result of the differences in the terrain and Le Nostre's splendid additions beyond the Parterre du Nord and Allée d'Eau. The transverse axis on this side of the chateau was extended beyond the Bassin du Dragon to terminate in the Bassin de Neptune. . . . When designing the Bassin de Neptune, Le Nostre obviously wanted to make it harmonize with the rest of the garden. This he achieved by creating the same monumental scale used earlier in the garden layout north of the chateau" (133).

8. Consider Hazlehurst's comments about Le Vau's *envelope.* Completed after Le Vau's death in 1670, this project enlarged and extended the chateau's garden facade. The Parterre en Broderie which had previously occupied the area directly adjacent to the chateau's garden facade did not complement the new structure (78 ff.). Accordingly, Hazlehurst reports, "to replace the Parterre en Broderie, which must have been considered too delicate in scale for the now heavy proportions of Le Vau's new facade, Le Nostre envisaged a water parterre that would combine delicacy with grandeur" (79). Yet that water parterre was in turn replaced by two *miroirs d'eau* of grand scale. Hazlehurst asserts that "By replacing the water parterre with the *miroirs d'eau,* a perfect equilibrium of parts was at last established among all the components decorating the central axis" (136).

9. Hyams, *History of Gardens,* 167.

10. Thacker, *History of Gardens,* 153.

11. Adams, *French Garden,* 88. He is referring to the total at Versailles, Trianon, and Marly combined.

12. Thacker, *History of Gardens,* 154; Hazlehurst, *Gardens of Illusion,* 83.

13. Thacker, *History of Gardens,* 152.

14. Hazlehurst, *Gardens of Illusion,* 105, 117.

15. Ibid., 110–11. Subsequent quotations from this book will be cited parenthetically in the text.

16. By 1684, this parterre was replaced by a much simpler and larger arrangement—the so-called Miroirs d'Eau—whose scale better matched Jules Hardouin-Mansart's reconstruction of Le Vau's garden front.

17. From Hazlehurst, *Gardens of Illusion,* n.40.

18. Hazlehurst explains that the Jardin Bas and Allée Royale were occluded when the vista was viewed from ground level—making it appear that the water parterre gave way immediately to the Grand Canal. Viewers who ascended to the second-floor terrace could see the Allée Royale, but the Jardin Bas remained concealed (136, 83).

19. *Saint-Simon at Versailles,* ed. Lucy Norton (New York: Harper and Bros., 1958), 262.

20. Geoffrey Trease, *The Grand Tour* (London: Holt, Rinehart, and Winston, 1967).

21. B. Sprague Allen, *Tides in English Taste,* vol. 2 (New York: Roman and Littlefield, 1969), 204.

22. Christopher Hibbert, *The Grand Tour* (New York: Putnam, 1969), 25.

23. Ibid., 90.

24. Trease, *Grand Tour,* 150.

25. J. H. Plumb, *Georgian Delights* (Boston: Little, Brown, 1980), 21.

26. Hibbert, *Grand Tour,* 16.

27. Trease quotes his journal entry: "Be Spaniard: girl every day," 174.

28. *Dictionary of National Biography,* suppl. vol. 4.

29. Trease, *Grand Tour,* 5. See also the various complaints compiled by Hibbert on pp. 35–40.

30. Hibbert, *Grand Tour,* 47, 135.

31. Ibid., 53.

32. Plumb, *Georgian Delights,* 23.

33. Christopher Hibbert claims that this is the art which reflects most clearly the influence of the grand tour (239).

34. Ibid., *English Taste,* vol. 1, 29.

35. Allen, 62–63. The reference is to the Villa Capra, nicknamed La Rotonda.

36. Bernard Denvir, *The Eighteenth Century: Art, Design, and Society 1689–1789* (New York: Longman, 1983), 11.

37. The full title of Stuart and Revett's work indicates the eighteenth-century attitude toward classical ruins. The tourist and his tutor would approach each site armed with "a mariner's compass and quadrant, and all things needful to measure the dimensions of the antiquities they would be shown" (Hibbert, *Grand Tour,* 141).

38. Begun in 1738 and 1748, respectively (Allen, *English Taste,* 232).

39. Trease, *Grand Tour,* 145.

40. Allen, *English Taste,* 66.

41. Hibbert, *Grand Tour,* 165.

42. Denvir, *Eighteenth Century,* 8.

43. Ibid.

44. Walpole's was sold by his spendthrift son to Catherine the Great, and the bulk of it remains in Russia today.

45. See Christopher Hussey, *The Picturesque* (London: Putnam, 1927), 27–29.

46. Isabel W. U. Chase, *Horace Walpole, Gardenist* (Princeton: Princeton University Press, 1943), 96.

47. Hussey, *Picturesque,* 126.

48. Malcolm Andrews, *The Search for the Picturesque* (Stanford: Stanford University Press, 1989), 73–74.

49. A "black convex glass used by artists to reflect the landscape in miniature and in doing so, to merge details and reduce the strength of colour so that the artist is presented with a broad picture of the same and a certain tonal unity. . . . Claude Lorrain is credited with the invention of the glass" (*Encyclopaedia Britannica,* 15th ed.,"Micropaedia," vol. 2, s.v. "Claude Lorrain glass").

50. Hussey, *Picturesque,* 28.

51. Chase, *Walpole,* 101.

52. Nikolaus Pevsner, *Academies of Art Past and Present* (Cambridge: Cambridge University Press, 1940), 82–83. Pevsner lists successive confirmations of the Guild's privileges in 1391, 1430, 1548, 1555, 1582, 1622, and 1639.

53. Ibid., 92.

54. Ibid., 87.

55. Ibid., 92.

56. André Fontaine, Preface to *Conférences inédites de l'Académie royale de peinture et de sculpture* (Paris, 1903), xvi.

57. Ibid., xix–xx. In 1655 a new constitution officially separated the Académie from the Maîtrise (xxvi).

58. In 1669 the academicians complained that the monthly lectures were too onerous to prepare and asked that their number be reduced to six per year. Colbert refused to permit this relaxation of the ritual (xxxvi).

59. Quoted by Fontaine (xxxii).

60. André Félibien, Preface to *Conférences de l'Académie royale de peinture et de sculpture de l'année 1667* (Paris, 1669).

61. Louis Hourticq, *De Poussin à Watteau* (Paris, 1921).

62. Fontaine, Preface, xxx.

63. Fontaine notes a loosening in the academy's practice beginning in 1678. It was in that year that the academicians took to rereading old lectures rather than preparing new ones each month (xxxix).

64. Rows of seats were added for the visitors and special places reserved for the academicians (Fontaine, Preface, xiv).

65. For example, see Pevsner, *Academies,* 187–93, 273 ff.

66. See Stephanie Ross, "Painting the Passions: Charles Le Brun's *Conférence sur l'expression,*" *Journal of the History of Ideas* 45: 25–49.

67. Published in 1669.

68. They argued that the Bible told of Rebecca offering water to Abraham's servant and then running to the well a second time to bring water to the camels. This, they claimed, showed that the camels were a considerable distance from the well and thus could be omitted from a painting of its immediate environs (Fontaine, Preface).

69. For example, did Poussin's painting of Christ curing the blind men represent the miracle at Jericho or that at Capernaum, for Christ had twice restored blind men's sight; did the same artist's representation of the Israelites receiving manna from heaven violate the biblical account, since the dew on the ground suggested that manna was falling in the morning, yet the Bible said it fell during the night and the Israelites woke to find it; did Carracci violate the principles of decorum by placing an ox and an ass in his nativity scene and thus detract from the Christ child's glory?

70. Thus Le Brun argued that line is superior because line is independent of color, because line represents what is real and essential, and because line depends only on the intellect. After Le Brun's death the colorists or *Rubénistes* led by Roger de Piles gained ascendancy in the Académie.

71. Pevsner, *Academies,* 125–26.

72. Ibid., 125.

73. One such proposal originated with the Society of Dilettanti, which was founded in 1734; another came from the Society of Artists, who split off in 1761 from the Society for the Encouragement of Arts, Manufactures, and Commerce in Great Britain to begin a series of exhibitions on their own (ibid., 184).

74. Sir Joshua Reynolds, *Discourses on Art,* ed. Robert R. Wark (New Haven: Yale University Press, 1975), Discourse 3 (pp. 44–45).

75. The word "gardenist" was coined by Horace Walpole. Isabel Chase uses it throughout her book *Horace Walpole, Gardenist* (see n. 46). I am using the term to single out the set of garden designers, enthusiasts, and connoisseurs who were so active in promoting the art of gardening in the eighteenth century. I intend the term to exclude garden laborers and others with no aesthetic stake in the gardens they viewed or tended.

76. Alexander Pope mentions the first passage and translates the second in his 1713 *Guardian* essay.

77. Christopher Thacker (*History of Gardens*) claims that this is "the first book in English to deal solely with gardening" (121).

78. As mentioned above, he did establish an Academy of Architecture in 1671, but this institution did not exist to educate young architects. Its members performed such tasks as inspecting historic buildings for damage, developing a distinctively French architectural order, and analyzing the nature of architectural *beauté.* See Ines Murat, *Colbert* (Charlottesville: University Press of Virginia, 1984), 128. The inclusion of landscape architecture within the discipline of architecture is, I suspect, a relatively recent phenomenon. In the seventeenth century, the botanical garden was the source for botanical (and medical!) instruction.

79. *Oxford Companion to Gardens* (Oxford: Oxford University Press, 1986).

80. Ibid.

81. Russell Page, *The Education of a Gardener* (London, 1962. Reprint, New York: Vintage Books, 1985), 16–17.

CHAPTER 3

1. Quoted in *The Genius of the Place: The English Landscape Garden, 1620–1820,* ed. John Dixon Hunt and Peter Willis (London: Paul Elek, 1975), 11.

2. See, for example, Jean H. Hagstrum, *The Sister Arts* (Chicago: University of Chicago Press, 1987), which takes these two passages as epigraphs.

3. *Ben Jonson: The Complete Poems*, ed. George Parfitt (New Haven: Yale University Press, 1975).

4. Hagstrum (*Sister Arts*) argues that Edmund Burke's account of the sublime, with its emphasis on obscurity and on the absence of detail, also contributed to the decline of literary pictorialism, 152–53.

5. Dean Tolle Mace, "*Ut Pictura Poesis:* Dryden, Poussin, and the Parallel of Poetry and Painting in the Seventeenth Century," in *Encounters: Essays on Literature and the Visual Arts*, ed. John Dixon Hunt (New York: W. W. Norton, 1971), 65.

6. Ibid., 59.

7. Commentators also say that the experience is like that of a succession of pictures. I shall discuss this in chapter 5.

8. Ronald Paulson, "The Eighteenth-Century Poetic Garden," *The Listener* 90 (1973), 878.

9. John Dixon Hunt, "Emblem and Expression in the Eighteenth-Century Landscape Garden," *Eighteenth-Century Studies* 4 (1971): 296.

10. Ronald Paulson, *Emblem and Expression: Meaning in English Art of the Eighteenth Century* (London: Thames and Hudson, 1975), 30.

11. Hagstrum, *Sister Arts,* 91.

12. Facsimile edition of *Iconologie,* Jean Baudouin's 1644 translation of Ripa (New York: Garland Publishing, 1976).

13. Elsewhere, Hagstrum notes that "virtues, vices, mental faculties, natural phenomena, countries, provinces, and cities all appeared as visual figures bearing their appropriate insignia" (Ibid., 148).

14. John Dixon Hunt, *The Figure in the Landscape: Poetry, Painting, and Gardening during the Eighteenth Century* (Baltimore: Johns Hopkins University Press, 1976), 71.

15. From a facsimile of the 1709 London edition of Cesare Ripa, *Iconologia; Or Moral Emblems* (New York: Garland Publishing, 1976), 77–78.

16. Ibid., 23–24.

17. I thank William Engel for this point.

18. See Roy Strong, *The Renaissance Garden in England* (London: Thames and Hudson, 1979).

19. Certainly *any* poem, through the spacing, length, and placement of its lines, visually communicates to its reader a sense of balance, measure, and pace. Some poems, however, are visual in a stronger sense. I have in mind a special subset of poems—calligrams or concrete poetry—where the actual shape of the poem on the page creates a symbol that contributes to the poem's overall meaning. Imagine a poem about Christmas whose lines form the silhouette of a fir tree, or a poem about flight whose stanzas coalesce as a bird or a plane. Poems such as these may make little claim to be significant works of art, perhaps because they stray from the central resources and strengths of poetry. But compare E. E. Cummings's poem "l(a," where the phrase "a leaf falls" is typeset vertically, with each pair of letters directly below the previous pair, or the same author's "r-p-o-p-h-e-s-s-a-g-r," where the letters are scrambled several times mid-poem, finally arriving at "grasshopper." The lines do not form silhouettes of falling leaves or leaping insects, but in each case the shape of the poem visually expresses its subject matter. Yet poems that are visual in this sense, where the look of the poem on the page contributes to its meaning, are very rare. In the characterization of poetry that follows, I am *not* trying to include such poems.

20. By appeal to sense and reference, or to accompanying ideas, or to rules for use. This brief sketch of the resources of poetry is meant to be neutral among competing accounts of meaning in natural language.

21. As a Catholic, Pope was prevented by the laws of the time from owning property. Thus he had to lease his estate.

22. I. R. F. Gordon, *A Preface to Pope* (London: Longmans Group, 1976), 101.

23. Note that with poetry, as with painting, young artists learned through imitation of exemplars from antiquity. Just as Pope practiced his poetic craft by translating and imitating the works of Virgil, Homer, Horace, Juvenal, and others, so painters learned by sketching antique sculpture, copying master drawings, and so on. Gardening cannot be learned in a comparable way: the great gardens of antiquity are not extant to serve as models. There are also problems with the very notion of copying another garden. See the discussion of Mara Miller's views on uniqueness in chapter 1, as well as the discussion of academies of gardening in chapter 2.

24. Gordon, *Pope,* 88. Gordon notes that not all Pope's attempts were equally successful.

25. Maynard Mack, *The Garden and the City: Retirement and Politics in the Later Poetry of Pope, 1731–1743* (Toronto: University of Toronto Press, 1969), 27.

26. Ibid., 28.

27. Compare Peter Martin's assessment: "The east-west central strip of Pope's garden, including the Great Walk, groves, bowling green, urns, and two smaller mounts, surrounded by a mixture of regularity and irregularity, illustrates that it was in some respects a transitional garden." Peter Martin, *Pursuing Innocent Pleasures: The Gardening World of Alexander Pope* (Hamden, CT: Archon Books, 1984), 58.

28. Mack, *Garden and City,* 28.

29. Hunt and Willis, *Genius of the Place,* 250.

30. See Naomi Miller, *Heavenly Caves: Reflections on the Garden Grotto* (New York: George Braziller, 1982).

31. Mack, *Garden and City,* 44.

32. Ibid., 37.

33. Ibid.

34. Hunt, *Figure,* 82.

35. "But really only Pope himself could have appreciated the rich associations with friend and topographical location that were offered by each specimen embedded into the grotto walls" (ibid.).

36. Hunt, *Figure,* 85. Elsewhere Hunt suggests that the poet's grotto, with its "variety of rooms" and "its essentially private iconography," acknowledges the "covert equation between the mind's activity and the contexts it visits during a philosophic stroll." See also Hunt, "Emblem and Expression," 306–7.

37. The sixteen worthies together with the inscriptions beneath the busts of each are presented in Edward Brayley and John Britton's guide, *The Beauties of England and Wales* (London, 1801). The sixteen worthies are: Alexander Pope, Sir Thomas Gresham, Inigo Jones, John Milton, William Shakespeare, John Locke, Sir Isaac Newton, Sir Francis Bacon, King Alfred, Edward Prince of Wales, Queen Elizabeth, King William III, Sir Walter Raleigh, Sir Francis Drake, John Hampden, and Sir John Barnard.

38. Hunt, "Emblem and Expression," 299.

39. Ibid., 300.

40. Hunt and Willis, *Genius of the Place,* 33–34.

41. Paulson, *Emblem and Expression,* 23.

42. Hunt and Willis, *Genius of the Place,* 38. Here is one example of an earlier garden program that places nearly unattainable demands on its viewers and interpreters. In his article "The Conundrum of Le Nôtre's *Labyrinthe*" (in *Garden History: Issues, Approaches, Methods,* ed. John Dixon Hunt [Washington: Dumbarton Oaks, 1992]) Michel Conan argues that the Labyrinthe, a bosquet developed at Versailles in the 1660s featuring a maze with thirty-nine fountains illustrating *Aesop's Fables,* is in fact a *carte du Tendre,* or map of sentimental geography like that presented in Mlle de Scudéry's novel *La Clélie.* Conan asserts that visitors to the labyrinth had to use complex mnemonic tricks to find their way through the bosquet and puzzle out the answer to the question "How to become an honest man?" Even consulting the numerous maps and diagrams Conan provides to illustrate his article, it is extremely hard to understand the relationships he maintains hold among various axes and segments of the labyrinth, each devoted to a different moral theme or question of moral conduct ("frailty of the human condition," "quest for glory," "foolishness," "illusion," etc.). It would

seem incredibly hard to even find one's way *out* of the labyrinth, let alone to discover that it "challenges the visitor to find the answer to a riddle that is nowhere expounded. Yet once you know that the Labyrinthe is providing a map of virtues an honest man should strive for and of defects he should flee, the riddle is self-evident" (142). If the Labyrinthe was really meant to function as Conan suggests, this much is sure: Whately would have hated it!

43. Hunt, "Emblem and Expression," 304.

44. Lawrence Whistler, Michael Gibbon, and George Clark, *Stowe: A Guide to the Gardens* (Buckingham: E. N. Hillier and Sons, 1974), 37.

45. Kenneth Woodbridge, *The Stourhead Landscape* (National Trust, 1982), 46.

46. Ibid., 47.

47. Paulson, *Emblem and Expression,* 29.

48. Woodbridge, *Stourhead,* 10.

49. Ibid., 60.

50. Paulson, *Emblem and Expression,* 30.

51. Max F. Schulz, "The Circuit Walk of the 18th-Century Landscape Garden and the Pilgrim's Circuitous Progress," *Eighteenth-Century Studies,* 15 (1981).

52. Ibid., 16.

53. Paulson, *Emblem and Expression,* 30.

54. Kenneth Woodbridge, "Henry Hoare's Paradise," *Art Bulletin* 47 (1965), 99.

55. Lionel Cust, *History of the Society of Dilettanti* (London: Macmillan, 1914), 9.

56. This would of course be easy to claim of many excavations.

57. Daniel F. Mannix, *The Hell Fire Club* (New York: Ballantine Books, 1959), 82.

58. John Plumb, "Secrets of West Wycombe," *House and Garden,* Nov. 1984.

59. Mannix, *Hell Fire Club,* 82.

60. Christopher Thacker, *The History of Gardens,* (Berkeley and Los Angeles: University of California Press, 1979), 204.

61. Mannix, *Hell Fire Club,* 5.

62. Donald McCormick, *The Hell-Fire Club: The Story of the Amorous Knights of Wycombe* (London: Jarrolds, 1958), 119.

63. E. W. Brayley, *The Beauties of England and Wales* (London, 1801), 360.

64. W. J. T. Mitchell, *Against Theory* (Chicago: University of Chicago Press, 1985), 2.

65. Ibid., 81.

66. "We argue that the design or intention of the author is neither available nor desirable as a standard for judging the success of a work of literary art." William K. Wimsatt and Monroe C. Beardsley, "The Intentional Fallacy," in *Philosophy Looks at the Arts,* ed. Joseph Margolis (New York: Charles Scribner's Sons, 1962), 92.

67. Kenneth Woodbridge, *Landscape and Antiquity: Aspects of English Culture at Stourhead, 1718 to 1838* (Oxford: Clarendon Press, 1970), 31–32.

68. Goran Hermeren, *Influence in Art and Literature* (Princeton: Princeton University Press, 1975).

69. A portion of the poem is quoted in Hunt, "Emblem and Expression," 300. The entire eulogy can be found in *Stowe: A Description of the House and Gardens of the Right Honorable Richard, Earl Temple, Viscount and Baron Cobham* (London, 1766). Hunt also cites Gilpin's *Dialogue on the Gardens at Stowe,* 3d ed. (1751).

70. Kimerly Rorschach, *The Early Georgian Landscape Garden* (New Haven: Yale Center for British Art, 1983), 76.

71. Ibid., 78 n.15.

72. James Turner, "The Structure of Henry Hoare's Stourhead," *Art Bulletin* 41 (1979): 68.

73. Ibid., 71–72.

74. Ibid., 70.

75. Ibid., 72.

76. Ibid., 75.

77. "The Grotto lies on the edge of a sheet of calm water at the foot of a thickly wooded hill, an exact counterpart to the harbor and the hanging wood described in the passage from which the first Grotto inscription is taken" (ibid., 74).

78. "Virgil's harbor is thus associated with moral integrity, and this in turn with rural retirement; in the landscape garden these metaphors are restored to concrete reality" (ibid., 76).

79. Ibid., 70, 75. See also n. 45, where Turner speculates that the statue is still at the bottom of the lake and claims to have dived to a depth of six feet in search of it.

80. Ibid., 76.

81. Ibid., 77.

82. Schulz, "Circuit Walk," 10.

83. Ibid., 9.

84. Ibid., 10.

85. Ibid., 16.

86. Ibid., 5.

87. Paulson, *Emblem and Expression,* 9.

88. Malcolm Kelsall, "The Iconography of Stourhead," *Journal of the Warburg and Courtauld Institutes* 46 (1983): 133.

89. One which functioned "to reconcile the Romans to the loss of liberty under the hands of the absolute ruler Augustus, and by showing a wise and religious lawgiver in Aeneas to flatter the Emperor to imitation" (ibid., 135). Kelsall bases this account on the commentaries accompanying the Pitt/Warton translation of the *Aeneid* which appeared in 1753 (135 n.7).

90. Ibid., 137.

91. Ibid.

92. Ibid.

93. "The first image of the garden therefore establishes as its central motifs natural religion and Augustan peace and invites one to consider the relation between the ancients' virtues idealistically portrayed and the virtues of a modern patrician. Such parallelism may be found at Stowe. But at Stourhead the relation between past and present is essentially dialectical" (ibid., 138).

94. Ibid., 139.

95. Ibid., 136.

96. Ibid., 140.

97. Ibid., 141.

98. Ibid., 142.

99. Ibid., 143.

100. In *Studies in Eighteenth-Century Culture,* vol. 11, ed. Harry C. Payne (Madison: University of Wisconsin Press, 1982).

101. Turner, "Sexual Politics," 349.

102. Ibid., 351.

103. Ibid.

104. Ibid., 357.

105. In *Studies in Eighteenth-Century Culture,* vol. 8, ed. Roseann Runte (Madison: University of Wisconsin Press, 1979).

106. Ibid., 117.

107. This accords with the argument of Fabricant's later paper "The Aesthetics and Politics of Landscape in the Eighteenth Century," to the effect that the eighteenth-century emphasis on prospects and lofty views was a way of appropriating the surrounding view. "Prospects, even when . . . not depicted didactically, possessed important ideological and symbolic overtones, due largely to the prospect viewer's lofty position and his consequent relationship to all objects within his scope of vision: a relationship epitomized in Arthur Young's assertion, after mounting a hill near Raby Castle, "You there command the whole." Carole Fabricant, "The Aesthetics and Politics of Landscape in the Eighteenth Century," in *Studies in Eighteenth-Century British Art and Aesthetics*, ed. Ralph Cohen (Berkeley and Los Angeles: University of California Press, 1985), 56.

108. Fabricant, "Binding and Dressing," 120.

109. Ibid., 122.

110. Roy Strong, in his book *The Renaissance Garden in England,* mentions two seventeenth-century gardens created by a most impressive woman, Lucy Harington, Countess of Bedford. Strong describes her as both cultivated and extravagant, in the vanguard of visual taste (120). Her garden at Twickenham Park, laid out in concentric circles, was emblematic of the pre-Copernican universe. See Strong's description (122). Later she created a garden at Moor Park described by Sir William Temple in his essay "Upon the Gardens of Epicurus" (143 ff.).

111. Even if historians were to learn of gardens designed by women in this era, Fabricant's claims would not be overturned should these gardens share the sexist and sexual characteristics she finds so salient at Rousham, Twickenham, and Stowe. That is, if women as well as men designed "sexist" gardens, this might only show that patriarchal conceptions of possession, power, and sexuality pervaded eighteenth-century society. Compare how a present-day feminist might respond upon learning that many of today's women engage in sexual fantasies involving rape and submission.

112. Fabricant, "Binding and Dressing," 126.

113. Nelson Goodman, *Ways of Worldmaking* (Indianapolis: Hackett, 1978), 27.

114. Ibid., 29.

115. Ibid., 35.

116. Richard Wollheim, "Pictorial Style: Two Views," in *The Concept of Style*, ed. Berel Lang (Philadelphia: University of Pennsylvania Press, 1979).

117. Ibid., 129–30.

118. Ibid., 130.

119. Ibid., 134–35.

120. Not just any interests, preferences, and so on, but those connected with the resources of his medium.

121. Wollheim, "Pictorial Style," 138.

122. Ibid., 135.

123. Ibid., 142.

124. "I cannot insist too strongly that what I say about individual style and the pictorial arts cannot simply be transferred to some other art without grave risk of falsehood, and possibly nonsense" (ibid., 131–32).

125. Jenefer Robinson, "General and Individual Style in Literature," *Journal of Aesthetics and Art Criticism* 43 (1984): 147–58.

126. Richard Woodbridge, "The Nomenclature of Style in Garden History," *Eighteenth-Century Life* 8, no. 2 (1983).

127. Strong discusses such Jacobean gardens as Somerset House, Greenwich, and Hatfield House, all designed by Salomon de Caus.

128. Woodbridge, "Nomenclature," 20.

129. Robinson, "General and Individual Style," 148.

130. Ibid.

131. Patrick Goode, *The Oxford Companion to Gardens* (Oxford: Oxford University Press, 1986), 454.

CHAPTER 4

1. Norman and Beryl Kitz, *Painshill Park* (London: Whittet Books, 1984), 17. Subsequent references to this work will be acknowledged parenthetically in the text.

2. Hamilton owed ten thousand pounds to another childhood friend, Lord Holland, who called in the debt when his own financial position worsened. Norman and Beryl Kitz detail Hamilton's financial difficulties as follows. Two sources of income—his positions as receiver general of His Majesty's revenues in Minorca from 1747 to 1756 and as deputy at the pay office to Paymaster General Henry Fox (Lord Holland) from 1758 to 1765—disappeared owing to military and political goings-on. See Kitz and Kitz, *Painshill*, 24, 45, 55–59, 85–86. And as the youngest son in a family of fourteen children, Hamilton lacked an independent income adequate to finance his garden ambitions. Accordingly, Painshill was put up for sale.

3. I am not using the term "painterly" in Heinrich Wölfflin's sense. In his book *Principles of Art History* (New York: Dover, 1950), he characterized Renaissance and Baroque paintings as linear and painterly, respectively. He explained painterly works as those by artists who see "in patches instead of lines" (11). I am not using the term "painterly" to indicate anything about patches, clumps, or the lack of fine detail. Rather, I deem painterly those gardens in which visual values predominate. Such gardens do not offer scenes merely as a means to achieve some denotative meaning.

4. Michael Symes, in a leaflet published by the Painshill Park Trust and distributed to garden visitors. And elsewhere, Symes writes that "Painshill is an associative garden, not a literary or allegorical one. There is nothing comparable to the specific literary references at The Leasowes, with its inscriptions and texts, to the emblematic and political groupings at Stowe, or to the Aenean Progress at Stourhead." "Nature As the Bride of Art: The Design and Structure of Painshill," *Eighteenth-Century Life* 8, no. 2 (1983): 67.

5. The venture was not a great financial success, nor was his later attempt at making tile and brick from clay excavated on the estate. Kitz and Kitz, *Painshill*, 35, 87.

6. "Julius Caesar, Augustus, Brutus, Caligula, Trajan, Geta, Hadrian, Lucius Verus, Dartinae, Albinus, Commodus, and Septimius Severus" (ibid., 67).

7. These included a Greek statue of Minerva, a Roman statue of Flora, and seventeen antique busts (ibid., 70).

8. Ibid., 13, 15. The Kitzes report that "Hamilton wanted to be able to paint in order to capture on canvas his visions of idealised landscape; he wanted to do this not as an end in itself but as a first step towards bringing those landscapes to life" (13). This claim does, however, seem both extravagant and unsupported.

9. In an appendix to their monograph, the Kitzes discuss Hamilton's collection of paintings. They state that he owned about 150 pictures (122). Nearly half the collection was put up for sale in 1773. The Kitzes argue that eighty entries in the Langford's auction catalog for March 11 and 12, 1773, came from Hamilton's collection; at least thirty-four of these were landscape scenes. Paintings retained by Hamilton were later listed in an inventory of his house in Bath. Of the eighty-eight paintings listed, fourteen are explicitly labeled landscapes, and eleven others are described as views of Painshill (125–27).

10. Ibid., 53.

11. "You have a view of a most elegant Gothic Temple. . . . Through it, as a vista, you command a charming lake of several acres which lies far under it in a valley. On a hill beyond it, beautifully clumped with old forest trees, a Hermitage, a Tower, a Doric Temple and a turkish Tent contend which shall please the beholder most" (Ibid., 76).

12. Thomas Whately, *Observations on Modern Gardening* (London, 1771), 185–86.

13. Kitz and Kitz, *Painshill,* 115.

14. Reported by Joseph Spence (*Anecdotes,* vol. 1, 252, sec. 606). The reference comes from "The Genesis of the English Landscape Garden," by S. Lang, in *The Picturesque Garden and Its Influence outside the British Isles,* ed. Nikolaus Pevsner (Washington: Dumbarton Oaks, 1974), 9.

15. *The Spectator,* ed. Donald F. Bond (Oxford: Clarendon Press, 1965), 414.

16. Quoted by Christopher Hussey in *The Picturesque* (London: Putnam, 1927), 128. Lang comments that the remark "was first reported by Uvedale Price and is probably apocryphal" (24).

17. "Gardening is entitled to a place of considerable rank among the liberal arts. It is as superior to land-skip painting as a reality to a representation" (Whately, *Observations,* 1).

18. Horace Walpole, *History of the Modern Taste in Gardening* (reprinted in The English Landscape Series, ed. John Dixon Hunt [New York and London: Garland, 1982]), 261.

19. Hussey, *Picturesque,* 128.

20. These were mentioned in the opening chapter. Views of the gardens at Chiswick were also painted by Jacques Rigaud in 1733, George Lambert in 1742, and John Donowell in 1753.

21. This too could be done in different ways. A painter could paint an actual scene, then embellish her *painted* landscape with a garden not present in the original. Or, she could paint a scene that was entirely imaginary, both garden and setting.

22. Ronald Paulson, *Emblem and Expression: Meaning in English Art of the 18th-Century* (London: Thames and Hudson, 1975), 19.

23. John Dixon Hunt and Peter Willis, eds., *The Genius of the Place: The English Landscape Garden, 1620–1820* (London: Paul Elek, 1975), 15. Hunt and Willis go on to downplay the influence of paintings.

24. Kenneth Woodbridge, *The Stourhead Landscape* (London: National Trust, 1982), 20.

25. Ibid., 25.

26. Geoffrey and Susan Jellicoe, Patrick Goode, and Michael Lancaster, eds., *The Oxford Companion to Gardens* (Oxford: Oxford University Press, 1986), 170.

27. Christopher Thacker, *The History of Gardens* (Berkeley and Los Angeles: University of California Press, 1979), 197.

28. H. F. Clark, *The English Landscape Garden* (Gloucester: Alan Sutton, 1980), 56.

29. *Oxford Companion,* 69. Clark makes a similar claim and illustrates it with a photograph (pl. 55) from *Country Life.*

30. Hussey, *Picturesque,* 130.

31. Walpole, *Modern Taste in Gardening,* 270.

32. Nelson Goodman makes this point emphatically. See *Languages of Art* (Indianapolis: Bobbs-Merrill, 1968), 4.

33. "An aspect is not just the object-from-a-given-distance-and-angle-and-in-a-given-light; it is the object as we look upon or conceive it, a version or construal of the object" (ibid., 9).

34. Ibid.

35. "Model," as opposed to "replica," carries the suggestion of differences in scale. Surely there are limits to cross-modal copying. In what media might one copy a gesture, an event, an attitude?

36. The relation in the other direction does not seem particularly problematic. A painting which copies a given garden depicts or portrays it. That is, for paintings (but not for gardens) the function "copy" is subsumed under the function "represent," although a painting could represent a scene or event without copying it.

37. See my paper "Art and Allusion," *Journal of Aesthetics and Art Criticism* 40 (1981): 59–70.

38. Jean Lipman and Richard Marshall, *Art about Art* (New York: E. P. Dutton in association with the Whitney Museum of American Art, 1978), 92.

39. The reference is to the theory of meaning developed in a series of papers by H. P. Grice beginning in 1957. These include "Meaning" (*Philosophical Review* 66 [1957], 377–88), "Utter's Meaning and Intention" (*Philosophical Review* 78 [1969], 147–77), and "Logic and Conversation" (*Syntax and Semantics*, vol. 3, ed. Peter Cole and Jerry L. Morgan [New York: Academic Press, 1975], 41–58).

40. Cf. Nelson Goodman's comments in "The Status of Style" (in *Ways of Worldmaking* [Indianapolis: Hackett, 1978]) to the effect that many different aspects of a work—its form, its subject, its message, its tone—can contribute to its style. Also compare Goran Hermeren's account of allusion: "In my earlier treatment of the notion of allusion, I have argued that it is possible to obtain a series of more or less strong concepts of allusion by combining the following conditions in different ways: (a) the artist who created X . . . intended to make beholders think of Y . . . (b) as a matter of fact, beholders contemplating X make associations with Y; and (c) the beholders recognize that this was what the artist wanted them to do" (*Influence in Art and Literature* [Princeton: Princeton University Press, 1975], 77).

41. Peter Kivy, *Sound and Semblance: Reflections on Musical Representation* (Princeton: Princeton University Press, 1984), 36, 40, 44, 68.

42. Roy Strong, *The Renaissance Garden in England* (London: Thames and Hudson, 1979), 116.

43. These examples are indebted to Anthony Savile's discussion, in *Aesthetic Reconstructions,* of paintings whose content might change in preplanned ways as their constituent pigments altered.

44. By Claude Gintz and Stephen Bann, respectively. See Claude Gintz, "Neoclassical Rearmament," *Art in America,* Feb. 1987, 111–17, and Stephen Bann, "A Description of Stonypath," *Journal of Garden History* 1, no. 2 (1981): 113–44.

45. Gintz, "Neoclassical Rearmament," 111.

46. The exhibit traveled to Glasgow, southern England, the Netherlands, and Belgium. See Bann, "Stonypath," 122.

47. E. H. Gombrich writes of "the road into the unknown that would enable [Cézanne] to 'redo Poussin from nature' through exploring alternative methods for suggesting a solid organizing world" (*Art and Illusion* [Princeton: Princeton University Press, 1969], 312).

48. Bann, "Stonypath," 132.

49. Gintz, "Neoclassical Rearmament," 112.

50. These are documented in the exhibition catalog, "Nature Over Again after Poussin: Some Discovered Landscapes" (University of Strathclyde, 1980).

51. Bann, "Stonypath," 122.

52. Whether a landscape artist's style or his entire oeuvre is picked out by Finlay's constructs is a rather artificial question, since the style can only be seen *in* the oeuvre, where it is realized or manifested. Moreover, it would be difficult to arrange a section of a garden so as to definitively refer to the landscapes of Claude yet not refer to the work of landscape artists like Richard Wilson who were deeply influenced by him. But in the cases under discussion, the addition of an inscribed signature disambiguates the reference and allows the garden/photo pair to refer unquestionably to a given artist and his oeuvre.

53. Thacker, *History of Gardens,* 187.

54. Derek Clifford, *A History of Garden Design* (New York: Praeger, 1966), 136.

55. Edward Hyams, *A History of Gardens and Gardening* (New York: Praeger, 1971), 238. Hyams goes on to claim, "There was no more question among the new English garden artists of copying French, Dutch or Italian paintings than there had been among Japanese garden artists of reproducing particular landscape paintings by Sung masters."

56. *Oxford Companion,* 310. Miss Stroud notes that Kent edited two volumes of *Designs of Inigo Jones, with Some Additional Designs,* published in 1727. Here again we have the sort of evidence needed to build a case about influence and intention.

57. Kenneth Woodbridge, "The Nomenclature of Style in Garden History," *Eighteenth-Century Life* 8, no. 2 (1983) [special issue, "British and American Gardens"], 22.

58. Symes ("Nature As the Bride of Art," 68–69) argues that it would be understandable if Hamilton, in creating his garden, "had tried to include some elements that suggested or embodied those qualities and characteristics that he absorbed while in Italy, in terms both of landscape and the use of buildings within a landscape. He may well have used the techniques of perspective and distancing to be found in landscape painting (but also in architecture and theatrical scenery)." In the end Symes endorses George Mason's reminder that Hamilton was "*previously* a gardener" before studying painting.

59. S. Lang, "Genesis of the English Landscape Garden," 3.

60. "The true progenitor of the landscape garden of its first and second phase was stage design and its written emanations, evolving from Vitruvius and particularly from the Renaissance tradition" (ibid., 29).

61. Malcolm Kelsall, "The Iconography of Stourhead," *Journal of the Warburg and Courtauld Institutes* 46 (1983): 137.

62. In *Art, Perception, and Reality*, ed. E. H. Gombich, Julian Hochberg, and Max Black (Baltimore: Johns Hopkins University Press, 1972), 95–130. Black's paper was delivered as part of the Thalheimer Lectures sponsored by the Johns Hopkins Philosophy Department in 1970.

63. See n. 81 below.

64. Gibson defines a faithful picture as "a delimited surface so processed that it yield[s] a sheaf of light-rays to a given point which is the same as would be the sheaf of rays from the original scene to a given point." From "A Theory of Pictorial Projection," quoted in Gibson's later paper, "The Information Available in Pictures," *Leonardo* 4 (1971): 28. Gibson expands upon his definition as follows: "That is, when the adjacent order of the points of color in the cross-section of one correspond[s] to the adjacent order in the cross-section of the other."

65. This theory emphasizes the *information* conveyed by light—the invariants of the optic array—rather than the bare "sheaf of light rays" mentioned above.

66. Irwin Rock, *Perception* (New York: Scientific American Books, 1984), 71.

67. M. H. Pirenne points out that many of the principles of natural perspective are defended in Euclid's *Optics,* though Euclid thought that straight visual rays were *emitted* by our eyes. See *Optics, Painting, and Photography* (Cambridge: Cambridge University Press, 1970), 61. Descartes endorsed a similar claim. Pirenne distinguishes natural perspective—the study of the visual angles objects subtend at the eye—from linear perspective—the pattern of lines given by the central projection of objects on a surface. He concludes that "Natural perspective is therefore more general in scope than linear perspective since each different surface gives a different section of the same pyramid of sight" 56–57.

68. Ibid., 77.

69. In fact the stereoscope, which allows for the viewing of strikingly realistic three-dimensional drawings or photos, operates on just this principle. The device isolates each eye and feeds a slightly different image to each. This creates the illusion of depth.

70. Ibid., 166.

71. Rock, *Perception,* 99.

72. Ralph Norman Haber, "Perceiving Space from Pictures: A Theoretical Analysis," in *The Perception of Pictures*, ed. Margaret A. Hagen (New York: Academic Press, 1980), 10.

73. Pirenne, *Optics,* 1.

74. Rock, *Perception,* 15ff. R. L. Gregory, in *Eye and Brain: The Psychology of Seeing* (New York: McGraw Hill, 1974), attributes this experiment to Scheiner. See p. 45.

75. Pirenne, *Optics,* 10, 44.

76. The supposition that we ourselves see, or some part of us sees, our retinal images seems to commit us

to a homuncular explanation of vision—one that posits a little person viewing the sights inside our head. Daniel Dennett somewhat playfully suggests that we posit a set of increasingly stupid homunculi and thereby discharge the intentional idiom.

77. *Perception,* 99.

78. Since many items that resemble one another to a high degree—for example, two 1949 pennies, or any pair of identical twins—do not represent each other: resemblance is not sufficient for representation. And, since our experience of paintings is so different from our experience of the scenes they depict (recall the many arguments rehearsed above), resemblance is not *necessary* for representation.

79. See *Languages of Art,* sec. 4, "The Theory of Notation"; also Kendall Walton, *Mimesis and Make-Believe: On the Foundations of the Representational Arts* (Cambridge: Harvard University Press, 1990), 298–99.

80. Goodman, *Languages of Art,* 36–37, 38.

81. Dominic Lopes, in his book *Understanding Pictures* (Oxford: Oxford University Press, 1996), warns that Goodman's theory of depiction should not be classified as conventionalist; this label wrongly implies that the associations between scenes and the symbols that represent them are wholly arbitrary. Lopes instead champions a compatibilist view on which linguistic models of depiction "do not rule out the possibility that pictures can be explained perceptually" (56). Entrenchment is a crucial notion for Goodman. Lopes maintains that just which symbol systems can and do become entrenched might depend, at least in part, on perceptual facts: "Nothing in the symbol model rules out pictures being correlated with and standing for their subjects because they resemble them, or provide for illusionistic experiences of them, or enable us to see things in them. . . . A theory of perception may, without inconsistency, explain pictures as both symbolic and perceptual" (57). I concur and suggest it would be less misleading to call Goodman's a semiotic or symbolic theory than a conventionalist one.

82. Goodman, *Languages of Art,* 35.

83. Richard Wollheim, *Art and Its Objects,* 2d ed. (Cambridge: Cambridge University Press, 1980), 151.

84. The first experiment with inverted retinal images was devised by the American psychologist G. M. Stratton. Later investigators extended Stratton's work, employing binocular inverted vision (Stratton had worn an inverting lens on one eye and kept the other eye covered) and vision displaced or rotated through prisms. A brief history of inverted image research is given by R. L. Gregory in his book *Eye and Brain: The Psychology of Seeing* (New York: McGraw-Hill, 1974), 204–10. Gregory reports that there remains some controversy regarding the degree of adaptation that occurs with inverted vision, for "the learning [may have] consisted of a series of specific adaptations overlying the original perception, rather than a reorganisation of the original perceptual system" (208).

85. Kendall Walton, *Mimesis as Make-Believe* (Cambridge: Harvard University Press, 1987), 299.

86. Goodman's account of representation ignores this point because Goodman discounts the visual experiences that representations cause us to have; he also overlooks other features of our intercourse with pictures. I have in mind capacities like the one Flint Schier calls "natural generativity." This is the ability of a person who has had some initial familiarity with a system of representation to go on to recognize novel pictures provided only that he or she could recognize the depicted objects in real life. (Clearly this is a pictorial version of Chomsky's linguistic competence.) Schier argues that "Natural generativity is what makes a symbol [system] iconic" (Flint Schier, *Deeper into Pictures: An Essay on Pictorial Representation* (Cambridge: Cambridge University Press, 1986), 43. The existence of such pictorial capacities and skills suggests that both our fluency with pictures and our ability to internalize the pictorial conventions current in our society depend on features and limits of human vision.

87. Gombrich, *Art and Illusion,* 313.

88. Ibid., 243.

89. "Seeing-in is a distinct kind of perception, and it is triggered off by the presence within the field of vision

of a differentiated surface. Not all differentiated surfaces will have this effect, but . . . when the surface is right, then an experience with a certain phenomenology will occur, and it is this phenomenology that is distinctive about seeing-in" (Richard Wollheim, *Painting as an Art* [Princeton: Princeton University Press, 1987], 46).

The famous quotation from Leonardo about looking at damp, stained walls goes as follows: "You should look at certain walls stained with damp, or at stones of uneven colour. If you have to invent some backgrounds you will be able to see in these the likeness of divine landscapes, adorned with mountains, ruins, rocks, woods, great plains, hills and valleys in great variety; and then again you will see there battles and strange figures in violent action, expressions of faces and clothes and an infinity of things which you will be able to reduce to their complete and proper form." Quoted in *Perceiving Artworks,* ed. John Fisher (Philadelphia: Temple University Press, 1980), 87.

90. "The two things that happen when I look at, for instance, the stained wall are, it must be stressed, two aspects of a single experience that I have, and the two aspects are distinguishable but also inseparable. They are two aspects of a single experience, they are not two experiences. They are neither two separate simultaneous experiences, which I somehow hold in the mind at once, nor two separate alternating experiences, between which I oscillate—though it is true that each aspect of the single experience is capable of being described as analogous to a separate experience." Wollheim, *Painting as an Art,* 46.

91. Ibid., 48.

92. Walton, *Mimesis,* 303. Walton elaborates on his claim as follows: "A game of pirates in which to crawl through a tunnel or to eat a watermelon is fictionally to climb a mast is unlikely to be at all rich or vivid." The "[visual] *vivacity*" of a game is defined as "the vivacity with which the participant imagines performing the visual actions which fictionally he performs" (296).

93. Ibid., 60.

94. Stanley Cavell, "Aesthetic Problems of Modern Philosophy" in *Must We Mean What We Say?* (New York: Charles Scribner's Sons, 1969), 78–79. As Cavell notes, it also shows her supreme among women, since "the moon, which other lovers use as emblems of their love, is merely her reflected light, and dead in comparison."

95. Gibson sets the stage by insisting that resemblance plays *some* role in pictorial representation; at the very least, pictures are experienced by us as resembling their subjects in certain respects. (This supports the supposition that perceiving pictures recruits some of the same perceptual mechanisms that we use to visually identify objects in the real world.) Goodman points out the possibility of competing systems of representation; it follows that judgments of realism might be due at least in part to our fluency in particular systems. Gombrich acknowledges the interactions of perceptual mechanism and cultural practice. His theory alerts us to complex ways in which the present practice of representation depends on both the history of art and the facts of human vision. Wollheim emphasizes the importance of twofoldness. With almost all pictures, we can be simultaneously aware of both the formal pattern or array and the object or scene represented. And finally, Walton highlights the spectator's imaginative response. Viewers need neither believe nor pretend that they are seeing the actual objects represented; rather, knowing they are viewing a representation, they work to identify what it is a representation of, using both their cognitive and imaginative faculties.

96. Of course, gardens might mirror other genres besides that of landscape painting. But if, for example, a garden were to function like a Dutch still life with a moral message, or like a portrait or conversation piece characterizing its owners, it would work much like the highly compressed and allusive emblematic gardens discussed in chapter 3.

97. Maggie Keswick, *The Chinese Garden: History, Art, and Architecture* (New York: Rizzoli, 1978), 34.

98. Cf. Keswick in *The Oxford Companion:* "The legendary Chinese Immortals were thought to live partly in the Western Mountains and partly on movable islands in the Eastern Sea which, like the Immortals themselves, dissolved into mist as human travelers approached" (112).

99. Thacker, *History of Gardens,* 45.

100. Ibid., 47.

101. Keswick, *Chinese Garden,* 37–38.

102. For some aesthetic effects of this agricultural revolution, see John Barrell's *The Idea of Landscape and the Sense of Place, 1730–1840: An Approach to the Poetry of John Clare* (Cambridge: Cambridge University Press, 1972).

CHAPTER 5

1. Walpole did not mention Rosa in his description of the hanging wood. Discussing Whately's distinction among different types of gardens (gardens, parks, farms, and ridings), Walpole remarks, "The third I think he has not enough distinguished. I mean that kind of alpine scene, composed almost wholly of pines and firs, a few birch, and such trees as assimilate with a savage and mountainous country. Mr. Charles Hamilton, at Pain's-hill, in my opinion has given a perfect example of this mode in the utmost boundary of his garden. All is great and foreign and rude; the walks seem not designed, but cut through the wood of pines; and the style of the whole is so grand, and conducted with so serious an air of wild and uncultivated extent, that when you look down on this seeming forest, you are amazed to find it contains a very few acres" (Horace Walpole, *The History of the Modern Taste in Gardening* [1770]. Reprint [New York and London: Garland, 1982], 274–75).

Whately himself described this section of Painshill in similar fashion: a spot "of the most uncultivated nature; not dreary, not romantic, but rude; it is a wood, which overspreads a large tract of very uneven ground; the glades through it are just cleared of the bushes and plants, which are natural to the soil; sometimes they are clothed on both sides with thickets; at other times they are only cut through the fern in openings; and even the larches, and the firs, which are mixed with beech on the side of the principal glade, are left in such a state of apparent neglect, that they seem to be the product of the wild, not decorations of the walk; this is the hanging wood" (Thomas Whately, *Observations on Modern Gardening* [1770]. Reprint [New York and London: Garland], 105).

2. Christopher Hussey speculates that Vanbrugh advised the elder Duncombe on the choice of a site, although the actual architect for the house was a local amateur, William Wakefield. See Christopher Hussey, *English Gardens and Landscapes 1700–1750* (London, 1967), 141.

3. Although Aislabie didn't formally acquire the abbey until 1768, Hussey writes that "the direct inspiration of the Rievaulx conception was no doubt the role assigned to Fountains Abbey in the scenery of Studley Royal" (ibid., 145).

4. Christopher Hussey, *The Picturesque* (London: Putnam, 1927), 17.

5. David Watkin, *The English Vision: The Picturesque in Architecture, Landscape, and Garden Design* (London: John Murray, 1982), vii.

6. William Gilpin, *An Essay on Prints* (London, 1781), xii.

7. John Dixon Hunt and Peter Willis, eds., *The Genius of the Place: The English Garden, 1620–1820* (London: Paul Elek, 1975), 337.

8. Malcolm Andrews, *The Search for the Picturesque: Landscape Aesthetics and Tourism in Britain, 1760–1800* (Stanford: Stanford University Press, 1989), 251. Subsequent references to this book will be cited parenthetically in the text.

9. This in turn helped displace the more cerebral and hitherto more respected genre of history painting.

10. See the much more detailed structural analysis of Claudean composition offered by John Barrell in *The Idea of Landscape and the Sense of Place 1730–1840: An Approach to the Poetry of John Clare* (Cambridge: Cambridge University Press, 1972), 47, and discussed below. Andrews also notes that William Gilpin criticized

these Claudean conventions but concludes that "Even so, Gilpin's structural conventions in landscape painting more often than not seem dependent on Claude's example (31).

11. Hussey, *Picturesque*, 68.

12. Nikolaus Pevsner, "Richard Payne Knight" in *Studies in Art, Architecture, and Design*, vol. 1 (New York: Walker & Co., 1968), 11, 13.

13. Marcia Allentuck, "Price and the Picturesque Garden," in *The Picturesque Garden and Its Influence Outside the British Isles*, ed. Nikolaus Pevsner (Washington: Dumbarton Oaks, 1974), 63.

14. Pevsner, "Richard Payne Knight," 18. Comparing *The Landscape* to Price's *Essay*, Pevsner concludes that Price "had thought far more on aesthetic theory than Knight." I disagree with this assessment.

15. Michael Clarke and Nicholas Penny, *The Arrogant Connoisseur: Richard Payne Knight, 1751–1824* (Manchester University Press, 1982), 9.

16. Allentuck, "Price," 59.

17. Hussey, *Picturesque*, 69.

18. Uvedale Price, *An Essay on the Picturesque,* (London, 1794). All further references to Price are from this edition and will be indicated parenthetically in the text. In what follows I shall continue to use the term "improving," as Price did, to refer to the art of landscape design.

19. Edward Hyams, *Capability Brown and Humphry Repton* (New York: Charles Scribner's Sons, 1971), 109. Hyams goes on to remark "It would have been a very considerable achievement for a landscape painter to have completed one hundred and twenty landscape paintings, all of them notable works of art, in a lifetime of painting. To have left behind for posterity as many or more landscape pictures, done not with paint or canvas but with nature's own materials on the face of England, is a staggering achievement and one which has never been equalled" (109).

20. Dorothy Stroud, *Oxford Companion to Gardens* (Oxford: Oxford University Press, 1986), 76.

21. Edmund Burke, *A Philosophical Inquiry into the Origins of Our Ideas of the Sublime and Beautiful* (Notre Dame: University of Notre Dame Press, 1968), pt. 1, sec. 7, p. 39. Subsequent references to this work will be indicated parenthetically in the text.

22. Ibid., pt. 2, 57–87, passim.

23. Burke says of sympathy that "It is by this principle chiefly that poetry, painting, and other affecting arts, transfuse their passions from one breast to another, and are often capable of grafting a delight on wretchedness, misery, and death itself" (44). Later, discussing imitation, he states, "Herein it is that painting and many other agreeable arts have laid one of the principal foundations of their power" (49).

24. "I likewise distinguish love, by which I mean that satisfaction which arises to the mind upon contemplating any thing beautiful, of whatsoever nature it may be, from desire or lust; which is an energy of the mind, that hurries us on to the possession of certain objects, that do not affect us as they are beautiful, but by means altogether different" (91).

25. He speaks of Burke as "a great master," and of the *Inquiry* as "that original work" (39).

26. "I felt that there were numberless objects which give great delight to the eye, and yet differ as widely from the beautiful as from the sublime" (Price, *Essay,* 39).

27. Price read Gilpin's *Essay on Picturesque Beauty* while working on his own *Essay,* and addressed a number of footnotes to points on which he and Gilpin disagreed. He is emphatic in his claim that "there is nothing more ill-judged, or more likely to create confusion (if we agree with Mr. Burke in his idea of beauty) than the joining of it to the picturesque, and calling the character by the title Picturesque Beauty" (42).

28. "I wish a more liberal and extended idea of improvement to prevail; that instead of the narrow mechanical practice of a few English gardeners, the noble and varied works of the eminent painters of every age and of every country, and those of their supreme mistress, Nature, should be the great models of imitation" (275).

Of course there is a danger that these two models—art and nature—could pull in different directions. But Price's remarks belong to a tradition dating back at least to Aristotle. Recall his advice to dramatists in the *Poetics* about tragic plot and character. The exhortation to imitate nature, but only nature at her most ideal, was codified in Alexander Pope's *Essay on Criticism:* "First follow Nature, and your judgment frame / by her just standard, which is still the same. . . . Those rules of old discovered, not devised, / Are Nature still, but Nature methodized."

29. See, for example, F. H. Hazlehurst's *Gardens of Illusion: The Genius of André Le Nostre,* or Horace Walpole's comments on the gardening of Alexander Pope.

30. Richard Payne Knight, *An Analytic Inquiry into the Principles of Taste* (London, 1805), 207. Further references to Knight are from this edition and will be indicated parenthetically in the text.

31. "Reason, in the strict sense of the word, has little or nothing to do with taste; for taste depends upon feeling and sentiment, and not upon demonstration or argument" (259).

32. Knight elaborates this thought as follows: "Nor are the gratifications, which such persons receive from these arts limited to their mere productions, but extended to every object in nature or circumstance in society, that is at all connected with them: for, by such connection, it will be enabled to excite similar or associated trains of ideas, in minds so enriched, and consequently to afford them similar pleasures" (146).

33. Later, in a different context, he claims that if we cast a plum pudding in the mold of a beloved's features, we won't find the result beautiful. This is offered as evidence that our response is due as much to the mind that feels it as to the properties the person displays (185).

34. In fact, in the opening passage of his chapter on imagination, he writes of intoxication, lunacy, and melancholy disposition as mere "excesses" of association.

35. To confirm this point, consult the travel literature of the time, which made frequent use of this shorthand in describing natural scenes. This is discussed in *The Picturesque*, by Christopher Hussey and in *Horace Walpole: Gardenist*, by Isabel W. U. Chase (Princeton: Princeton University Press, 1943).

36. Other associationists were aware of this problem. For example, Archibald Alison, in his *Essay on the Nature and Principles of Taste* (1790), acknowledges great variation in people's judgments of the beautiful and the sublime but insists that an aesthetic response is characterized by emotional unity. The leading emotion which triggers and unifies the response places *some* constraints on the extent of association. See Peter Kivy's discussion of Alison in *The Seventh Sense* (New York: B. Franklin, 1976), chap. 11. I thank Peter Kivy and Dabney Townsend for help on this point.

37. Price, quoted in Hussey, *Picturesque,* 73.

38. "Sensual pleasure arising from viewing objects and compositions, which we call picturesque, may be felt equally by all mankind in proportion to the correctness and sensibility of their organs of sight; for it is wholly independent of their being picturesque, or *after the manner of painters*" (152).

39. He goes on to add that "all change not so violent as to produce a degree of irritation in the organs absolutely painful is pleasing" (426).

40. "Indeed, in all matters of taste and criticism, general rules appear to me to be, like general theories in government and politics, never safe but where they are useless" (232).

41. Hyams, *Brown and Repton,* 119–20.

42. Stroud, in *The Oxford Companion to Gardens,* p. 467.

43. Laurence Fleming and Alan Gore, *The English Garden* (London: Michael Joseph, 1979), 149.

44. Stroud, *Oxford Companion.*

45. Hyams, who calls such wooded hills Repton's signature (133), quotes the passage from Repton about this technique: "In recommending that the hills should be planted, I do not mean that the summits only should be planted by a patch or clump; the woods of the valley should on the contrary seem to climb the hills by such connecting lines as may neither appear meagre nor artificial" (132).

46. Christopher Thacker, *The History of Gardens* (Berkeley and Los Angeles: University of California Press, 1979), 227.

47. Dorothy Stroud deems Hafod, laid out by Knight's cousin Thomas Johnes, the "most truly picturesque creation" (*Oxford Companion*, 170). She also mentions Fonthill Abbey and Mount Edgecumbe. Price's and Knight's own estates of course deserve mention in this regard. See below, n. 59.

48. Humphry Repton, "A Letter to Sir Uvedale Price, Esq.," reprinted as a footnote to the Appendix of Repton's *Sketches and Hints on Landscape Gardening* (London, 1794). Subsequent references to both works, the "Letter" and *Sketches and Hints,* will be indicated parenthetically in the text.

49. Uvedale Price, *Letter to H. Repton, Esq., on the Application of the Practice As Well As the Principles of Landscape-Painting to Landscape-Gardening,* in *Sir Uvedale Price on the Picturesque,* ed. Sir Thomas Dick Lauder (London, 1842), 119–20. Subsequent references to Price's *Letter* will be indicated parenthetically in the text.

50. He goes on to explain: "Whoever has examined with attention the landscapes of eminent painters, must have observed how much art and study they have employed, in contriving that all the objects should have a mutual relation—that nothing should be detached in such a manner as to appear totally insulated and unconnected" (180).

51. The Wye became famous for a scenic tour leading from Ross-on-Wye to Chepstow and culminating in a view of Tintern Abbey, made famous in Wordworth's poem. See Andrews, *Search for the Picturesque,* chap. 5.

52. I am not sure of the date of the edition of *Sketches and Hints* in which this citation occurs, but it had nine chapters as opposed to the seven chapters plus appendix featured in the first (1794) edition. The brief appendix was obviously expanded into chapters 8 ("Affinity between Painting and Gardening") and 9 ("Sources of Pleasure in Landscape Gardening").

53. The principles of landscape gardening that Repton cites are as follows: (1) display the natural beauties and hide the natural defects of every situation, (2) give the appearance of extent and freedom by disguising or hiding the boundary, (3) conceal every interference of art . . . by which the scenery is improved, making the whole appear the production of nature only, and (4) all objects of mere convenience or comfort, if incapable of being made ornamental, . . . must be removed or concealed (*Sketches and Hints*, 42). Repton contrasts these with four principles of ancient gardening: (1) use lofty walls to exclude every surrounding object, (2) use orna-mentation to make the walls more conspicuous, (3) display the efforts of art by which nature has been sub-dued, and (4) place objects of convenience as near the house as possible. As I claimed above, these two types of gardens differ in naturalness. The "ancient" gardens, according to Repton, featured high surrounding walls with conspicuous ornamentation; beds and basins were rectilinear or geometric, trees were clipped, and out-buildings were placed close to the main house (43 ff.).

54. The remaining argument concerns specialization and expertise. Basically a sarcasm-laden argument from analogy, it proceeds as follows. Since Price urges every gentleman to become his own landscape garden-er, why not, Repton suggests, encourage them to do other things as well? "With equal propriety might every gentleman become his own architect, or even his own physician: in short, there is nothing that a man of abil-ities may not do for himself, if he will dedicate his whole attention to that subject only. But the life of man is not sufficient to excel in all things; and, as 'a little knowledge is a dangerous thing,' so the professors of every art, as well as that of medicine, will often find that the most difficult cases are those where the patient has begun by *quacking himself*" (74 n.).

55. Repton goes on to add "therefore, to give an accurate portrait of the gardener's improvement would require pictures from each window."

56. Repton says of the remarks making up chapter 7 of this edition of *Sketches and Hints* that they were written considerably earlier: "I shall transcribe a few passages from mss., written long before I saw [Mr. Knight's] poem [*The Landscape*], although the inquiry was originally suggested by conversations I had, both

with Mr. Knight and Mr. Price, at their respective seats in the county of Hereford" (*Sketches and Hints*, 53). I don't know whether these remarks of Repton's were previously published, but they must, in light of the admission just quoted, date from before 1794.

57. To convince us of this, Price proposes a thought experiment: he invites us to consider the effect on any composition, "either real or painted, were all the near objects swept away and only distant ones left" (131).

58. At the very least there is a conflict, because a painting is best seen from a fixed vantage point, while a natural landscape is usually seen by an ambulatory viewer. (This was Repton's first point, above.) In light of such facts, Repton proposes a normative principle that overrides our aesthetic concerns: utility and convenience must not be sacrificed to picturesque effect.

59. *Sketches and Hints*, Appendix, 77. Compare the following descriptions of Price's and Knight's estates, Foxley and Downton, from this same volume. On Downton:

A narrow, wild, and natural path, sometimes creeps under the beetling rock, close by the margin of a mountain stream. It sometimes ascends to an awful precipice, from whence the foaming waters are heard roaring in the dark abyss below, or seen wildly dashing against its opposite banks; while, in other places, the course of the river Terne being impeded by natural ledges of rock, the vale presents a calm, glassy mirror, that reflects surrounding foliage. The path, in various places, crosses the water by bridges of the most romantic and contrasted forms; and, branching in various directions, including some miles in length, is occasionally varied and enriched by caves and pleasing horrors of the scene. Yet, if the same picturesque objects were introduced in the gardens of a villa near the capital, or in the more tame, yet interesting pleasure grounds which I am frequently called upon to decorate, they would be as absurd, incongruous, and out of character as a Chinese temple from Vauxhall transplanted into the Vale of Downton (65)

On Foxley:

Foxley is less romantic than *Downton,* and therefore Mr. Price is less extravagant in his ideas, and willing to allow some little sacrifice of picturesque beauty to neatness, near the house; but by this very concession he acknowledges, that real *comfort,* and his ideas of *picturesqueness,* are incompatible (77).

60. "The landscape painter may consider men subordinate objects in his scenery, and place them merely as *figures,* to adorn his picture" (77).

61. Rules, the argument goes, belong in the academy; they generate formulaic and derivative works of art.

62. Repton, *Sketches and Hints,* 57.

63. John Barrell, *The Idea of Landscape and the Sense of Place: An Approach to the Poetry of John Clare* (Cambridge: Cambridge University Press, 1972), 7–9. Barrell goes on to argue that visual and verbal structures can be comparable, and that Claudean structure can be discerned in the landscape descriptions of many eighteenth-century poets. Barrell maintains that James Thomson successfully adapted Claude's compositional techniques, but that later poets borrowed Claudean conventions less successfully. See chapter 1, "The Idea of Landscape in the Eighteenth Century," sec. 4.

64. Anne Bermingham, *Landscape and Ideology* (Berkeley and Los Angeles: University of California Press, 1986), 10. Other artists whose work Bermingham includes in this genre are listed in a footnote: "John Crome, John Sell Cotman, and the other Norwich painters as well as the work of David Cox, William Delamotte, Peter De Wint, George Lambert, George Robert Lewis, John Linnell, and Cornelius and John Varley, artists who, while not directly influenced by Gainsborough and Constable, nevertheless did paint native, rural scenes" (197 n. 5).

65. Though the influence of the Dutch landscape school would no doubt be indicated in terms of tonality and brushwork as well as motif. See Bermingham, 34 ff.

66. Alice Recknagel Ireys, *Garden Design* (New York: Prentice-Hall 1991).

67. William Lake Douglas, Susan R. Frey, Norman K. Johnson, Susan Littlefield, and Michael Van Valkenburgh, *Garden Design: History, Principles, Elements, Practice* (New York: Simon and Schuster, 1984), chap. 4, passim.

68. Russell Page, *The Education of a Gardener* (1962). Reprint. (New York: Vintage Books, 1985), 16–17.

69. Admittedly, Russell Page is just one case, but a particularly representative one since he is heir to many of the traditions of British landscape design explored in this book.

Henry Shapiro has pointed out a passage from Hume that has a bearing on this debate. In his essay "Of Simplicity and Refinement in Writing," Hume states, "However different the tastes of men, their general discourse on these subjects is commonly the same. No criticism can be instructive which descends not to particulars, and is not full of examples and illustrations. It is allowed on all hands, that beauty, as well as virtue, lies always in a medium; but where this medium is placed is the great question, and can never be sufficiently explained by general reasonings." In *Eighteenth-Century Prose by the Most Eminent English Authors,* ed. Louis I. Brevold, Robert K. Root, and George Sherburn (New York: Thomas Nelson and Sons, 1932), 654.

70. Cp. Bermingham, *Language and Ideology*: "Price's plan for the picturesque garden initially depended on the examples of the great landscape painters. . . . Nevertheless, as he developed his category of the picturesque and suggested specific picturesque effects landowners might use in their gardens, he relied on examples from nature as much as art. Price's argument, then, tended to move the source of the picturesque away from the picturesque in painting to the picturesque in nature. . . . The picturesque garden, precisely because it depended on the maturing effects of time and on not entirely calculable accidents, was fated to remain little more than an impractical ideal. It never substantially altered the practices of gardening" (68).

71. Morris Brownell, *Alexander Pope and the Arts of Georgian England* (Oxford: Oxford University Press, 1978). Brownell maintains that Pope was the first to apply the word "picturesque" in English to natural description (104).

72. Ibid., 85. Brownell later claims that "The unmistakable conclusion to be drawn from the evidence of Pope's sensibility to landscape and the idea of the landscape garden derived from it, is that the picturesque was for him a complex and meaningful aesthetic of natural scenery" (98). Brownell goes on to characterize this aesthetic as follows: "A taste for landscape visualized in terms of painting or stage design, containing the pictorial values of colour, light, and shade, organized according to perspective and 'a Picture for a point of Sight,' composed in terms of the painter's sense of ground, contrast, and balance, poetically significant and expressive of emotions which can be distinguished from sublime or romantic responses to landscape" (85).

73. Pope did actually employ the term several times in notes to his translation of the *Iliad.* But as John Dixon Hunt explains in his essay "*Ut Pictura Poesis, Ut Pictura Hortus,* and the Picturesque," the meaning of "picturesque" at this time was grounded in seventeenth-century theories of *ut pictura poesis* (107); that is, it concerned the comparison between painting and poetry, and in particular, the way these two arts could both fulfill the Aristotelian injunction to tell a tale of significant human action. See John Dixon Hunt, *Gardens and the Picturesque: Studies in the History of Landscape Architecture* (Cambridge: MIT Press, 1992), 105–39, passim.

74. Hyams, *The English Garden* (New York: Harry N. Abrams), 30.

75. Hunt, "*Ut Pictura Poesis.*" Presumably such an audience would also feel at home with movements that supplanted the picturesque—the romantic emphasis on feeling and emotion, and the modern emphasis on uninterpreted formal qualities. And in fact, Hunt warns against a "proleptic" reading of the picturesque, one which sees it merely as prefiguring the movements which succeeded it. See the essay "The Picturesque Legacy to Modernist Landscape Architecture" in Hunt, *Gardens and the Picturesque.*

76. Andrews sums up the moral consequences of the picturesque as follows: "Thus the long tradition of the *paysage moralisé,* the landscape designed for interpretation and instruction as well as for visual enjoyment, gives way to what might almost be called a *paysage amoralisé,* if not *démoralisé*" (59).

77. Andrews again: "The Picturesque painter often goes to absurd depths to find the lowest possible angle on his subject" (61).

CHAPTER 6

1. John Dixon Hunt and Peter Willis, eds., *The Genius of the Place: The English Landscape Garden, 1620–1820* (London: Paul Elek, 1975), 314.

2. Peter Martin, *Pursuing Innocent Pleasures: The Gardening World of Alexander Pope* (Hamden, CT: Archon Books, 1984), 40.

3. Gordon, *Pope,* 80.

4. F. Hamilton Hazlehurst, *Gardens of Illusion* (Nashville: Vanderbilt University Press, 1980), 53.

5. It would perhaps be more accurate to attribute control to the garden designers rather than ascribe agency to the gardens themselves. Gardens do of course have many of their powers in virtue of features knowingly instilled by their designers. But we can also think of many cases where gardens affect their viewers in ways that the designers didn't anticipate or bring about.

6. Compare the ringing phrases with which Walpole introduces Kent: "At that moment appeared Kent, painter enough to taste the charms of landscape, bold and opinionative enough to dare and to dictate, and born with a genius to strike out a great system from the twilight of imperfect essays. He leaped the fence, and saw that all nature was a garden." Quoted in Hunt and Willis, *Genius of the Place,* 313.

7. Hunt and Willis, *Genius of the Place,* 314.

8. Martin, *Innocent Pleasures,* 32.

9. Kenneth Woodbridge, "Henry Hoare's Paradise," *Art Bulletin* 47 (1965): 83.

10. Hunt and Willis, *Genius of the Place,* 315.

11. Ronald Paulson, *Emblem and Expression: Meaning in English Art of the 18th-Century* (London: Thames and Hudson, 1975), 22.

12. Ronald Paulson, "On the Eighteenth-Century Poetic Garden," *The Listener* 90 (1973): 880.

13. Norman and Beryl Kitz, *Painshill Park* (London: Whittet Books, 1984), 75 ff.

14. Quoted in *The English Garden,* by Laurence Fleming and Alan Gore (London: Michael Joseph, 1979), 114.

15. Paulson, "Poetic Garden," 879.

16. John Dixon Hunt, "Emblem and Expression in the Eighteenth-Century Landscape Garden," *Eighteenth-Century Studies* 4, no. 3 (1971), 304.

17. For example, recall the discussion in chapter 5 of Richard Payne Knight's *An Analytical Inquiry into the Principles of Taste.*

18. Mary Warnock, *Imagination* (London: Faber and Faber, 1976), 20 ff. Warnock argues that the imagination does this by grouping together ideas related by resemblance, continuity, and causal connection.

19. Thus Kant calls this a function of the transcendent imagination.

20. Essays 411–21, in *The Spectator,* ed. Donald F. Bond (Oxford: Clarendon Press, 1965). Subsequent references to Addison's papers on "The Pleasures of the Imagination" in this edition of *The Spectator* will be cited parenthetically in the text.

Each issue of the *Spectator* contained a single essay. The paper was printed six days a week, Monday through Saturday, and was sold at various shops throughout London. The central conceit behind the periodical was that a fictional persona, Mr. Spectator, together with six members of his club, would offer reflections on London life. One topic alone was excluded, that of contemporary politics (Addison and Steele were, nonetheless, stauch Whigs). Bond describes the six club members as follows: "an old-fashioned country squire [Sir Roger de Coverley], a member of the Inner Temple and amateur of the stage, a successful merchant in the city of London, a retired army officer, an elderly beau and man of the world, and a 'very philosophick' clergyman" (from the editor's Introduction, xix).

21. Quoted in Hunt and Willis, p. 141.

22. Recall similar claims by James Turner and Carole Fabricant, discussed in chapter 4 above.

23. Arnold Berleant, *Art and Engagement* (Philadelphia: Temple University Press, 1991).

24. Rachel and Stephen Kaplan, "Restorative Experience: The Healing Power of Nearby Nature," in *The Meaning of Gardens*, ed. Mark Francis and Randolph T. Hester, Jr. (Cambridge: MIT Press, 1990), 241–42. The Kaplans label these four aspects of restorative experience "Being Away," "Fascination," "Extent," and "Compatibility." See also their book *The Experience of Nature: A Psychological Perspective* (Cambridge and New York: Cambridge University Press, 1989). I am not convinced by the Kaplans' claims about compatibility; I see no reason to think gardening immune to the various frustrations that beset all of our other daily enterprises.

25. Kaplan and Kaplan, "Restorative Experience," 241.

26. See, for example, Anne Raver, "Patients Discover the Power of Gardens," *New York Times,* Dec. 29, 1994. An earlier article by William K. Stevens ("Want a Room with a View? Idea May Be in the Genes," ibid., Nov. 30, 1993) discusses benefits to cheerfulness and mental creativity as well as to health more narrowly construed.

27. Jay Appleton, *The Experience of Landscape* (New York: Wiley, 1975). See also his article "Prospects and Refuges Revisited," *Landscape Journal* 3, no. 2, 91–103.

28. Appleton, "Prospects and Refuges Revisited," 93.

29. For an example of a popular application of Appleton's views, consider the following excerpt from a review by Michiko Kakutani of John D. Barrow's book *The Artful Universe:* "The savanna environment inhabited by [our] early ancestors, he suggests, left us with a predisposition towards habitats offering both shelter and 'clear, unimpeded views of the terrain,' the sort of landscape widely reproduced in parks and gardens today. He adds that contemporary architecture that employs these features (i.e., sloping ceilings, overhangs, gables, and porches, combined with balconies, bays and picture windows) has a natural appeal, while the sort of modern urban architecture that relies upon exposed walkways, blind corners and monotonous facades can lead to 'depression, crime and emotional disequilibrium.'" *New York Times*, December 29, 1995. I hope that what I have written so far makes it clear that the category "parks and gardens" is too varied to stand as the equivalent to some one type of savanna landscape for which humans might have a genetic preference.

30. A great deal of the criticism directed at *Sociobiology* concerned Wilson's claim that there exist human genes for such types of behavior as altruism and aggression.

31. Michael Van Valkenburgh, *New York Times,* Oct. 13, 1991, sec. 6, pt. 2 (*Home Design Magazine*), p. 46.

32. Nigel Nicolson in "The Garden of Sissinghurst Castle," a commemorative booklet produced for the National Trust by the *Illustrated London News,* 4, 5.

33. My colleague Henry Shapiro has persuaded me that invitation and enclosure or immersion are quintessentially sexual concepts. I grant that the rich and enticing gardens discussed in this book can indeed be seen as imbued with sexuality. And in fact there are probably gardens to analogize every taste in sex, every construal of sexuality—heterosexuality or homosexuality, dominance or submission, conquest or communication, the pursuit of pleasure or the search for a lost primal unity. The views of Carole Fabricant and James Turner discussed earlier suggest further ways in which landscape can be sexualized. This is a vast topic. Clearly, I cannot do it justice here, but invite readers to pursue these lines of thought.

34. Mara Miller, in *The Garden as an Art* (Albany: SUNY Press, 1993), identifies a related visual appeal of gardens: they encourage us to alternate between wide, sweeping views of the space we enter and closer investigation of individual details—the perceptual equivalent of a zoom lens on a modern-day camera. "One of the peculiar pleasures of the garden is the shift of focus from one distance to another" (48).

35. I owe this phrase to Henry Shapiro.

36. William Shenstone, in his posthumously published "Unconnected Thoughts on Gardening," divided gardening into three species: (1) kitchen gardening, (2) parterre gardening, and (3) landskip, or picturesque gardening. The latter he defined as gardening that pleased the imagination through scenes of grandeur, beauty, or variety. This clearly recalls Addison's categories of greatness, beauty, and novelty. See *The Works in Verse and Prose of William Shenstone, Esq.* (London, 1764).

37. I thank Mara Miller for calling this to my attention. She discusses Langer's use of this concept in *The Garden as an Art*. Subsequent references to Susanne Langer's *Feeling and Form* (New York: Charles Scribner's Sons, 1953) will be cited parenthetically in the text.

38. Daniel N. Lapedes, ed., *McGraw Hill Dictionary of Physics and Mathematics* (New York: McGraw-Hill, 1978).

39. H. J. Gray and Alan Isaacs, *A New Dictionary of Physics* (London: Longman Group, 1975).

40. Ibid.

41. As one textbook notes, "The photon involved in this interchange of momentum is a *virtual* (unobservable) *photon*, since it violates conservation of energy, and it may be considered a mathematical construct without direct physical reality" (F. W. Van Name, Jr., *Modern Physics* [Englewood Cliffs, NJ: Prentice-Hall, 1962]). Compare this account from *A New Dictionary of Physics:* "Because of the uncertainty principle it is possible for the law of conservation of mass and energy to be broken by an amount dE providing this only occurs for a time dt such that $dE\,dt \leq h/4$ pi. This makes it possible for particles to be created for short periods of time where their creation would normally violate conservation of energy. These particles are called virtual particles" (567).

42. For realists, as opposed to constructivists, theoretical terms refer to entities that are presently unobservable but which may someday come to be detected—have their existence confirmed—as science progresses.

43. One caveat here; recall that Danto declared all works of art to be representational. Within his system, then, we would need an additional marker to flag the distinction between (1) paintings (and gardens!) that represent in the usual sense—that is, that refer to and inform us about particular scenes, and (2) those that are abstract or purely formal yet still make a statement and require interpretation.

44. And also of seeing-in, the perceptual ability he characterizes as prior, both logically and historically, to representation (Richard Wollheim, *Painting as an Art* [Princeton: Princeton University Press, 1987]), 47.

45. Arthur Danto, *The Transfiguration of the Commonplace* (Cambridge: Harvard University Press, 1981).

46. Nicholas Wolterstorff, *Worlds and Works of Art* (Oxford: Clarendon Press, 1980). Subsequent references to this work will be indicated parenthetically in the text.

47. Which Langer discussed under the headings "discursive" and "non-discursive."

48. Of course, a similar painting *could* illustrate a doomsday science-fiction tale. Context would greatly influence our interpretive strategies.

49. This is attested by the fact that many of them come to us from comments made by Pope's friends.

50. With this last point especially, we must endorse the second of Wolterstorff's two interpretive schemes, the one relativizing things to what the artist's contemporaries would have assumed. "When an author composes a narrative with the intent of making it available to others he writes with a certain audience in mind. Much of what he says and how he says it is conditioned by what he assumes to be true of that audience. In particular, much of it is conditioned by what he assumes the bulk of that audience to believe. . . . I suggest that many of us do our extrapolating along the lines of what we take to be those expectations of authors" (122–23).

51. "Often elucidation and extrapolation are both called *interpretation*. But it should be clear that they are decidedly distinct activities. Of course there is no sharp line between cases of them" (116).

52. Cp. Hume's comments in his essay "Of the Standard of Taste" regarding the ways works of art are received by people from different eras and nations. An eighteenth-century Englishman, an eighteenth-centu-

ry Frenchman, and a twentieth-century American woman would no doubt have strikingly different experiences of Stowe or Rousham or Painshill.

53. Wolterstorff acknowledged some of the paradoxes that befall his notion of the world of a work of art in virtue of the fact that anything is entailed by a contradiction. The mechanisms of elucidation and extrapolation of possible garden experiences would have to be set out in more detail to prevent the early accumulation of contradictory aesthetic judgments—e.g., whether a certain bloom is garish, a particular layout pleasing, a given plantation overbearing, etc.—since the claims entailed by such contradictions would bloat the contents of the virtual world. In a much-anthologized paper, Frank Sibley argues that aesthetic terms are not condition-governed. If aesthetic claims are not necessitated by the perceptual and factual judgments underlying them, then different viewers might frequently make different, perhaps even contradictory, claims about one and the same garden. At the very least, different interpretations of a given garden would have to reside in or constitute different (virtual) worlds. That is, if we think of interpretations as structured in terms of a base and superstructure—the base containing perceptual, factual, and perhaps some aesthetic claims—then the world of a garden might encompass only the base. Incompatible interpretations of a given garden could then be represented as branching supervenient garden worlds.

While there are clearly problems to be solved regarding Wolterstorff's notion of the world of a work of art, it is important to note that they apply equally to all the arts, not just to the art of gardening. And, we might find some clues about how to handle these problems by studying recent accounts of the semantics of possible worlds, especially claims about the accessibility of one world from another.

54. In *Reconceptions in Philosophy and other Arts and Sciences* by Nelson Goodman and Catherine Z. Elgin (Cambridge and Indianapolis: Hackett, 1988). Quoted in *Aesthetics: A Critical Anthology*, ed. George Dickie et al. (New York: St. Martin's Press, 1989), 553.

55. Roger Scruton, *The Aesthetics of Architecture* (Princeton: Princeton University Press, 1979), 87. Subsequent quotations from this work will be acknowledged parenthetically in the text.

56. In *The Garden as an Art*, Mara Miller makes many observations about the ways in which gardens affect our perception of time. For example, she points out that gardens inevitably bring our attention to the daily, seasonal, biological, and even geological cycles that govern the growth and decay of living things (38 ff.). When we return to gardens we have visited before, we recall previous times there, yet gardens refer us to future visits as well: "The first crocus implies the hyacinths and forsythia, the first rosebud its own blossoming" (115). On the other hand, Miller claims that unlike other arts, gardens have an internal temporality "continuous with normal, everyday time . . . [and therefore reveal] the temporal structure of human living" (166).

57. The details can be found in *Languages of Art* (Indianapolis: Bobbs Merrill, 1968), where Goodman characterizes art and the aesthetic in terms of relations of symbols in symbol systems. All arts for Goodman exploit the symbolic relations representation, expression, and exemplification. Some arts like literature and music are notational; the symbols comprising them come from a system which is syntactically and semantically disjoint, syntactically and semantically finitely differentiated, and semantically unambiguous (see pp. 127–57). Notational arts are allographic. They cannot be forged because the notation provides a standard of correctness for work identity. Neither painting nor gardening is a notational art in Goodman's sense.

58. Ibid., 229. This is the feature Goodman tries to capture, much more technically, with talk of syntactic density and repleteness. Admittedly, some variations don't matter aesthetically, for instance, how much the Hokusai print weighs, or a shopping list lightly penned on the reverse side by the print's present owner. To eliminate examples of this sort, Goodman would appeal to a work's pictorial properties, which he defines recursively on p. 42.

CHAPTER 7

1. William Howard Adams, *Nature Perfected: Gardens through History* (New York: Abbeville Press, 1991), 329, 334.

2. Arthur Danto, "The End of Art," in *The Philosophical Disenfranchisement of Art* (New York: Columbia University Press, 1986), 86. All further references to this essay will be cited parenthetically in the text.

3. George Dickie, "What is Art? An Institutional Analysis," in *Art and Philosophy,* ed. W. E. Kennick (New York: St. Martin's Press, 1979), 89.

4. Compare the movement in photography known as Appropriation, in which artists like Sherrie Levine photograph other (famous) photographs.

5. I believe that a work may cease to be recognized as art—and thus cease to count as art—when transferred from one culture to another. Therefore my question about the loss of the status "work of art" should be limited to works that remain within the artworld that promoted them.

6. Nelson Goodman, *Languages of Art* (Indianapolis: Bobbs-Merrill, 1968), 41.

7. The revocation of Anthony Blunt's knighthood after he was convicted of spying seems to be an analogous case. I thank Henry Shapiro for calling it to my attention. As I interpret it, this case involves the realization that what had been assumed to be one of Blunt's "constitutive" properties—honor—had never been present at all. On this view, the knighthood was wrongly awarded and thus properly revoked.

8. I grant that the institution of divorce produces plenty of pain, suffering, unhappiness, and inconvenience of its own.

9. Arthur Danto has challenged my claim that tapestry is a dead art (private communication), and Henry Shapiro has offered Graham Sutherland's tapestry of Christ in the new Coventry Cathedral as a counterexample to my claims. But I will stick to my guns here. Although there may be plenty of present-day artists working with fiber in various ways, I don't see that their works collectively carry weight in the artworld, or have a place in the public's imagination, in any way comparable to that of drama during Shakespeare's time, painting in the impressionist era, film in the 1940s, and so on.

10. *The Genius of the Place,* ed. John Dixon Hunt and Peter Willis (London: Paul Elek, 1979), 1.

11. I omit a third view which Danto considers—art as expression—because it doesn't permit a linear view of art history.

12. Ralph Norman Haber, "Perceiving Space from Pictures" in *The Perception of Pictures,* vol. 1, ed. Margaret A. Hagen (New York: Academic Press, 1980). The paper "Photography, Vision, and Representation" by Joel Snyder and Neil Walsh (*Critical Inquiry,* Autumn 1975) persuasively argues the same point. Differences between picture perception and the perception of natural scenes were also discussed in chapter 4.

13. For example, see *The Transfiguration of the Commonplace* (Cambridge: Harvard University Press, 1981), 8–32.

14. Danto, *Transfiguration,* 26.

15. Ibid., 29.

16. Ibid., 151.

17. Ibid., 23.

18. In his book on musical representation, Peter Kivy points to an interesting eighteenth-century source of this insight, a little-known manuscript by the economist Adam Smith. See Kivy, *Sound and Semblance: Reflections on Musical Representation* (Princeton: Princeton University Press, 1984), 90.

19. In the paper "Depiction and Description" (*Philosophy and Phenomenological Research* 43, no. 1 [1982]) and again in "The End of Art," Danto contrasts mimesis and diegesis—imitation and description or narrative. Both are modes of representation; they represent in different manners.

20. "When we think of description as against mimesis, we may immediately notice that it is not at all clear

that there is any room for the concept of progress or of technological transformations at all" ("The End of Art," 98).

21. Danto does acknowledge moral or political progress, for example, when taboos are lifted or mores change. While such changes allow new things to be said, Danto notes that pictures as well as words are the beneficiaries.

22. After all, what makes one description "better" than another? Falsehoods and inaccuracies aside, what grounds are there for declaring that one description more successfully reproduces natural appearances? One might try comparing the completeness of narrative passages. But no description can capture every aspect of the world, nor is there any reason to think that the more complete description is necessarily the better one. The same comment applies to stylistic differences, differences in tone and point of view, and so on.

23. Arthur Danto, "Approaching the End of Art," delivered at the Richard Rudner Memorial Symposium at Washington University, St. Louis, MO, on March 20, 1987. All references are to a publicly circulated 27-page version of the manuscript.

24. "The history of art as the discovery of perceptual equivalences did not come to an end with cinema, but the history of painting came to an end so far as it was regarded as the mimetic art par excellence" (ibid., 36).

25. Stephen Bungay, *Beauty and Truth: A Study of Hegel's Aesthetics* (New York: Oxford University Press, 1984). Further references to this work will be cited parenthetically in the text.

26. "Art is an end in itself which reconciles the opposition between mind and nature, by being the self-expression of mind in the form of a natural, sensuous medium. It is through art, and only through art, that *truth* is revealed in a sensuous form" (ibid., 36).

27. Ibid., 29. Cp. the claim that "art is an expression of self-awareness, and a means of expanding it" (33).

28. "The content or Thought which is the soul of the work, completely determines its form, so as to infuse it with significance" (ibid., 40).

29. "Only a certain sphere of Truth, at a certain stage, is open to representation in a work of art; its own determination must require it to take on a sensuous form" (ibid., 76). For example, Hegel compares the religion of the ancient Greeks—whose gods could be represented in human form—with Christianity—whose God is pure spirit.

30. The progression from art to religion to philosophy takes us from intuition to representation to pure Thought. Bungay, p. 32.

31. "The Last Work of Art: Artworks and Real Things," originally published in *Theoria* 39 (1973); reprinted in *Aesthetics: A Critical Anthology*, ed. George Dickie and Richard J. Sclafani (New York: St. Martin's Press, 1977), 551–62. Henceforth referred to as "Artworks and Real Things."

32. Danto, *Transfiguration,* p. 82.

33. Ibid., p. 79.

34. Ibid., p. 77.

35. Ibid., 125.

36. The allusion is of course to Samuel Johnson's act of kicking a stone and then declaring, "Thus I refute Berkeley."

37. Danto, "Art, Evolution, and History," in *The Philosophical Disenfranchisement of Art* (New York: Columbia University Press, 1986), 205.

38. "Artworks and Real Things," 561.

39. "Approaching the End of Art," 24.

40. Ibid., 13.

41. Ibid., 31.

42. Since literature is not an art which shapes a sensuous medium, it will not end with the appearance of truths which transcend that medium. Nevertheless, this highest of all the arts is still subject to changing rela-

tions between Beauty and Truth. Two of Bungay's remarks about drama indicate literature's course: "Drama has its roots in our self-understanding, and the forms of drama alter as our self-understanding alters" (178). In a society "which understands the human subject to be influenced by upbringing and environment, unconscious drives, and the message encoded in its DNA, the scope for heroic action is small indeed. In such a society, art has been overtaken by thought, and those ancient forms of Beauty, found wanting by the demands of Truth, will be abandoned" (178).

43. "Artworks and Real Things," 558.

44. Despite the evidence I have been citing that Danto treats the arts on a par, one recent work, his collection of essays entitled *The Philosophical Disenfranchisement of Art,* challenges this view. In the papers "Philosophy as/and/of Literature" and "Philosophizing Literature," Danto argues that philosophy is not literature and that literature is not philosophy. (See the paragraph introducing essay 8.)

In "Philosophy as/and/of Literature," Danto argues that philosophy is not literature because philosophy makes truth claims (136 ff.). Building on Aristotle's distinction between poetry and history, Danto argues that philosophy aspires to be not just universal but necessary as well (154), while literature is universal in the special sense of being about each reader who experiences it in a "metaphoric and allusive way" (154). Literature is thus transfigurative; it transforms its reader "who in virtue of identifying with the image recognizes what he is" (156). Philosophy, by contrast, seeks "really to reveal us," not just metaphorically (156, 161).

In "Philosophizing Literature" Danto further characterizes literature by claiming that it embodies ideas, makes them incarnate. What this amounts to never becomes very clear. Danto does offer these further clues: embodiment differs from exemplification (182); some ideas are too abstract for embodiment (182); texts which embody ideas are not transparent, they contribute something of their own to the understanding of their topics (183); such texts set an example before us (183); embodiment is somehow connected with intuition (183).

A novel which embodies a philosophical idea would be philosophical literature (181), but apparently few philosophical ideas invite such treatment. Danto does give a few examples, drawn from the dialogues of Plato (*Lysis* on friendship, *Meno* on recollection, *The Symposium* on love) as well as Descartes's *Meditations* (which embodies the search for clear and distinct ideas) and Locke's *Essay* (which embodies the abstract concept of understanding), (182). Thus philosophy and literature are distinguished by their differing relations to truth, differing modes of universality, and differing use of embodiment.

Do these distinctions mean that literature cannot end by *becoming* philosophy? Presumably painting and philosophy are just as distinct, yet Danto happily predicts the collapse of the one into the other. I don't know whether there are grounds in Hegel's system for treating the futures of painting and literature as skewed. It may be that the distinctions Danto draws between philosophy and literature do not preclude that literature will end as painting has. That is, Danto's distinctions might characterize a *present* difference, one which will be transcended when the end of literature merges these two activities into one.

This reading of Danto is belied by one passage. Namely, by Danto's claim that the task of differentiating philosophy from literature has become an urgent problem for art "because of art having come so close to becoming its own philosophy that it seemed to require a rescue by philosophy in order that art should not lose its identity in philosophical reflection upon itself. Literature might simply have turned into philosophy in an act of self-transcending" (173). However, since this passage negates the story Danto tells about painting as well as the one I am trying to piece together about literature, I am inclined to discount it.

45. "Approaching the End of Art," 14–15.

46. This is the whole point of Danto's Hegelian story: "Its own philosophy is what art aims at, so that art fulfills its destiny by becoming philosophy at last"; "art's philosophical history consists in its being absorbed ultimately into its own philosophy" ("The End of Art," 81, 110). Danto also seems to endorse transformation in the other direction. Compare what he says of his paper "Artworks and Real Things": "In a way the paper is part of its own subject, since it becomes an artwork at the end" (551).

47. Here is how Danto describes the posthistorical artworld: "A point has been reached where there can be change without development, where the engines of artistic production can only combine and recombine known forms" ("The End of Art," 85).

48. "A 1986 Gallup survey conducted for the National Gardening Association showed that for the third year in a row, gardening is the No. 1 outdoor leisure activity in the United States" (*New York Times,* June 4, 1987, p. 17).

49. Alan Sonfist, ed., *Art in the Land: A Critical Anthology of Environmental Art* (New York: E. P. Dutton, 1983).

50. Michael McDonough, "Architecture's Unnoticed Avant-Garde" (ibid., 233).

51. Clement Greenberg, "Avant-Garde and Kitsch," in *Art and Culture* (Boston: Beacon Press, 1961).

52. Danto, "The End of Art," 111.

53. Christopher Thacker, *The History of Gardens* (Berkeley and Los Angeles: University of California Press, 1979), 278.

54. "The dangers of fraud, and of trust, are essential to the experience of art." Stanley Cavell, "Music Discomposed," in *Must We Mean What We Say?* (New York: Charles Scribner's Sons, 1969), 188–89. Cavell explains the situation in music a little more fully as follows: "The possibility of fraudulence, and the experience of fraudulence, is endemic in the experience of contemporary music; . . . its full impact, even its immediate relevance, depends upon a willingness to trust the object, knowing that the time spent with its difficulties may be betrayed" (188).

55. I discuss his argument in the paper "Chance, Constraint, and Creativity: The Awfulness of Modern Music," *Journal of Aesthetic Education* 19, no. 3 (1985): 21–35.

56. Jane Owen, *Eccentric Gardens* (New York: Villard Books, 1990).

57. I first learned about this garden from Tom Leddy's paper "Gardens in an Expanded Field," *British Journal of Aesthetics* 28 (1988): 327–40. Little Sparta is also discussed in the following works: Claude Abrioux, *Ian Hamilton Finlay: A Visual Primer* (Edinburgh: Reaktion Books, 1985); Claude Gintz, "Neoclassical Rearmament," *Art in America,* Feb. 1987: 111–17; Stephen Bann, "A Description of Stonypath," *Journal of Garden History* 1, no. 2 (1981): 113–44.

58. Finlay sought tax exemption for an outbuilding he converted into a gallery. Later he remodeled it as a garden temple dedicated to Apollo ("His music; His missiles; His muses") and demanded the tax exemption appropriate to religious buildings. The Strathclyde Regional Council refused these requests, precipitating an ongoing struggle.

59. Mark Rosenthal, "Some Attitudes of Earth Art: From Competition to Adoration," in *Art in the Land,* ed. Alan Sonfist. Many writers analyze earth art in terms of gestures, but Rosenthal offers a typology of earth art very similar to mine. He proposes five categories: (1) Gestures in the Landscape (2) Enclosures in the Landscape (3) Modest Gestures in the Landscape (4) Nature for Itself (5) Idealized Landscape.

I initially added a seventh category to my typology—Didactic and/or Conceptual Gardens. I was thinking here of the work of Helen and Newton Harrison, many of whose exhibits would fit as well in a science museum as in a museum of fine art. Their art is intended to draw attention to the ecological crisis confronting us. As Grace Glueck reports, their projects "deal in story form with such ecological matters as seabed resources and fishing, the impact of big agriculture on the California desert, the damming of the Colorado River system, the possibility of glacial melt, the plethora of sulfuric acid rain" (*Art in the Land,* ed. Sonfist, 178). The Harrisons are famous for discovering how to keep rare Sri Lankan crabs happy in captivity. (The secret is to produce waves in the tank to mimic their native monsoons.) A related set of works might include ideal gardens and environmental works that are planned but never funded or executed.

60. It has been suggested, with some justice, that my treatment of art in this chapter is sexist. I acknowledge two aspects in which my discussion is indeed sexist, but I maintain that this is an unavoidable result of analyz-

ing the artworld of an inherently sexist society. The first "locus" of sexism involves the artists cited in my account of environmental art. It simply is the case that those artists creating massive earthworks in remote locations in the sixties and seventies were predominantly male. And/or that male artists creating such works received more attention than female artists creating comparable works. This is in turn reflected in the primary and secondary literature available to inform nonspecialists about the contemporary artworld. We do now have Nancy Holt, Mary Miss, Maya Lin to range alongside Michael Heizer, Robert Smithson, Walter De Maria. One might, however, object that these female artists are doing a quite different kind of work than the males first cited. And this leads to the second "locus" of sexism in my account—my taxonomy that classes some environmental works as "masculine gestures." Here I defend myself by appeal to the sex-role stereotypes in place in our society right now. It just is the case that we do—perhaps metaphorically—classify as male things that are large, bold, energetic, expansive; we classify as female things that are gentle, shy, diminutive. It does not follow that these are inevitable or "hard-wired" gender traits; it does not even follow that they apply within all ethnic and social groups in our society. (See, for example, Patricia Hill Collins's work on the stereotyping of black women as emasculating matriarchs.) But, given that these generalizations are current in our society and provide an easy way to refer to a certain cluster of traits, I have felt free to use them in my exposition.

61. This account, like many of the others to follow, was drawn from Sonfist's anthology. Carol Hall's article "Environmental Artists: Sources and Directions," which describes the recent work of eighteen of the most renowned environmental artists, was especially helpful.

62. Elizabeth C. Baker describes *Complex One* in considerable detail in her article "Artworks on the Land" (in *Art and the Land,* ed. Sonfist, 73–84). The work consists of a 20 X 110 X 140-foot pyramidal mound, framed by a set of cantilevered concrete piers. From a distance, *Complex One* reads as a single rectangular plane framed by bands of concrete. As the viewer approaches, this illusion fades. The mound actually inclines backwards forty-five degrees, and the concrete columns jut out in front of it.

63. From 1966 on, Turrell worked in the Mendota Hotel in Ocean Park, California. Two front rooms sealed off from outside illumination served as his studio spaces and housed a variety of "projection pieces," works created by projecting bright halogen and later xenon light sources into the all-white rooms. Light projected onto adjacent flat walls was perceived as a three-dimensional cube hovering in the corner and shifting in response to the viewers' movement. A later series of works, the *Mendota Stoppages,* evolved when Turrell opened up his studio and explored relations of light between the inside and outside spaces. Craig Adcock (cited below) deems these site-specific works (88), since for each performance Turrell manipulated apertures to introduce light images from various sources (street lamps, neon signs, lights of passing cars and buses, the nighttime sky, and, ultimately, random activity of the viewers' retinas) into the interior.

Turrell was evicted from his studio in 1974. Seeking to create light-and-space works similar to the *Mendota Stoppages* in a natural environment, Turrell began exploring the surrounding desert for a site. An amateur pilot, he used a Guggenheim grant to buy fuel and for seven months flew over the western United States seeking a site "with the specific phenomena he wanted to engage artistically: . . . celestial vaulting and its counterpart in the concave earth illusion. . . . He needed a crater or a butte that rose from a surrounding plain to a height between 600 and 1,000 feet. . . . When he found Roden Crater . . . it met his requirements almost perfectly." It took several years of negotiating with the owners to arrange the purchase of the crater. See *James Turrell: The Art of Light and Space*, by Craig Adcock (Berkeley and Los Angeles: University of California Press, 1990), 154–55; also 85 ff. and 111 ff.

64. From Eleanor Munro's article "Art in the Desert," *New York Times,* Dec. 7, 1986. Turrell himself summarizes his ambitions for *Roden Crater* as follows: It "is located in an area of exposed geology, the Painted Desert, where you feel geologic time. You have a strong feeling of standing on the surface of a planet. Within that setting, I am making spaces that will engage celestial events. Several spaces will be sensitive to starlight and will be literally empowered by the light of stars millions of light years away." Quoted in Adcock, *James Turrell,* 158.

65. Elizabeth Baker writes, "The experience of visiting the works is a complicated one, no small part of which is the difficulty of getting there and the exoticism of locale and life-style. Things can become intensely anecdotal: you learn about local economics, land purchasing in the West, enormous government land reserves, atomic test sites, snakes, trucks, and desert climates. All this, especially in the course of short visits, tends to overwhelm, so at a certain point it becomes necessary to separate the art experience from the general experience" (79–80). Eleanor Munro concurs. She offers the following anecdote: "As we drove toward the town of Overton, jumping off place for the Heizer work [*Double Negative*], the temperature was pushing 120. We stopped at a gas station to ask if anyone knew the road. A well-oriented highway patrol officer with a four-wheel drive sized up our situation and growled, 'I'd rather take you up than have to go find you and bring you out'."

Munro concludes her article with a set of warnings: "Travelers should bear in mind that sites are in semi-wilderness away from emergency facilities. . . . Fill the gas tank and check oil at nearest station stops and never be without containers of drinkable water. . . . Wear high-topped heavy shoes—this is rattlesnake and scorpion country—head covering and sunscreen."

66. She states that "*The Lightning Field* is slowly grasped. . . . Perceptually it strains your attention, your sense of intervals; its boundaries are not clear once you are more than one or two units inside it. The distance between poles is so great you strain to locate the next one—and especially the one beyond that. But psychological and supraperceptual factors seem crucial here" (81). Baker wrote this after viewing a small test grid of thirty-five poles which was erected before the finished work.

67. For example, the five diagonally arrayed trenches that make up Heizer's work *Dissipate* look like a hard-edged minimalist composition, while the five circular excavations and surrounding tire tracks that constitute *Five Conic Displacements* (1969) remind me of nothing so much as Robert Motherwell's series of *Elegies for the Spanish Republic*.

68. Kate Linker, "Michael Singer: A Position in, and on, Nature," in *Art in the Land,* ed. Sonfist, 185.

69. Rosenthal applies this term to Long's work in "Some Attitudes of Earth Art: From Competition to Adoration."

70. Hall, "Environmental Artists," 34.

71. John Beardsley, *Probing the Earth: Contemporary Land Projects* (Washington, DC: Smithsonian Press, 1977), 52. Beardsley's volume is the catalog for an exhibition on earthworks that was on view at the Hirshhorn Museum and Sculpture Garden, the La Jolla Museum of Contemporary Art, and the Seattle Art Museum in 1977 and 1978.

72. Rosenthal, "Some Attitudes," 67.

73. *Running Fence* was 24.5 miles long, while *Surrounded Islands* draped 35 tons (6.56 million square feet) of pink polypropylene around eleven islands in Biscayne Bay spreading over seven miles.

Despite the impression generated by some photographs, Christo and Jeanne-Claude point out that their works are "always amongst people in sites previously managed by human beings for human beings, with barns, churches, temples, gas stations—all near a major airport" (personal correspondence, 24 March 1997).

In catagorizing Christo and Jeanne-Claude's works as I did, I am trying to emphasize certain affinities to the performing arts. Since their works are installed and then dismantled, it seems quite possible they could organize a repeat performance of the same work, titled for example, "Running Fence, Sonoma, and Marin Counties, California, 1998–2000." I do not, however, mean to imply that the workers who install Christo and Jeanne-Claude's creations are in any sense performers playing a role, or that they are adding interpretive dimensions to the works.

74. Hall, "Environmental Artists," 29.

75. Adcock, *James Turrell,* 158.

76. Described in *Public Art: New Directions*, by Louis G. Redstone with Ruth R. Redstone (New York: McGraw-Hill, 1981), 38.

77. Rosenthal, "Some Attitudes," 71.

78. From a description of *Pass* by Beej Niereengarten-Smith, Director of Laumeier Sculpture Park, in the brochure "Meg Webster: Recent Work/Recent Acquisitions."

79. Melinda Wortz, "Surrendering to Presence: Robert Irwin's Aesthetic Integration," *Artforum,* Nov. 1981, 64.

80. Arthur Danto, "Art-in-Response," 147. This essay appears in the catalog *Robert Irwin* (Los Angeles: Museum of Contemporary Art, 1993), ed. Russell Ferguson, published for a 1993 exhibition.

81. Ibid., 150.

82. Ibid., 151.

83. Quoted in Lawrence Weschler, "Playing It as It Lays and Keeping It in Play: A Visit with Robert Irwin" (another essay in the same catalog), 162. In a complex flow chart meant to show the integration of design and art considerations in the overall airport experience, Irwin listed the design goals as (1) resolving problems and (2) minimizing anxiety and the art goals as (1) celebrating opportunities and (2) maximizing richness. Each of these in turn headed a branching tree with further goals and considerations.

Irwin's glosses and justifications for his overall airport scheme recall some of the points made in an earlier chapter about gardens' control of their visitors' experiences. For example, Irwin insists that artists need to be in on the design process from the very beginning in order to make arguments for what he calls quality (i.e., quality of experience). He says, "If you give an engineer a set of criteria which does not include a quality quotient . . . he will then basically put the road straight down the middle. He has no reason whatsoever to curve it. But if I can convince him that quality is absolutely a worthwhile thing and we can then work out a way in which the road can be efficient and also wander down by the river, then we have essentially both—he provides quality in the sense that the road works, I provide quality in that it passes by the river" (163).

84. Danto, "Art-in-Response," 147.

85. These parks were written up in recent issues of *Artforum* and *Art in America.*

86. Goran Hermeren, *Influence in Art and Literature* (Princeton: Princeton University Press, 1975).

87. "If X influenced the creation of Y with respect to a, and if B created Y, then B's contact with X was a contributory cause of the creation of Y with respect to a" (ibid., 93).

88. Robert Irwin, *Being and Circumstance: Notes toward a Conditional Art* (Larkspur Landing, CA: Lapis Press, 1985).

89. Irwin says of site-*specific* art: "Our process of recognition and understanding of the 'work of art' is still keyed (referenced) to the oeuvre of the artist. Familiarity with his or her history, lineage, art intent, style, materials, techniques, etc., are presupposed; thus, for example, a Richard Serra is always recognizable as, first and foremost, a Richard Serra" (ibid., 27). I am not convinced that a site-*determined* work would be without such stylistic markers, for even were an artistic response entirely elicited by a site, it would still be the response (action) of a particular individual and would be colored by that person's beliefs, desires, interests, habits, and so on.

90. In his essay "Art-in-Response" (446) Arthur Danto classifies Christo and Jeanne-Claude's environmental works as site-dominant rather than site-generated. Unlike Irwin, these artists impose an artistic will on an existing site, he says, referring to islands skirted with pink plastic, landscapes dotted with umbrellas, structures wrapped in plastic, oil drums piled up in the form of a mastaba. While Christo and Jeanne-Claude do add artificial elements to the landscape, perhaps even in a manner and on a scale that justify Danto's use of the word "impose", I think Danto slights the extent to which these works are nevertheless responsive to the landscapes they inhabit. Pink skirts wouldn't encircle just any landscape feature—nor even just any islands—to the same effect. Similarly, a running fence traversing a suburban neighborhood or a twenty-four-mile straight and level track wouldn't resemble the pieces that were in fact created.

91. Described in Jonathan Carpenter, "Alan Sonfist's Public Sculptures," in *Art in the Land,* ed. Sonfist, 152.

Bibliography

Abrioux, Yves. *Ian Hamilton Finlay: A Visual Primer.* Edinburgh: Reaktion Books, 1985.

Adams, William Howard. *The French Garden, 1500–1800.* New York: George Braziller, 1979.

———. *Nature Perfected: Gardens through History.* New York: Abbeville Press, 1991.

———. *Grounds for Change: Major Gardens of the Twentieth Century.* Boston: Little, Brown, 1993.

Adcock, Craig. *James Turrell: The Art of Light and Space.* Berkeley and Los Angeles: University of California Press, 1990.

Addison, Joseph. "The Pleasures of the Imagination." In *The Spectator,* ed. Donald F. Bond. Oxford: Clarendon Press, 1965.

Allen, B. Sprague. *Tides in English Taste (1619–1800).* 2 vols. New York: Rowman and Littlefield, 1969.

Allentuck, Marcia. "Price and the Picturesque Garden." In *The Picturesque Garden and Its Influence outside the British Isles,* ed. Nikolaus Pevsner. Washington, DC: Dumbarton Oaks, 1974.

Altschuler, Bruce. *Noguchi.* New York: Abbeville Press, 1994.

Andrews, Malcolm. *The Search for the Picturesque.* Stanford: Stanford University Press, 1989.

Appleton, Jay. *The Experience of Landscape.* New York: Wiley, 1975.

Bann, Stephen. "A Description of Stonypath." *Journal of Garden History* 1, no. 2 (1981): 113–44.

Bardi, P. M. *The Tropical Gardens of Burle Marx.* New York: Reinhold, 1964.

Barrell, John. *The Idea of Landscape and the Sense of Place, 1730–1840: An Approach to the Poetry of John Clare.* Cambridge: Cambridge University Press, 1972.

Batey, Mavis, and David Lambert. *The English Garden Tour: A View into the Past.* London: John Murray, 1990.

Beardsley, John. *Probing the Earth: Contemporary Land Projects.* Washington, DC: Smithsonian Press, 1977.

Bermingham, Ann. *Landscape and Ideology: The English Rustic Tradition, 1740–1860.* Berkeley and Los Angeles: University of California Press, 1986.

Black, Max. "How Do Pictures Represent?" In *Art, Perception, and Reality,* ed. Maurice Maundelbaum. Baltimore: Johns Hopkins University Press, 1972.

Brownell, Morris R. *Alexander Pope and the Arts of Georgian England.* Oxford: Clarendon Press, 1978.

Bryson, Norman. *Vision and Painting: The Logic of the Gaze.* New Haven: Yale University Press, 1983.

Bungay, Stephen. *Beauty and Truth: A Study of Hegel's Aesthetics.* New York: Oxford University Press, 1984.

Burke, Edmund. *A Philosophical Enquiry into the Origin of Our Ideas of the Sublime and Beautiful,* edited by James T. Boulton. Notre Dame: University of Notre Dame Press, 1968.

Carlson, Allen. "Is Environmental Art an Aesthetic Affront to Nature?" *Canadian Journal of Philosophy* 16, no. 4 (1968): 635–50.

———. "On Appreciating Agricultural Landscapes." *Journal of Aesthetics and Art Criticism* 43, no. 3 (1985): 301–12.

Carroll, Noel. "Historical Narratives and the Philosophy of Art." *Journal of Aesthetics and Art Criticism* 51, no. 3 (1993): 313–26.

Cavell, Stanley. "Aesthetic Problems of Modern Philosophy." In *Must We Mean What We Say?* New York: Charles Scribner's Sons, 1969.

Chase, Isabel W. U. *Horace Walpole, Gardenist.* Princeton: Princeton University Press, 1943.

Clark, H. F. *The English Landscape Garden.* Gloucester: Alan Sutton, 1980.

Clarke, Michael and Nicholas Penny. *The Arrogant Connoisseur: Richard Payne Knight, 1751–1824.* Manchester: Manchester University Press, 1982.

Clifford, Derek. *A History of Garden Design.* New York: Praeger, 1963.

Crawford, Donald. "Nature and Art: Some Dialectical Relationships." *Journal of Aesthetics and Art Criticism* 42, no. 1 (1983): 49–58.

Danto, Arthur. *The Transfiguration of the Commonplace.* Cambridge: Harvard University Press, 1981.

———. *The Philosophical Disenfranchisement of Art.* New York: Columbia University Press, 1986.

Denvir, Bernard, ed. *The Eighteenth Century: Art, Design, and Society, 1689–1789.* London and New York: Longman, 1983.

Dickie, George. "What Is Art: An Institutional Analysis." In *Art and Philosophy,* ed. W. E. Kennick. New York: St. Martin's Press, 1979.

Fabricant, Carole. "Binding and Dressing Nature's Loose Tresses: The Ideology of Augustan Landscape Design." In *Studies in Eighteenth-Century Culture,* vol. 8, ed. Roseann Runte. Madison: University of Wisconsin Press, 1979.

———. "The Aesthetics and Politics of Landscape in the Eighteenth Century." *In Studies in Eighteenth-Century British Art and Aesthetics,* ed. Ralph Cohen. Berkeley and Los Angeles: University of California Press, 1985.

Ferguson, Russell, ed. *Robert Irwin.* Los Angeles: Museum of Contemporary Art, 1993.

Fisher, John, ed. *Perceiving Artworks.* Philadelphia: Temple University Press, 1980.

Fleming, Laurence, and Alan Gore. *The English Garden.* London: Michael Joseph, 1979.

Foss, Michael. *The Age of Patronage: The Arts in England, 1660–1750.* Ithaca: Cornell University Press, 1971.

Francis, Mark, and Randolph T. Hester, Jr., eds. *The Meaning of Gardens.* Cambridge: MIT Press, 1990.

Gilpin, William. *An Essay on Prints.* London, 1781.

Gintz, Claude. "Neoclassical Rearmanent." *Art in America,* Feb. 1987: 111–17.

Girouard, Mark. *Life in the English Country House.* Harmondsworth: Penguin Books, 1980.

Gombrich, E. H. *Art and Illusion.* Princeton: Princeton University Press, 1969.

———. *The Image and the Eye: Further Studies in the Psychology of Pictorial Representation.* Ithaca: Cornell University Press, 1982.

———. "The Renaissance Theory of Art and the Rise of Landscape." In *Norm and Form: Studies in the Art of the Renaissance.* London: Phaidon, 1966.

Goodman, Nelson. *Languages of Art.* Indianapolis: Bobbs-Merrill, 1968.

Gregory, R. L. *Eye and Brain: The Psychology of Seeing.* New York: McGraw Hill, 1974.

Hagen, Margaret A., ed. *The Perception of Picture.* Vol. 1, *Alberti's Window: The Projective Model of Pictorial Information.* New York: Academic Press, 1980.

Hagstrum, Jean H. *The Sister Arts: The Tradition of Literary Pictorialism and English Poetry from Dryden to Gray.* Chicago: University of Chicago Press, 1958.

Harris, John. *The Artist and the Country House.* London: Sotheby Parke Bernet, 1979.

Hazlehurst, F. Hamilton. *Gardens of Illusion: The Genius of André Le Nostre.* Nashville: Vanderbilt University Press, 1980.

Hermeren, Goran. *Influence in Art and Literature.* Princeton: Princeton University Press, 1975.

Hibbert, Christopher. *The Grand Tour.* New York: Putnam, 1969.

Hipple, Walter John, Jr. *The Beautiful, the Sublime, and the Picturesque in Eighteenth-Century British Aesthetic Theory.* Carbondale: Southern Illinois University Press, 1957.

Hobhouse, Penelope, and Elvin McDonald, eds. *Gardens of the World: The Art and Practice of Gardening.* New York: Macmillan, 1991.

Hudson, Roger, ed. *The Grand Tour, 1592–1796.* London: Folio Society, 1993.

Hunt, John Dixon. "Emblem and Expressionism in the Eighteenth-Century Landscape Garden." *Eighteenth-Century Studies* 4, no. 3 (1971): 294–317.

———. *The Figure in the Landscape: Poetry, Painting, and Gardening during the Eighteenth Century.* Baltimore: Johns Hopkins University Press, 1976.

———. *Gardens and the Picturesque: Studies in the History of Landscape Architecture.* Cambridge: MIT Press, 1992.

Hunt, John Dixon, and Peter Willis, eds. *The Genius of the Place: The English Landscape Garden, 1620–1820.* London: Paul Elek, 1975.

Hussey, Christopher. *The Picturesque.* London: Putnam, 1927.

———. *English Gardens and Landscapes.* London: Country Life, 1967.

Hyams, Edward. *Capability Brown and Humphry Repton.* New York: Charles Scribner's Sons, 1971.

———. *A History of Gardens and Gardening.* New York: Praeger, 1971.

Irwin, Robert. *Being and Circumstance: Notes toward a Conditional Art.* California: Lapis Press, 1985.

Jackson, John Brinckerhoff. *The Necessity for Ruins.* Amherst: University of Massachusetts Press, 1980.

Jacques, David. *Georgian Gardens: The Reign of Nature.* Portland, OR: Timber Press, 1984.

Kelsall, Malcolm. "The Iconography of Stourhead." *Journal of the Warburg and Courtauld Institutes* 46 (1983): 133–43.

Kemal, Salim, and Ivan Gaskell, eds. *Landscape, Natural Beauty, and the Arts.* Cambridge: Cambridge University Press, 1993.

Keswick, Maggie. *The Chinese Garden: History, Art, and Architecture.* New York: Rizzoli, 1978.

Kitz, Norman, and Beryl Kitz. *Pains Hill Park: Hamilton and His Picturesque Landscape.* London: Whittet Books, 1984.

Kivy, Peter. *Sound and Semblance: Reflections on Musical Representation.* Princeton: Princeton University Press, 1984.

Knight, Richard Payne. *An Analytical Inquiry into the Principles of Taste.* London, 1805.

Lang, S. "The Genesis of the English Landscape Garden." In *The Picturesque Garden and Its Influence outside the British Isles,* ed. Nikolaus Pevsner. Washington, DC: Dumbarton Oaks, 1974.

Langer, Susanne. *Feeling and Form.* New York: Charles Scribner's Sons, 1953.

Leddy, Tom. "Gardens in an Expanded Field." *British Journal of Aesthetics* 28, no. 4 (1988): 327–40.

Lee, Rensselaer W. *Ut Pictura Poesis: The Humanistic Theory of Painting.* New York: W. W. Norton, 1967.

Lehrman, Jonas. *Earthly Paradise: Garden and Courtyard in Islam.* Berkeley and Los Angeles: University of California Press, 1980.

Lipman, Jean, and Richard Marshall. *Art about Art.* New York: E. P. Dutton, in association with the Whitney Museum of American Art, 1978.

Lopes, Dominic. *Understanding Pictures.* Oxford: Oxford University Press, 1996.

Maccubbin, Robert P., and Peter Martin, eds. "British and American Gardens." A special edition of *Eighteenth-Century Life* (vol. 8, no. 2 [1983]).

Mack, Maynard Mack. *The Garden and the City: Retirement and Politics in the Later Poetry of Pope.* Toronto: University of Toronto Press, 1969.

Malins, Edward. *English Landscaping and Literature, 1660–1840.* London: Oxford University Press, 1966.

Mannix, Daniel P. *The Hell Fire Club.* New York: Ballantine, 1959.

Margolis, Joseph. *Texts without Referents.* Oxford: Basil Blackwell, 1989.

Martin, Peter. *Pursuing Innocent Pleasures: The Gardening World of Alexander Pope.* Hamden, CT: Archon Books, 1984.

Miller, Mara. *The Garden as an Art.* Albany: State University of New York Press, 1993.

Miller, Naomi. *Heavenly Caves: Reflections on the Garden Grotto.* New York: George Braziller, 1982.

McCormick, Donald. *The Hell-Fire Club: The Story of the Amorous Knights of Wycombe.* London: Jarrolds, 1958.

Moore, Charles W., William J. Mitchell, and William Turnbull, Jr. *The Poetics of Gardens.* Cambridge: MIT Press, 1988.

Owen, Jane. *Eccentric Gardens.* New York: Villard Books, 1990.

Pace, K. Claire. "Some Eighteenth-Century Discussions of Landscape." *Journal of the History of Ideas* 40, no. 1 (1979): 141–55.

Page, Russell. *The Education of a Gardener.* Reprint. New York: Vintage Books, 1985.

Paulson, Ronald. "On the Eighteenth-Century Poetic Garden." *The Listener* 90 (1973): 878–80.

———. *Emblem and Expression: Meaning in English Art of the 18th Century.* London: Thames and Hudson, 1975.

Pevsner, Nikolaus. *Academies of Art Past and Present.* Cambridge: Cambridge University Press, 1940. Reprint. New York: Da Capo Press, 1973.

———. "The Genesis of the Picturesque." *Studies in Art, Architecture, and Design.* Vol. 1, *From Mannerism to Romanticism.* New York: Walker, 1968.

Pirenne, M. H. *Optics, Painting, and Photography.* Cambridge: Cambridge University Press, 1970.

Plumb, J. H. *Georgian Delights.* Boston: Little, Brown, 1980.

Pollan, Michael. *Second Nature: A Gardener's Education.* New York: Dell, 1991.

Price, Martin. "The Picturesque Moment." In *From Sensibility to Romanticism: Essays Presented to Frederick A. Pottle,* ed. Frederick W. Hilles and Harold Bloom. New York: Oxford University Press, 1965.

Price, Uvedale. *An Essay on the Picturesque.* London, 1794.

———. *Letter to H. Repton, Esq.* In Sir *Uvedale Price on the Picturesque,* ed. Sir Thomas Dick Lauder. London, 1842.

Repton, Humphry. *Sketches and Hints on Landscape Gardening.* London, 1794.

———. "Letter to Uvedale Price, Esq." (Published as an Appendix to *Sketches and Hints.*)

Reynolds, Joshua. *Discourses on Art,* ed. Robert R. Wark. New Haven: Yale University Press, 1975.

Robinson, Jenefer. "General and Individual Style in Literature." *Journal of Aesthetics and Art Criticism* 43, no. 2 (1984): 147-158.

Rorschach, Kimerly. *The Early Georgian Landscape Garden.* New Haven: Yale Center for British Art, 1983.

Schier, Flint. *Deeper into Pictures: An Essay on Pictorial Representation.* Cambridge: Cambridge University Press, 1986.

Schulz, Max F. "The Circuit Walk of the Eighteenth-Century Landscape Garden and the Pilgrim's Circuitous Progress." *Eighteenth-Century Studies* 15, no. 1 (1981): 1–25.

Sonfist, Alan, ed. *Art in the Land: A Critical Anthology of Environmental Art.* New York: E. P. Dutton, 1983.

Snyder, Joel, and Neil Walsh Allen. "Photography, Vision, and Representation." *Critical Inquiry* 2, no. 1 (1975): 143–69.

Sparshott, Francis. *The Theory of the Arts.* Princeton: Princeton University Press, 1982.

Strong, Roy. *The Renaissance Garden in England.* London: Thames and Hudson, 1979.

Stuart, David C. *Georgian Gardens.* London: Robert Hale, 1979.

Stuart, Jan. "Ming Dynasty Gardens Reconstructed in Words and Images." *Journal of Garden History* 10, no. 3 (1990): 162–72.

Symes, Michael. "Nature as the Bride of Art: The Design and Structure of Painshill." *Eighteenth-Century Life* 8, no. 2 (1983): 65–73.

Thacker, Christopher. *The History of Gardens.* Berkeley and Los Angeles: University of California Press, 1979.

Trease, Geoffrey. *The Grand Tour.* New York: Holt, Rinehart, and Winston, 1967.

Treib, Marc, ed. *Modern Landscape Architecture: A Critical Review.* Cambridge: MIT Press, 1993.

Tuan, Yi-fu. *Topophilia.* Englewood Cliffs, NJ: Prentice-Hall, 1974.

———. *Dominance and Affection: The Making of Pets.* New Haven: Yale University Press, 1984.

Tunnard, Christopher. *A World with a View: An Inquiry into the Nature of Scenic Values.* New Haven: Yale University Press, 1978.

Turner, James. "The Structure of Henry Hoare's Stourhead." *The Art Bulletin* 21, no. 1 (1979): 68–77.

Turner, James G. "The Sexual Politics of Landscape: Images of Venus in Eighteenth-Century English Poetry and Landscape Gardening." In *Studies in Eighteenth-Century Culture*, vol. 11, ed. Harry C. Payne. Madison: University of Wisconsin Press, 1982.

Walpole, Horace. *The History of the Modern Taste in Gardening.* Reprint, New York and London: Garland, 1982.

Walton, Kendall. *Mimesis as Make-Believe: On the Foundations of the Representational Arts.* Cambridge: Harvard University Press, 1990.

Wartofsky, Marx W. "Art History and Perception." In *Perceiving Artworks,* ed. John Fisher. Philadelphia: Temple University Press, 1980.

———. "Picturing and Representing." In *Philosophy Looks at the Arts,* ed. Joseph Margolis. Philadelphia: Temple University Press, 1987.

Watkin, David. *The English Vision: The Picturesque in Architecture, Landscape, and Garden Design.* London: John Murray, 1982.

Whately, Thomas. *Observations on Modern Gardening.* London, 1770. Reprint, New York and London: Garland, 1982.

Wollheim, Richard. *Art and Its Objects.* Cambridge: Cambridge University Press, 1980.

———. *Painting as an Art.* Princeton: Princeton University Press, 1987.

Wolterstorff, Nicholas. *Works and Worlds of Art.* Oxford: Clarendon Press, 1980.

Woodbridge, Kenneth. "Henry Hoare's Paradise." *Art Bulletin* 47 (1965): 83–116.

———. *Landscape and Antiquity: Aspects of English Culture at Stourhead, 1718–1838.* Oxford: Clarendon Press, 1970.

Wroth, Warwick. The London Pleasure Gardens of the Eighteenth Century. Hamden, CT: Archon Books, 1979.

Index

WITHDRAWN

FASKEN LEARNING RESOURCE CENTER

9000063354